The Genesis of Tragedy

and the

Sacred Drama

of

Eleusis

(1936)

> Contents: The Theatre of Antiquity in India and Greece; The Renaissance of the Classic and Romantic Theatre; The Theatre of the Future Psyche in the Three Worlds; The Genesis of the Hindu Theatre Through Sacred Dance; The Genesis of Greek Tragedy; The Life and Works of Aeschylos; The Life and Work of Sophokles—Oedipus and the Sphinx; The Mystery of Eleusis; and The Sacred Drama of Eleusis.

Edouard Schure

ISBN 0-7661-0020-0

> Request our FREE CATALOG of over 1,000
> # Rare Esoteric Books
> ## Unavailable Elsewhere
>
> Freemasonry * Akashic * Alchemy * Alternative Health * Ancient Civilizations * Anthroposophy * Astral * Astrology * Astronomy * Aura * Bacon, Francis * Bible Study * Blavatsky * Boehme * Cabalah * Cartomancy * Chakras * Clairvoyance * Comparative Religions * Divination * Druids * Eastern Thought * Egyptology * Esoterism * Essenes * Etheric * Extrasensory Perception * Gnosis * Gnosticism * Golden Dawn * Great White Brotherhood * Hermetics * Kabalah * Karma * Knights Templar * Kundalini * Magic * Meditation * Mediumship * Mesmerism * Metaphysics * Mithraism * Mystery Schools * Mysticism * Mythology * Numerology * Occultism * Palmistry * Pantheism * Paracelsus * Parapsychology * Philosophy * Plotinus * Prosperity & Success * Psychokinesis * Psychology * Pyramids * Qabalah * Reincarnation * Rosicrucian * Sacred Geometry * Secret Rituals * Secret Societies * Spiritism * Symbolism * Tarot * Telepathy * Theosophy * Transcendentalism * Upanishads * Vedanta * Wisdom * Yoga * *Plus Much More!*

Kessinger Publishing, LLC
U.S.A.
http://www.kessingerpub.com

CONTENTS

INTRODUCTION - - - - - - page 11

FIRST PART

THE INITIATORY THEATRE

FIRST EPOCH: THE THEATRE OF ANTIQUITY IN INDIA AND IN GREECE

The Sacred Dancing Girl and the Indian Theatre. The Mystery of Dionysos and the Sacred Drama of Eleusis - - - - - - page 19

SECOND EPOCH: THE RENAISSANCE OF THE CLASSIC AND ROMANTIC THEATRE

Shakespeare and the Laic Theatre. Calderon and Ecclesiastical Drama. The Classical Theatre in France. The Romantic Theatre in France - page 28

THIRD EPOCH: THE THEATRE OF THE FUTURE— PSYCHE IN THE THREE WORLDS

Legendary and Philosophical Drama: The Occult in Goethe and in Richard Wagner. The Theatre of the Future. Psyche in the Three Worlds - - - - - - - page 69

CONTENTS—*continued*

SECOND PART

THE GENESIS OF TRAGEDY AND THE DRAMA OF ELEUSIS

CHAPTER I

THE GENESIS OF THE HINDU THEATRE THROUGH SACRED DANCE. THE DRAMA OF SAKUNTALA

Psychology of the Contemporary Theatre. Outline of the Evolution of the Theatre in Three Thousand Years. The Dance in Primitive India. The Heroic Idyll: 'Sakuntala'. The Essence of Dramatic Emotion - - - - page 123

CHAPTER II

THE GENESIS OF GREEK TRAGEDY

The Mystery of Dionysos and the Dithyramb. The Adolescence of Aeschylos at Eleusis. The Persian Wars: The 'Persae' of Aeschylos - page 155

CHAPTER III

THE LIFE AND WORK OF AESCHYLOS

The 'Prometheus' of Aeschylos and the Promethean Idea. The 'Oresteia'. The Poet's Exile in Sicily - - - - - - - - page 178

CONTENTS—*continued*

CHAPTER IV

THE LIFE AND WORK OF SOPHOKLES—OEDIPUS AND THE SPHINX—ANTIGONE AND THE ETERNAL-FEMININE

The Athens of Perikles and the Genius of Sophokles. The Theatre of Sophokles: The Law of Nemesis and the Wisdom of Delphi. 'Oedipus Tyrannus' and the Riddle of the Sphinx. 'Oedipus at Colonus': Purification by Suffering. 'Antigone': Revealer of the Eternal-Feminine and of Universal Love - page 203

CHAPTER V

THE MYSTERY OF ELEUSIS—PSYCHE IN THE THREE WORLDS—THE FUTURE OF THE THEATRE

The Sacred Drama of Eleusis. Origin of the Sacred Drama of Eleusis. The Sorrow of Demeter and the Initiation of Triptolemos (First Act of the Sacred Drama) - - - - - page 240
Persephone in the Lower World (Second Act of the Sacred Drama) - - - - - page 253
The Sacred Marriage: The Meeting of Persephone with the New Dionysos (Third and Last Act of the Sacred Drama) - - - - page 255

THIRD PART

THE SACRED DRAMA OF ELEUSIS

page 267

INTRODUCTION

THE INITIATORY THEATRE IN HUMAN EVOLUTION

THE studies contained in this volume are the exact reproduction of the five lectures I delivered early in 1925 at the Société de Géographie, in Paris, on the subject of *Le Théâtre initiateur, son passé, son présent, son avenir.* Let me state at the outset that this book realizes only the first part of the programme here announced. To be dealt with as a whole, the vast subject would require two other volumes, the one on *Le Théâtre néo-classique et romantique,* the other on *Le Théâtre de l'avenir* as resulting from the vital aspirations latent in the nineteenth and twentieth centuries. I very much doubt whether I shall be able to carry through so rash a project which would include the entire history of the theatre and establish its laws in accordance with its dual descending and ascending development and its rhythmic movement throughout the ages. If I cannot realize my dream, at all events I intend to give a sketch of the grandiose tableau appearing before my gaze at the beginning of the present work.

The following pages will be a sort of rapid vision of this synthetic conception, condensed in a series of living epitomes as well as an attempt to set forth a new

INTRODUCTION

aesthetic and a view of the world history of the Theatre. With this explanation, let us return to our origins.

. . . .

Many years ago, I happened to be at Florence, working at a poem on Empedokles, the philosopher-magician of Agrigentum, who ended his triumphant career by suicide on Mount Etna. Tradition attributes his death to his investigations into the causes of terrestrial fire. With poetic licence, I supposed that Empedokles had received his first initiation from a priestess of the two Great Goddesses (Demeter and Persephone), whose cult flourished in Sicily in the sixth century before Christ. This prophetess had died, consumed by her passion for the initiate who had become her master. But after the burning of her body on the funeral pile, the soul of Elpenor had remained in communion with Empedokles, instilling into him the sublime truths of the world of the Gods. To this revelation the philosopher, now Archon of Agrigentum, owed all his power and might. A dangerous privilege, for pride proved to be his downfall! His disciples having asked him whence came the wonderful truths he taught them, he answered that he was indebted to his own reason alone. Immediately the golden lyre, set up on his house-top, through which the soul of Elpenor spoke to him every evening at sunset, became silent. The spring of inspiration being exhausted, Empedokles lost his courage, his strength and his reason. The light of divine truth was extinguished, he became mad, and, in despair, flung himself into the crater of the volcano.

With this poem and all its circumstances in mind, I

INTRODUCTION

went every morning to the Uffizi library to consult the ancient authors who had dealt with the mysteries of Eleusis to which, from earliest youth, I had been irresistibly attracted. The municipal library, standing in the heart of Florence, behind the Museum, on the banks of the Arno, not far from the Palazzo Vecchio which proudly erects its slender campanile, sentinel-wise, above the elegant city—all this constituted a favourable framework to my meditations. One day, lost in the labyrinth of the mysteries contained in the pages of Plato and Porphyry, Iamblichus and Apuleius, my inward vision suddenly extended its bounds beyond the horizon.

That which fascinated me in the history of Empedokles was the poignant enigma of the Beyond offered to the individual human being in his emotional life. But what a bewildering scope does this problem assume when referred to the whole of mankind! What is its origin, what is its destination? From what abyss has it escaped to plunge into what annihilation, or into what eternity? What relation does it bear to the cosmic powers at work behind the apparent chaos of the universe in the production of so magnificent a harmony! In the dense darkness where wallows the noisy materialism of the age, it is no longer a question simply of restoring the bond between the Visible and the Invisible in the case of the individual, but of proving how fertile is the influence of this omnipotent Beyond upon the whole history of humanity.

This thought filled me with an ardent desire to trace the connection between the revelation of Eleusis and that of the Christ.

To throw a bridge between the Paradise lost and the

INTRODUCTION

Earth plunged in darkness, was it not necessary to reconstruct the magnetic chain of the various religions, to recast Hellenism and Christianity into their original unity, to reconcile in their primordial and final harmony the entire religious traditions of East and West? Then, as in a flash, I glimpsed the light that illumines the mighty founders of religions, from the Himalayas to the plain of the Iran, from Sinai to Tabor, from the crypts of Egypt to the sanctuary of Eleusis. Those powerful evokers of Gods, those mighty framers of human souls, Rama, Krishna, Hermes, Moses, Orpheus, Pythagoras, Plato and Jesus, appeared before me in a homogeneous group. How diverse in form, appearance and colour! Nevertheless, the eternal Word thrilled in all alike. To be in unison with them was to hear 'the Word which was in the Beginning', it was to ascertain, by experience, *the continuity of inspiration in history as an historical fact.*

Might not this rapid, this instantaneous vision of consciousness become a new bridge to traverse the abyss separating heaven from earth? At all events, I had found my *Novum Organum.*

From this dazzling truth which obtained its illumination direct from the centre of things, what individual illuminations were kindled; from this solar axiom, what multiple traditions! As it is impossible to mention all, I will dwell upon one alone. For after this it seemed to me that an evolution of the theatre must correspond with this religious and philosophical evolution of humanity, wherein were manifested the spiritual powers that give it direction.

The theatre! What a strange phenomenon, what

INTRODUCTION

an amazing puzzle is this *camera oscura* wherein is reflected the entire outer and inner world of things! A singular duplication of life, now its grotesque caricature, now its sublime transfiguration. Does it not seem as though the theatre were the magic mirror of the human soul in action and in process of becoming, the most potent lever of the imagination and the sensibility? In the hands of genius, it is the most enchanting creator of beauty and enthusiasm. In the hands of the inexperienced and the perfidious, it is a sink of corruption and defilement. In very truth, Melpomene can be an admirable healer, the most powerful moulder of souls, or else the most subtle and terrible of poisoners.

But how is one to apprehend the progress and the law of theatrical aesthetics in the labyrinth of nations and literatures, the pandemonium of invasions and revolutions, the never-ending struggles between races and civilizations, the conflicts between peoples and systems? After years of study and research, meditation and effort, after innumerable trials and the experience of a lifetime, the result is set down in this book, though it comprises no more than the third of the work projected.

From this preliminary outline, however imperfect be the résumé, the reader will be able to form some idea of the conception as a whole.

FIRST PART

THE INITIATORY THEATRE

FIRST EPOCH

THE THEATRE OF ANTIQUITY IN INDIA AND IN GREECE

The Sacred Dancing Girl and the Indian Theatre

IT might be imagined *a priori* that the theatre was born of an imitation of external life because it is a reflection of its doings and its happenings. This, however, is not so. Wherever it appears, it has sprung originally from the arcana of the interior life, from a poetical incantation. Especially is this apparent in India and in Greece, where drama issued forth from the profoundest mysteries of religion.

One need only read the *Vishnu Purana* to see how important is the rôle played by the sacred dancing girl (the *devadasi*) in religious life and Hindu art. The poetical legend of Krishna shows that the religious dance was the very source of Art in India during its heroic epoch, and remained its centre and inspiration on to the period of decadence when theatrical art developed. When young Krishna, the incarnation of the god Vishnu and a type of the perfect initiate, has overcome the dragon, the symbol of animal passions, he retires to the shepherds of Mount Meru to meditate upon his lofty mission. There, beneath the stately cedars, in the dewy night of the tropical moon, he

THE GENESIS OF TRAGEDY

teaches sacred dances and music to the wives and daughters of the Gopis. Not, however, for the mere pleasure of movement does he tell them how to bend their supple limbs to the sounds of tambourines and stringed instruments, but rather in order to symbolize the deeds of Gods and Heroes. The epic which Krishna has recited to them, these marvellous visions within his own soul, revolving panoramically in his memory, are not interpreted by these nimble *ballerine*, for the dancing girls are silent. There is neither dialogue nor dramatic action; the dance reproduces no single episode of the divine epic. Krishna, however, teaches this primitive corps de ballet to express by gestures and attitudes the leading Sentiments and Ideas of these tales. Thus do the Gopis interpret the wrath of Indra against the god of darkness, Rama's devotion to his father, and the grief of Sita when separated from her husband.

We have not yet come to real drama, but to expressive dancing, plastic lyricism. The inspired dancer gives life to the epic story just as cinema pictures illustrate the luminous legend depicted on the screen. Subsequently, with the juxtaposition of the two arts, the epic story and the moving dance will blend into the living word, real action and the objective representation of the drama.

But why does Krishna take women and not men to interpret the sacred art? There are transcendent reasons for this. The Rishis of pre-Vedic times, founders of the cult of Agni, the sacred Fire, saw the world through the Eternal-Masculine, the creative Spirit, which in truth is Androgyne and includes the Eternal-Feminine as its ineffable quintessence. Brahmanic

THE INITIATORY THEATRE

India, on the other hand, and above all Krishna, its great inspirer, saw the world through the Eternal-Feminine, the plastic force of Nature. To understand the profound significance of the Eternal-Feminine and of woman both in the Brahmanic religion and in Hindu poetry we must supplement the legend of Krishna by the no less significant myth of the Apsaras.

Such Vedic hymns as the *Ramayana* and the *Mahabharata* relate that Indra, the Solar God, is surrounded by celestial nymphs or Apsaras, supra-terrestrial souls of radiant beauty, who serve him as messengers and mediators with men. Sometimes they are sent by the Gods to aid and inspire the great sages, and then again to test and tempt them when these ascetics threaten the very existence of the Gods by the intense profundity of their meditations. If, as almost always happens, the ascetics succumb to the temptation, then, from the union of the Rishi with the Apsara is born some hero or king. Occasionally the ascetic resists, because by his own might he conceives and creates a more lovely Apsara than that of the Gods. Then this superior being becomes the spouse of a perfect monarch as in the case of Urvasi. Thus, in Hindu mythology, the Apsaras represent exceptional souls, born in a higher world, who, as *Heavenly intruders*, come down into earth life to help forward human evolution.

Manifestly the temple dancing girl played in the social life of primitive India the same rôle that the Apsara plays in Hindu mythology. She is the interpreter of the Gods to men, the mediator between the divine and the earth world. Accompanying, vivifying and illustrating the poetical recitations of the Hindu

THE GENESIS OF TRAGEDY

rhapsodies, these dancing girls were for centuries the representatives of sacred Art, realizing in some sort the presence of the Gods upon Earth, whether on the improvised stages of the nomad Aryans of Iran, in front of the pagodas of India, or on the terraces of those gigantic temples with the pyramids of Gods on their roofs.

When subsequently there came about a development of the Hindu drama, perhaps following the example of the Greek theatre imported by Alexander the Great into Bactria, the ancient legends were introduced, and the Apsara, the celestial nymph, continued to play an important part. In *The Nymph and the Hero* of Kalidasa, Urvasi is an Apsara incarnated on earth. In the *Sakuntala* of the same poet, the heroine is the daughter of an Apsara. In another work, Sita, falsely accused by Rama of conjugal infidelity, allows herself to be consumed on her funeral pile, in the trial by fire, and receives a transfigured apotheosis wherein she is received by the goddess of the Ganges and by the goddess of the Earth.

Thus the theatre makes its début in the history of civilization with a religious drama which takes place in a region intermediate between heaven and earth. It is a sort of innocent and paradisiac idyll enacted far above the zone of violent passions where unbridled Hatred and Love, Voluptuousness and Death hold grim and horrible sway. Here are wafted the soft breezes of the Himalayas which breathe upon the peaks of tropical forests, but there can be heard neither the roar of wild beasts nor the shrill quizzing call of the mocking bird.

Those who doubt the important rôle played by the

THE INITIATORY THEATRE

dancing girl in Indian religion and poetry, should visit the temples of Angkor-Tom and Angkor-Watt in Cambodia, where the wide stretching Mekong, a mighty over-flowing sheet of water, fertilizes impenetrable virgin forests. In these colossal and forsaken pagodas, surrounded by luxuriant vegetation, the entire epic story of the *Ramayana*, carved in high relief, extends over gigantic walls as far as the eye can see. Rama's mighty army is represented as engaged in the conquest of Ceylon. Chariots on chariots, horsemen on horsemen, a great multitude, with apes fighting at the side of men, hurl themselves forward in headlong onset. Above the frightful mêlée appear the Apsaras, the airy messengers of Indra. They hang in belts along the frieze, dying away in the thick of the fight. With their bell-shaped robes they give the impression of celestial butterflies flitting above the human pandemonium. Dainty as dragon-flies, they even now evoke, before our wondering gaze, the supernatural and inspiring rôle of the sacred dancing girl in Hindu art and drama.

The Mystery of Dionysos and the Sacred Drama of Eleusis

> Regrettez-vous le temps où le Ciel sur la Terre
> Marchait et respirait dans un peuple des Dieux?

These admirable lines of Alfred de Musset proudly express the sovereign magic and immortal charm of Greek mythology. In this glowing expanse of speaking symbols, all the cosmic powers—the many-coloured rays of the one supreme God—have their legitimate

THE GENESIS OF TRAGEDY

place, from the elementary forces of visible Nature to the loftiest archetypes of creative Spirit.

In this stupendous cycle, vast and world-embracing, Dionysos represents the desire for bodily manifestation. Glowing genius of Incarnation, multiform and irresistible stream of life, he invades and permeates all beings, stirring them to life and action, Dionysos is the frenzy of life, the genius of Individuality. Apollo, his brother, is the sun of the divine world, the God of Dream and Inspiration, the Logos of celestial intelligence and of all Archetypes, the radiant manifestation of immutable eternal Beauty.

Apollo and Dionysos form a complete opposition, for one controls the spiritual, the other the material world. Nevertheless they are not enemies, they work together throughout the universe in fraternal and indefatigable collaboration—and without them the universe would not be possible. It was doubtless for this reason that, according to the Greeks, the God of the Muses and the God of the Bacchantes reign facing each other on the twin peaks of Parnassos.

The religious organiser of primitive Greece was the Doris Orpheus, son of a priestess of Apollo. His powerful though ultra-sensitive nature was in marvellous accord with his soul,—a tuneful lyre. He blended and fused both deities in his life and work. He elaborated Apollonian thoughts with Dionysiac enthusiasm. Orpheus was the founder of the Orphic mysteries, the creator of the myth of Dionysos torn to pieces by the Titans and restored to life by Athene. This myth is a summary of the entire cosmic evolution, i.e., of the dispersion of the deity throughout the visible world and its

THE INITIATORY THEATRE

return to eternal and infinite harmony by the sufferings of incarnation.

It is a striking fact that the Greek theatre—and through it the whole of the modern theatre—should owe its birth to the myth of Dionysos. It indelibly marks the profound significance of the theatre for all time. The history of the Greek theatre contains, in striking epitome, that of the past, present and future theatre. A sonorous voice like that of the God Pan proclaims its lofty mission even from its birth-wail. Before it became the tragedy of Aeschylos, Sophokles and Euripides, the Greek theatre was an itinerant dithyramb. The Satyrs bewailing the death of Dionysos and then celebrating his resurrection with cries of joy, a god emerging from a vat of crushed grapes in a fume of intoxication—such was the singular origin of tragedy.

With Dionysos there breaks out into Art, Poetry and the Theatre, an idea unknown to India: the idea of the necessity of Grief, of progress by Struggle, of the purification of the Soul by Suffering. At first, Dionysos alone represents this idea, but soon it multiplies in endless ways. Beasts, men and Gods are soon to express it and appear on the proscenium of the theatre of Athens. Thus was literally to be verified the saying of Orpheus: 'Men are born from the tears of Dionysos and the Gods from his smile.'

And so the Greek theatre offers us a spectacle quite unknown to the Hindu theatre; that of the struggle of men with one another and even of the struggle of man with the Gods, an inevitable consequence of freedom. This struggle reaches its culminating point in the *Prometheus Bound* of Aeschylos, as does the idea of expiation by glorified suffering in the *Oedipus at Colonus* of Sophokles, whereas his *Antigone* suggests the redemptive power of the Eternal-Feminine.

. . . .

Although Greek tragedy constantly caused the Gods to intervene in the progress of scenic action and the fluctuations of the human consciousness, it gave no clear idea, in the theatre of Dionysos, of the origin and the future destiny of the soul. Both the present and the hereafter of life remained an insoluble enigma. The impenetrable veil of the Mysteries covered this hereafter. The political power of the time (the Areiopagos) and the spiritual authority (the Eumolpides of Eleusis), at one in this as in all fundamental questions of government, regarded these problems as too serious to be discussed before the masses. The wisdom of antiquity, however, represented by the Eumolpides, looked upon the sacred drama of Eleusis as an infinitely suggestive symbolical image of the ulterior destiny of the Soul and of its eternal goal, by showing its relation to the whole of cosmic evolution. It is this sacred drama that we have attempted to reconstruct in the final chapter of the present work.

A synthesis of the utmost importance is involved in this juxtaposition and this opposition.

In tragedy and in the mystery of Eleusis, ancient Greece set before the world a dual realization: the terrestrial realisation of the Divine by the *Promethean Idea* and its celestial realization by the *Eleusinian Idea*, which is that of the deliverance and the fulfilment of human destinies in the future life.

THE INITIATORY THEATRE

Now conflict and struggle and rapprochement, the endless combinations and ever new attempts to blend harmoniously these two ideas, constitute the basis of the whole of human history, and of the history of the theatre.

Thus it may be asserted that, in its tragic art and its Eleusinian synthesis, the Hellenic genius gives us a preliminary outline and enables us to guess at the solution of the problem.

SECOND EPOCH

THE RENAISSANCE OF THE CLASSIC AND ROMANTIC THEATRE

Shakespeare and the Laic Theatre

THE disappearance of the theatre of antiquity from the world stage dates from the day when the Emperor Constantine adopted Christianity as the official religion of the Roman Empire. We must take a mighty leap over ten centuries of history before we again find an art theatre worthy of the name, transferring ourselves suddenly into the new civilization that had formed in Western Europe, in the sixteenth century, throughout England, Spain and France.

What had taken place during this millennium of history, perhaps the most stormy years in the evolution of mankind?

First of all, the lingering death-struggle of the ancient civilization through the corruption and decomposition of the Roman Empire which had lost its authority along with its faith. Then successive barbaric invasions had spread over the corrupt world of antiquity. Finally, Christianity had restored the aspect of things by substituting the worship of the One God for that of many Gods. A far deeper revolution, however, had taken

THE INITIATORY THEATRE

place in the interior world of the Soul, finding expression in two phrases of heart-stirring power. Under the reign of Tiberius, a pilot, sailing along the coasts of Syria, heard loud lamentation and a clamorous outcry: *Great Pan is dead!* At the same period, in the catacombs proscribed Christians, before being thrown to the circus beasts, concluded their prayers with the exclamation: *Christ is risen from the dead!* The first of these cries announced the end of the cult of Nature, consequently the breach of communion with the cosmic powers that animate Nature. The second expressed the new impulses of the human soul towards the limitless empire of the Invisible, and this cry, like a flash of light, pierced the darkness of the soul and opened up glorious perspectives upon the mighty Beyond. Such an epoch had to find expression in ogival (pointed) architecture, in the *Imitation of Jesus Christ,* and in Dante's *Commedia Divina,* but it was unable to create a dramatic art. This can be born only when reality has come to real grips with an idea. The theatre was to return to civilization through the phenomenon of the Renaissance which restored humanity to Hellenism, i.e., to Nature through the cult of Science and Beauty.

After the fierce and sanguinary Wars of the Roses, the English theatre, under the reign of Elizabeth, flourished exceedingly. This theatre was essentially laic in character; its exponents were legion. In the dense forests of Merry England before the days of Puritanism, these jovial or melancholy poets both great and insignificant, grew like an army of oaks and mushrooms. They are summed up in one man, who

THE GENESIS OF TRAGEDY

surpasses all the rest in mental stature, the great and incomparable Shakespeare.

There is something enigmatical in the dual nature of his personality. A butcher's son, there is nothing about this young poacher, who has become a talented actor and a poet of renown, to distinguish him from his confrères, unless it be a suppleness of disposition, a degree of skill and amiability that charms all and is universally acknowledged. As a poet, however, he surpasses his rivals not only in the scope but in the nature of his genius. He is an inspired seer of the first rank. His seership, however, is different from that of Homer, Aeschylos or Sophokles. Still less does it resemble that of the Eumolpides, the priests who initiated the drama of Eleusis and fixed their gaze, over beyond the world of souls, on to that of the divine Archetypes. Shakespeare, when writing his dramas in a sort of poetic trance, is a gigantic mirror of real life, a medium thrilling with sympathy, a seer of the whole of terrestrial mankind, from the man of the plebs and the glebe on to princes and kings. He is familiar alike with the heroes of Roman history and with the rulers of England. With like impartiality and apparent dispassion he mirrors the various aspects of life which may now be a clownish farce, now a sentimental comedy and again a sombre tragedy—and is often all of these at once. This spectacle unfolds beneath his eyes not as a chaos, but in its organic and majestic ensemble.

So vividly has Shakespeare evoked the dominant human types and the *grandes passions* that all the representations made thereof since his day appear cold in comparison. Where has the vertiginous altitude of

THE INITIATORY THEATRE

absolute power been better described than in *Julius Caesar*; passion of freedom than in Brutus and mass fickleness than in Mark Antony's oration? Where has the conception of crime, in the very depths of the human consciousness, been staged as in Macbeth's meeting, on the heath, with the three witches, the weird sisters and filthy hags of destiny? Where has the viper of jealousy unrolled its coils as in *Othello*? Where has love dreamed in moonlight shade or shuddered in mortal despair as in *Romeo and Juliet*? Where have the thirst after pleasure and regal licentiousness reached such delirious heights and agonized longings as in *Antony and Cleopatra*? Who like Shakespeare in the person of Iago has depicted hardened wickedness? What has ever expressed remorse for crime like the tiny spot of blood on the white hand of Lady Macbeth in the famous somnambulistic scene at the beginning of the last act—that spot on the little hand which 'all the perfumes of Arabis will not sweeten'? No one like Shakespeare has shown us the series of reactions and psychic ungearings which leads to madness all human passions when reason does not keep watch over them and they are not controlled by the will. This delirium of insanity reaches its height in the storm scene, in the third act of *King Lear*, when the impetuous blasts of fretful elements on the bare heath lash and pursue the hapless old man exposed to their fury by the ingratitude of his daughters. When the fallen king clasps to his breast the sublime Cordelia, the only one of his daughters who has been faithful to him throughout, one has the feeling that the world is crumbling in ruin.

THE GENESIS OF TRAGEDY

There is affirmed and justified the psychology and moral philosophy of the Shakespearean drama. Its formula is that man is the framer of his destiny. If he overcomes his passions, he retains self-mastery; vanquished by them, he commits moral suicide. Here is a new concept, one but dimly suspected by the drama of antiquity: man's responsibility for his most trifling deeds. Nevertheless, this does not perceptibly diminish the pessimism of Shakespearean philosophy. Human freedom is extremely relative. For though man may determine his own destiny, he can modify it but slightly between birth and death. While the outer world does not crush him, it imposes strict limits on him. If his fate depends largely on his character, whence comes this character? Shakespeare's melancholy outlook upon life is wholly expressed in that of his creations into which he has instilled most of his own thought.

In the drama of *Hamlet* the chords of his own soul vibrate most painfully. It is generally considered that this character expresses impotence in action through the weakness of the will. Nothing could be more untrue. Hamlet is the most chivalrous soul, the most finely tempered and truly prince-like of his time. His undaunted courage is proof of the delicacy of his feelings. In revealing to him the crime of his brother, the usurping Claudius, Hamlet's father imposes on his son a formidable mission. The latter devotes himself to it with all the might at his command. The reason he is tardy in its accomplishment is not lack of moral power but the very profundity of his thinking. What gives pause to his avenging arm is no pusillanimous dread but rather extreme scruples of conscience and the need to

THE INITIATORY THEATRE

know things in their very essence. To make quite certain that the ghost was indeed his father's and had not deceived him, he had the murder scene played by actors in the presence of the king, thus causing the latter to betray himself involuntarily. The reason why he does not kill him after this is that he fears to do his mission badly by sending to the other world the repentant king whom he finds kneeling in prayer. When, after the gruesome grave-diggers' scene, Laertes reproaches Hamlet for having slain his father and caused the death of his sister Ophelia, Hamlet answers the challenge with frenzied courage and the utmost violence. This tragic meeting of the brother and the lover at the tomb of poor Ophelia, where the exasperated Hamlet tells Laertes that, in spite of everything, he has loved Ophelia more than anyone, is superbly audacious. Here, the soul of the Prince of Denmark shows itself in all its idealism. That which arrests his impulses and paralyses his actions is no degenerate or feeble cowardice, it is the pettiness of humanity, the irremediable wretchedness of life. It is this consciousness of the impossibility of happiness that makes him say to Ophelia: 'Get thee to a nunnery.' He has seen too much of the worst side of things, and has pierced through and through the cunning and tenebrous soul of man. But he has not fathomed the great mystery, he has not solved the awful problem of the Beyond; and this is his cankerworm, his bitterest torment. 'To be or not to be—that is the question. . . . To die—to sleep; . . . perchance to dream. . . .' And, in spite of all, Hamlet does his duty by killing the king at the right time. Himself wounded by the poisoned blade of Laertes, he can die in peace. For now he will

THE GENESIS OF TRAGEDY

hold the key to the great enigma. And the faithful Horatio, the only friend to understand him, might fittingly end the play with Hamlet's own lines which seem to soar above the entire theatre of Shakespeare: 'There are more things in heaven and earth, . . . Than are dreamt of in your philosophy.'

We assert that, though a gloomy pessimism broods over Shakespeare's dramas, the world of occult powers wraps them about like a wan twilight occasionally illumined by dazzling flashes.

More profoundly than anyone did Shakespeare descend into the bog and quagmire of life, into the depths of the human heart wherein crawl terrifying monsters. Our globe, in Shakespeare's imagination, appears as some misty earth whereon writhes perturbed mankind beneath a tempest-laden sky which occasionally becomes darkened with the most threatening blackness. Through this dense layer, however, glint and beam strange and variegated lights. These are rays from another world invisible to mortal sight, one that is a near accomplice of our own passions, that overshadows and besets us with the vastness of its mystery. These beams pass through the fissures and crevices of our earthly 'carapace', casting into our dark prison-house now the reflections of an inferno more frightful than our own perverse and refractory world, now the consoling vision of a far-away heaven. Such was the lamentable ghost of Hamlet's father, such the blood-stained spectre of murdered Banquo; such the witches of Macbeth, larvae inciting to ambition along with their mistress Hekate, the potent worker of Evil. Such too were the souls of the victims of Richard III, who appeared at night be-

THE INITIATORY THEATRE

tween the camps of the two rival kings. It is the eve of the decisive battle; Richard III and Richmond lie asleep in their tents. To the crowned monster, Richard the assassin, these ghosts exclaim: 'Despair and die!' To the innocent and noble Richmond, they murmur: 'Live and flourish! . . . Awake and win the day!' Such, finally, the elementals of flowers and forests, the Elfs and Sylphs, and the tricksy merry Puck who come to bless the happy and reconciled pairs of lovers at the end of *Midsummer Night's Dream*.

We thus see that the world of the Gods which plays so important a part in the dramaturgy of the world of antiquity, has not altogether disappeared in the Shakespearean drama, upon which it casts a light that is both disturbing and suggestive.

In his last drama, *The Tempest*, which he wrote shortly before retiring to his native town, Shakespeare rose to still greater heights. Here we have the symbolic drama and enter the domain of white magic. The magician Prospero, rightful Duke of Milan, left shipwrecked by his brother on a desert island, succeeds in gaining power over the elemental forces that animate and people the lower regions of nature, the Elves and Sylphs. By means of the tuneful Ariel, he tames Caliban, the symbol of a coarse humanity still plunged in all kinds of bestial excesses. He employs Nature's mysterious forces, and, through Ariel, the invisible musical instrument, restores to each other—and inspires mutual love in—his daughter Miranda and Ferdinand, the son of his hostile brother. These simple noble-hearted souls, united in a perfect couple, represent a higher humanity evolved by the powers invisible.

THE GENESIS OF TRAGEDY

And so it must be recognized that whereas on the one hand Shakespeare, the inspired poet and mighty seer, carried drama down into the deep abyss of sin and crime, on the other hand, he has proved that it is the destiny of the theatre to rise again, with all the power acquired in its hurtling descent, to the sublime heights of the Gods, of the one undying Spirit.

Calderon and Ecclesiastical Drama

While it was the mission of England (Celtic, Norman and Saxon) to create the laic drama for the modern world, the ethnical temperament of Spain (Iberian, Visigothic and Moorish) predestined her to create the ecclesiastical drama in the vast concert of the European theatre.

In the English temperament there is a blend of violence and sentimental reverie, of positive egoism and audacious utopianism, which enables it to enfold all human contrasts and at the same time to penetrate very far into the life of the soul. By a miracle impossible to explain, this soul is both universal and incongruous. On the other hand, the soul of Spain is fierce and narrow, inclining her to action that is violent and concentrated, though always intermittent. A blend of the sombre harshness of the Iberians, of the majestic gravity of the Visigoths, of Catalanian gaiety, Castilian pride and Andalusian languor—in short, of Oriental magniloquence and Saracen splendour (for the victor always borrows something from his vanquished enemies), it had need of the most imperious discipline to keep these

THE INITIATORY THEATRE

contradictory elements under subjection. It found them first in its Latin tradition, then in the Roman Catholic Church, the terror of the Inquisition, the subtle government of the Jesuits. The Cid and the king Don Pedro help Spain to triumph over the Moors; Ferdinand the Catholic enables her to crush feudal anarchy. Hernando Cordez conquers South America; Charles the Fifth aspires after world dominion. Owing to the naval defeat of the Armada under the fanatical Philip II, Spain fails in her struggle with England. Then, all of a sudden, after amazing and fascinating the world with her greatness, Spain sinks into a torpor from which she emerges only by fits and starts.

In literature, art and religion, she oscillates between extremes. She gives birth to a Don Juan and to a Santa Teresa, enthusiastically acclaiming both alike. She passes from the Cid to Don Quixote, from Goya to Murillo. From the terrifying *corrida* where the torero, all bedizened with gold lace, thrusts his sword into the neck of the roaring bull before a delirious populace, she rushes desperately to the Calvary where a God is bleeding on the cross. The same kind of frenzy is seen in voluptuousness and vice as in asceticism and ecstasy. Such a temperament could not fail to produce extraordinary and powerful results upon the theatre, under an absolute monarchy, surrounded by all the luxury of a haughty feudal system and a brilliant chivalry.

This phenomenon took place at the beginning of the seventeenth century, under the reign of Philip IV, just at the moment when the blazing sun of the heroic monarchy was on the point of eclipse and was shedding

THE GENESIS OF TRAGEDY

its dying beams upon a Spain still enamoured of the spirit of chivalry. Tirso de Molina, Alarcon and others have given masterpieces to the Spanish theatre. Lope de Vega and Calderon mark the apex of this development.

The individuality of Shakespeare is impossible to grasp; it is a chameleon continually changing colour. He is the great Seer of history, the faithful mirror of all human characters, the quivering medium through which mighty men of genius speak to us. However diligently we may seek, he himself eludes us just when we think we hold him. This is not so with Calderon; he stands out as a strong individuality on the swarming and picturesque background of a society stirred by the deepest passions.

Don Pedro Calderon de la Barca belonged to a distinguished though indigent family. His vocation for tragedy manifested itself at an early age. A suggestive legend tells us that he wept thrice in his mother's womb before birth. It may be that we owe this paradox to his pessimism for he puts into the mouth of one of his characters the following harsh maxim. 'Man's greatest crime is that of being born.' From nine to fifteen he was educated by Jesuits, who bent his subtle intellect to the mastery of logic and criticism. From fifteen to twenty he studied at the university of Salamanca. He had already written more than one play, and he now plunged headlong into a care-free and joyous theatrical career. There has come down to us a strange confession of his regarding this juvenile and somewhat foolish period: his reply to a lady who had asked him for his portrait. He answers with the wit and the impertinence

THE INITIATORY THEATRE

of a Grazioso. 'A liking for the theatre took me behind the scenes. . . . I have been . . . and shall be for all time . . . a parasite, a poet, a squire. Oh sublime patience of Job, has anyone ever experienced a greater combination of calamities? Saddled with these three professions, one could scarcely imagine, I suppose, that any mother-in-law would want me as a husband for her daughter.' In consequence, he never married, though he lived a very gay life, modestly confessing that he contents himself with two mistresses at once. He prefers two who are ugly to one who is beautiful. He must have a brunette and a blonde, a titled lady and a peasant girl. According to him, Plato is wrong when he claims that the man who loves two women loves neither of them.

Such is the first Calderon, a shameless wit. The second Calderon is a fashionable nobleman, attached to the Court, devoted to literature and to fighting, who spends ten years in Italy, writes superb dramas, but is even prouder of having fought in Catalonia and been made a favourite of Philip IV. He is fifty years old when the king appoints him knight of Santiago. Shortly afterwards, he receives tonsure and enters the congregation of the native monks of Madrid, becoming their head chaplain three years afterwards. Throughout these weighty functions and imposing honours, however, he continues to write for the theatre his finest *autos sacramentalès*.

And so we have the third Calderon transcending the first two. The priest is still a nobleman and a dramatic author. He dies in the odour of sanctity, grave though not austere, courteous and charitable, adored by king

THE GENESIS OF TRAGEDY

and people, and is interred in his royal tomb with the red cross of Santiago embroidered on his breast, as a knight of letters, a prince of poetry. No wonder that he receives funeral wreaths from Milan, Rome and Naples, that Madrid laments him as her greatest poet and honours him with regal obsequies.

The whole of Spain marches past in the theatre of Calderon: valet and hero, bandit and alcade, nobleman and king, abigail, country girl and noble dame. All the pride and passion of the Spanish soul glows in these plays. We know that he wrote nearly a hundred tragedies and comedies; two of these sum up his entire philosophy: *The Physician of His Honour* and *Devotion to the Cross*.

The former, with its suggestive title, is also the drama of jealousy, wherein the Spaniard goes to the farthest limits of subtlety and violence. Calderon depicts jealousy in all its inquisitorial cruelty, though remaining mistress of itself even in the ferocity of its vengeance.

In the flower of his youth, the Infanta Don Enrico, brother of Pedro the king, makes the acquaintance of a maiden of rare beauty and of even greater qualities of soul, Dona Mencia de Acuna. Their first mutual glance kindles a passionate love. Dona Mencia, however, knowing that she cannot aspire to the rank of queen, considering herself too lowly to be a wife and too highly born to be a mistress, resists temptation. For several years she has contrived to erect a mountain of snow between herself and the prince. Finally, to make the barrier impassable and in obedience to her father's orders, she has married a nobleman of high lineage, Don

THE INITIATORY THEATRE

Guttiere Alfonso de Solis, without the Infanta knowing anything of it. Nothing further can be done to extinguish the dangerous spark of forbidden love. But destiny takes upon itself to kindle it anew and convert it into a devouring furnace.

Don Guttiere and Dona Mencia live to all appearance quite happy in a villa in the outskirts of Seville. He idolizes his wife; she does her best to return his love. As it happens, during a journey, Don Enrico's horse, galloping at full speed, falls to the ground at the door of the *quinta* where the married couple live retired. The Infanta is carried unconscious and severely injured into the young wife's dwelling where he awakes without knowing where he is. Dona Mencia and Don Enrico recognize each other. Their brief conversation thrills with emotion and restrained passion. When the lady tells him that she is married, the Infanta starts up from his couch, forgetting his wound. Don Guttiere, entering the room, offers the prince hospitality, with every mark of respect due to his rank. Don Enrico, however, sombre and perturbed, instantly takes his departure on a horse offered him by his host. Don Guttiere has neither seen nor heard anything equivocal; Dona Mencia's attitude has been perfectly dignified and haughtily correct. It suffices, however, that the suspicious hidalgo has seen together these two beings who love each other with a violent though virtuous passion, to arouse within his bosom the blackest thoughts, the most sinister projects.

The drama begins with this scene of violent—even tragic—calm. Soon we see the volcano seething beneath its mantle of ice.

THE GENESIS OF TRAGEDY

In the monologue of Mencia before the unconscious Infanta we glimpse the proud and tender soul of the heroine who is to be the victim of this love. 'Why cannot I, O heaven, without honour demurring, give myself up to the pleadings of my heart! Why cannot I cry aloud and break the prison of icy silence wherein lies buried the passionate fire which, now reduced to ashes, is no more than a ruin saying: Here was love!' All the power and force of expressed passion breathes in these words. How piercingly the heart's cry is heard in this silence! And now this school of silence becomes the crucible wherein the soul comes to a true knowledge of itself by stifling its passions beneath the might of the will. 'The soul,' says Dona Mencia, 'is its own touchstone, like the diamond. Gold comes out pure from the crucible, diamond is tested by diamond, and metals by fire; so is my honour tested by itself. Let me win my own victory over myself, for it is by trial that one reaches perfection. Pity me, O heaven, let me live silent since it is in silence that I die!' Enrico too, before leaving, says to Mencia: 'Troy is on fire. Aeneas of my senses, I will pluck them from the flames.' His will, however, is infirm and his resolve will not endure. Guttiere, the jealous husband, represents the egoism of honour; his delicate susceptibilities inculpate his wife's most secret thoughts. 'Love and honour,' he says, 'are passions of the soul; he who offends love in love thereby offends honour. The insult felt by the heart is felt also by the soul.'

The impassioned drama now being enacted between the crafty Guttiere and the noble-hearted Mencia is not that of a husband trying to take his wife in the very act

THE INITIATORY THEATRE

of adultery, but rather that of an inexorable inquisitor who is determined, at whatsoever cost, to violate the secret of a conscience. We need consider only the two main scenes of this mortal duel between fierce jealousy and innocent love. By intrigue, Don Enrico, in the husband's absence, and at night-time, finds his way into the garden where lies Dona Mencia, lulled to slumber by a melancholy romance sung by her waiting-maid. Without concealing her love, she beseeches him to leave. Of a sudden, voices are heard at the door of the villa: her husband has unexpectedly returned. Mencia succeeds in effecting the escape of the Infanta through a secret door, by skilfully extinguishing a torch. All the same, Guttiere finds a strange dagger in the room, the one which the Infanta had dropped in his flight. From this time onward, the husband is convinced that his wife either is or might be guilty. But he gives no sign, rather does he show more passionate tenderness than before. He contrives the most cunning of counter-tests; he too, in turn, steals at nightfall into the garden where his wife is in the habit of slumbering in languorous ease beneath a rose shrubbery. He approaches like a thief or a lover and, in low tones and disguised intonation, murmurs a few words of love in his sleeping wife's ear. Dona Mencia awakes in profound darkness and exclaims: 'What is this, your Highness, would you have me die a second time? Reflect that Guttiere may return at any moment. Quick, leave me, Highness, I beg of you!' Is not this single word, Highness, to the mind of the suspicious husband, an irrefutable proof of his wife's treachery? He departs, with death in his soul and vengeance gnawing at his heart, as though the

THE GENESIS OF TRAGEDY

lovers had spent the night together and he had seen them in each other's arms.

Here he is, then, immured for ever by this vision in the torture of jealousy and the hell of damnation. The wretched Don Guttiere has become a miserable spy prowling around two lovers on the point of attaining to supreme bliss. To crown everything, when hiding behind a curtain he has heard the Infanta say to his father Don Pedro the king who vainly reproves him: 'Love is omnipotent, successful in all things!' Himself in love, he understands how true the saying is. Thereupon his maddened fury breaks all restraints; sinister is the plot he contrives. He causes a terror-stricken surgeon to bleed Dona Mencia to death. By this means, he himself will not commit the crime, and no one will know anything. The death will be regarded as an accident. He shuts up his wife in his Seville house, and, before handing her over to her executioner, leaves on Dona Mencia's table the following note: 'Love adores thee but honour detests thee; this is why the one kills thee and the other warns thee. Thou hast but two hours to live; as thou art a Christian, save thy soul; thou canst not possibly save thy life.' This cruel drama is carried out on the sinister stage where the blood-stained body of Dona Mencia is seen stretched on the ground while the avenged husband proclaims the disquieting moral of the play: 'I am the physician of my own honour and I purpose to restore it to life by bleeding. It is blood that heals everything now-a-days.'

King Pedro, informed of this unexpected death, questions Don Guttiere, who attributes it to an accident. A lover of justice, he divines the real story but pretends

THE INITIATORY THEATRE

to believe the criminal whom at heart he excuses, merely commanding him to marry Leonor, a woman to whom he had formerly paid court though he abandoned her in favour of Dona Mencia. We on this side of the Pyrenees look upon this as a very slight expiation. Shakespeare, dealing with the same subject, would have had banditti of the Sierra to put Don Guttiere to death, obsessed by the spectre of a blood-stained wife. Calderon, however, had to conform to the inflexible code of honour of which his play is the haughty and sombre tragedy. Dona Mencia, the victim alike of conjugal fidelity and of her own repressed love, is one of the most moving figures on the stage. She unites ineffable tenderness with a silent courage which braves everything. Whereas, according to the legend, the house of Don Guttiere de Solis, in Seville, bears the impress of a blood-stained hand, from the marble tomb of Dona Mencia we imagine we see rising a dark cypress tree around which a rose bush is closely entwined.

. . . .

While *The Physician of his Honour* exalts Spanish pride in all its harsh hauteur, *Devotion to the Cross* equally magnifies the religious fanaticism of Spain. The following are the ultra-romantic facts upon which this play, the most original and striking of all Calderon's works, is built.

An old nobleman, Curio, in his youth wished to kill his wife whom he unjustly suspected of infidelity. He drags her to a cross-road in a lonely forest, where stands a great wooden cross. Just as Curcio is drawing his sword to perpetrate the crime, Rosmira seeks refuge at

THE GENESIS OF TRAGEDY

the foot of the cross and miraculously disappears. Returning home, Curcio finds his wife in bed, where she has been delivered of a female child who bears on her breast a miraculous sign, a cross of blood and fire woven into the very fibres of her flesh and leaving an indelible mark on the skin.—Now, before returning to the house, Rosmira had brought forth, in the self-same wood, another male child who was picked up by a shepherd, and whose breast also is marked with the same sign. These twins, Eusebio and Julia, brought up apart from each other and ignorant of their common origin and the strange relationship that existed between them, are the two heroes of the play. The sign of the cross mysteriously imprinted upon their flesh is, as it were, the stamp of Providence, whose invisible hand is to control their destiny.

In the first act we see Eusebio, the son of Curcio and Rosmira, adopted by another man and unknown by his true father. Eusebio has become enamoured of Julia. They love each other and are engaged to be married without knowing that they are brother and sister. Lisardo, Julia's lawful and officially recognized brother, challenges Eusebio to a duel and is killed. Eusebio, now the murderer of his fiancée's brother, is condemned to death and compelled to flee. Curcio, the girl's father, forces her to take the veil.

In the second act, Eusebio has become a robber chieftain of unbridled passions. The violence of his character is expressed in the sentence: 'I wish my crimes to be as infinite as my punishments.' After many adventures, he scales the walls of the convent and

THE INITIATORY THEATRE

reaches Julia's cell. In a scene of rare boldness and impetuous passion, he appeals to her in the name of their former love. At first she resists, but soon allows herself to be swayed by a feeling which has never left her. On the point of yielding to temptation, however, as Eusebio is tearing away the nun's scapulary he sees on her throbbing bosom the cross of blood and fire. The bandit seducer starts back; this sign is the only thing he respects, it is the finger of God. This cross is like the opening of a wound on the body of Christ, a mouth of blood and fire which exclaims: 'Back! Thou shalt not touch this woman. . . . She belongs to me!' . . . Terror-stricken, Eusebio hurries from the spot.

In Julia, the very opposite takes place. Passion, once unleashed in a woman's heart, knows no bounds. Up to the present, she has simply been a woman in love, resigned to an eternal sacrifice, wearing a penitent's hair-cloth. Now, she has quaffed the mortal poison in the breath of desire, in her lover's presence. No longer does she comprehend her destiny, for she has lost alike her God and her love. How can she still endure her captivity? Better become a demon. Leaving her prison by way of the ladder left by the cowardly fugitive, she exclaims: 'I trample under foot all respect for the world, for man and God, when I plunge into this mighty turbulent vortex. I am an evil angel hurled headlong from heaven, and, unwilling to repent, I lose all hope of returning!' Alone, groping in the dark, she is terrified and would like to regain her refuge, but peasants have removed the ladder. To what strange fate is she now condemned. Well, she will express the

THE GENESIS OF TRAGEDY

whole of her passion and mad resentment. She will be free, an adventuress, a bandit heroine. Disguised as a huntsman, sword by side, she will seek out Eusebio in his lair, affront him and challenge him to a duel. Driven to despair, she is no more than an arrow shot from a bow, a spent thunder-bolt.

In this violent and breathless drama, everything is carried to extremes right on to the dénouement. In the bandit's den, Eusebio defends himself with lion-like courage. Curcio, Julia's father who has been informed of his daughter's disappearance from the convent, tracks down the seducer with a company of hired men. Julia, disguised, masked and armed to the teeth like a real bandit, has also gone there, awaiting an opportunity either to kill her treacherous lover or to be killed by him. Then we have ambuscades and fights, marches and counter-marches, and surprise encounters. Finally they all meet at the fateful cross-ways, at the foot of the great wooden cross, where began this mysterious drama whose entangled and blood-imbrued threads are here to be unravelled. Curcio, who has mortally wounded the bandit chief without suspecting that he was his son, recognizes in him the twin brother of his daughter when he discovers the birthmark on his breast, the cross of blood and fire. Eusebio dies as a good Christian after confessing to a priest whose life he had once saved. To crown the wonder of this ending, Julia, the nun who has broken her vows and whose father wished to slay her in his indignation at her witchcraft, flings herself against the trunk of the great tree whose branches overshadow the gloomy spot. Distracted, she clings to the life-saving Cross. Immediately the unhappy and

THE INITIATORY THEATRE

guilty Julia disappears from sight.—A miracle! exclaims the priest.

It would be impossible to praise too highly the amazing dramatic skill, the wealth of imagination with which Calderon succeeded in representing this drama, which is more symbolical than real, though the onrush of passion and the imaginative eloquence prevent certain episodes from seeming too improbable. To understand the intended meaning, however, we must remember the solemn words uttered by Eusebio before he dies, when, exhausted by his wounds, and aware that the end is near, he says: 'Halt before the saving cross, that, though men inflict on me speedy death, it may give me life eternal. Tree whereon heaven would ripen the true fruit, healing balm for that which brought about man's fall, flower of the new paradise, arch of light whose message over a boundless sea proclaimed the peace of the world, planet worthy of adoration, fruit-bearing vine, harp of the new David, tabernacle of a second Moses, I am a sinner and implore thy favour in justice since God suffered on thy sacred wood only for the purpose of redeeming sinners. Thou owest me thy protection, for even though I had been the only one in the wide world, God would have died for me alone. For me, then, dost thou exist. O cross! Had I not been a sinful man, God would not have died upon thee. My natural devotion, holy cross, even entreated thee not to permit me to die unconfessed.'

Such is the controlling thought of this tragedy and of the entire theatre of Calderon: Grace without Effort, by absolute submission and passive obedience. It is the

THE GENESIS OF TRAGEDY

Cross as an external sign that performs all miracles, sets its mark on the twins, controls their destiny, directs or arrests the arrow or the bullet, and finally saves the world. It represents the Church, and sole guardian and dispenser of salvation. Let it be acknowledged that in all the external signs—and especially in all religious rites—there is great magic working upon human imagination, and sometimes occultly on things that lack sensibility; also that Jesus Christ is the greatest person in history and that no power, human or divine, attains to the mystery of Golgotha. On the other hand, it must be confessed that in the drama of Calderon, *the interior world of the soul* is almost totally neglected, that nothing there happens except from without and by an arbitrariness which is unexplained. A moment's repentance suffices to redeem a life of crime. In a word, *salvation by the cross* replaces *the development and evolution of the soul*.

This doctrine was that of the Church in Calderon's time; it remains so even now, with few exceptions.

Now, the esoteric reserves of Christianity, as contained in the Gospel of Saint John and in the Book of Revelation hold cosmic and psychic mysteries that are far more vast and profound than those taught by the modern Church. And the understanding of these mysteries is the only means of entering into this sphere of the Beyond. This very penetration is possible only by individual effort and freedom of intuition. Of this the Church is well aware, but she will not permit it because she wishes to be the sole custodian of the keys of Heaven and Hell. However it be, at the present time the world

THE INITIATORY THEATRE

is powerfully attracted by these problems and will sooner or later impose on science new methods of investigation, and on the Church an expansion of her symbols and rites—though this by no means implies an abandonment of faith but rather its fulfilment. The conquest of the Beyond will come about only by intensive cultivation of the interior life of the Soul combined with the development of the Intellect. These reforms will compel both poetry and the theatre to create a new aesthetic.

The merit of the drama of Calderon consists in the fact that it expresses, in all their power and intransigence, the discipline of the Roman Church and one of the most imposing phases of the human mind.

To give a complete idea of his genius, something should be said of his many and brilliant plays. Here we see, in kaleidoscopic flutter and clash, the whole of XVIII century Spanish society with its wealth of costumes and characters, its prepossessing abigails and its sly and crafty *graziosos*.—On the twelfth of June, 1639, under the reign of Philip IV, *Circe* was performed in the splendid royal park of *Buon-Retiro*. The stage was an island with its clump of trees and its grottoes in the middle of a pond. The scattered spectators moved about the island in barques bedecked with flags, reminding one of those amorous couples in Watteau's *Embarquement de Cythére* who indulge in gay delights and gallant fêtes. Just as Circe, issuing from her cave, appears half-naked in all her seductive beauty with her troop of nymphs, before Ulysses and his companions, the sky is suddenly blackened by a formidable storm, and a terrible hurricane sweeps over all these enchantments. In the twinkling of an eye the beautiful magician and her train, as well as the scattered barques with their spectators in streaming plumes and mantillas, disappear beneath a storm of dust and rain —a fitting image of life and a résumé of the Spanish play.

Calderon's tragedy gives one the impression of a magnificent catafalque erected in a sumptuous hall of the Escurial. Over against the black drapery stands a gigantic silver cross, shining with sinister brilliance and scattering horror and dread throughout the solitude of the deserted palace. It is the seal of the Inquisition on the grave of the absolute Power.

The Classical Theatre in France

By reason of its incomparable perfection, neo-classic tragedy held sway over Europe for two centuries. In spite of all our political and literary revolutions, it never lost its prestige, and one may truly say, with Jules Lemaître, that Racine is the diamond of French literature. It may be that the Celtic soul which, deep in the Gaul of the druids and in the Breton bards still projected its dream-like figures and flashes of its mysteries into the fancy-creating souls of troubadours and trouvères, is absent from an art dominated by reason and eloquence. The essential forces, however, that moulded the French soul—Christianity, Chivalry and the Renaissance—collaborated in the birth of tragedy. To crystallize it, all that was needed was the brilliant society of the seventeenth century and the intelligent

THE INITIATORY THEATRE

protection of the most fascinating and seductive of kings.

The beauties of tragedy in Corneille and Racine are so widely known and have been analyzed with such subtle skill by the most competent critics, from Sainte-Beuve to Jules Lemaître, and even by excellent poets like Auguste Dorchain, that it would be superfluous to dwell further upon them. We shall simply examine what distinguishes French from Greek tragedy, noting the gap which may have justified the search after a broader ideal, beyond the one so clearly conceived and so perfectly realized.

Bathed in the atmosphere of mythology, Greek tragedy is still saturated with the world of the Gods and with the symbolism and the psychic marvels which they represent. Not only do these Gods frequently appear in person—even in the plays of the sceptical Euripides—but the choruses, who constantly invoke them, testify to their invisible presence. In neo-classical tragedy we still have Gods—whether Pagan Gods or the God of the Christians—but these sovereign powers are relegated to some vague far-away region. They no longer enter into the plot but occupy some abstract place behind the scenes; and this gives them something that is conventional. They are replaced, so to speak, by the moral that dominates the tragedy. The drama which was once mystical has become purely psychological, the divine powers speaking only through the conscience and the reason of the heroes themselves.

The sense of the divine in human consciousness speaks with strong and loud voice in Corneille, a rough honest Norman. No one surpassed him in a sense of heroism. In his magnificent flights of imagination, he combines the religious fevour of the *Chanson de Roland* with the grandiloquent pride of Spanish chivalry. Love was no stranger to his life, though it was always controlled by reason; consequently, the perpetual theme of his tragedies is the triumph of duty over passion. In the *Cid*, the sentiment of honour proves superior to the most passionate love, alike in hero and heroine. In *Horace*, the fierce cult of patriotism stifles brotherly love. In *Cinna*, we see the cruel and ambitious Octavius transformed into the wise and generous emperor who pardons the ungrateful traitor and crushes him with the words:

Je suis maître de moi comme de l'univers.

Though the two metamorphoses of sovereign and conspirator somewhat astonish us by their abruptness, they are expressed in such noble terms that we fall under the charm and are ourselves converted. In *Polyeucte*, Corneille's masterpiece, it is religious feeling that overcomes love both in the man and in the woman. Polyeucte, a famous Armenian has been married only a fortnight to Pauline whom he loves passionately. But he has become secretly converted to Christianity by his friend, an old man named Néarque. Summoned by his faith to a public confession of the God of the Christians on the very day following his marriage, he does so unhesitatingly, thus repudiating the Pagan idols, condemning himself to certain death and renouncing a beloved wife. Pauline, in love with Sévère, crushed this love the moment she became the wife of Polyeucte whom she has married, in obedience to her father's orders. Another miracle; although Pauline has remained a Pagan, the sacrilege of Polyeucte against the Gods of his native land does not shock her. On the contrary, it arouses her sympathy for the condemned man. Finally, the execution of her husband converts her, as by a flash, to the God of the heroic martyr. This conversion is summed up in the well-known line of Pauline:

Je vois, je sais, je crois; je suis désabusée!

Here we reach the height of the sublime, but also the limit of the art of Corneille, and of French tragedy in general. Corneille rises at a bound to the threshold of the great mystery but he does not cross the door. Strictly confined to the visible world, wherein reason is sole mistress, he does not enter the sphere of pure feeling and clairvoyant intuition where reign other powers that inspire us at the great crises of life. To enable us to understand how the love-smitten Polyeucte became converted to Christianity, more than a sermon is needed. Again, the conversion of Pauline to the Christian faith presupposes an accumulation of feelings and sensations that is absent from the drama. Its spring lies in the mystic phenomenon, but the very phenomenon itself eludes the spectator. In a word, the neo-classical drama moves in the domain of surface effects or secondary causes, it cannot penetrate that of deep primary causes. Its emotion, moreover, gives us a potent sensation of their counter-effects in admirably progressive order, but it leaves behind in the heart a craving after the supreme springs of life and the soul.

In his marvellous plays, Racine penetrated deep into the world of passion whose surfaces Corneille did no more than touch. Everything pre-disposed Racine to so ardent an initiation: his ultra-sensitive temperament, his intimacy with the genius of Greece, and more especially with the court of Louis XIV, whose favourite poet he was. Beneath elegance of manner and refinement of wit, this society concealed the most violent passions and sometimes frightful crimes of black magic. Better than from any number of books, the author of *Bérénice*, of *Phèdre* and of *Britannicus* learned to know the variety of human types by cultivating the acquaintance of such persons as the great Condé, the parvenu Fouquet and Louis XIV himself. And what of the captivating charms of the ladies of Versailles? The graceful and tender figures of Henrietta of England, of La Valliére and of the haughty and formidable Montespan taught him more about the exquisite allurements and the tortuous profundities of the fair sex than did all the ancient and modern writers.

Although *Britannicus* is one of the most powerful historical tragedies known, and *Bajazet* one of the most striking political dramas, Woman and Love constitute the centre of the theatre of Racine. There is an invincible attraction in this subject as he meditates upon this great problem of life, this fiery centre where human destinies appear and disappear. His feminine creations are divided into two groups; on the one hand, sweet virgins and unhappy lovers like Andromaque, Aricie, Iphigénie, Monime, Julie; on the other, such Furies of passion as Hermione, Ariphile, Phèdre and Roxane. The one common element of the former, in the diversity of their delicate gradations, is the fugitive grace, the modesty and decorum that mask their

THE INITIATORY THEATRE

tender and profound feeling like a strip of slender gauze flung about ravishing forms. What distinguishes the others is the irresistible impetuosity of desire, the determination for absolute possession, the unbridled tyranny of one soul over another which along with overheated sense allurement, according to La Rochefoucault, constitutes the very foundation of amorous passion.

As Jules Lemaître has very rightly stated, there is nothing of the idealist about the *grandes amoureuses* of Racine. Treachery, rejected love or jealousy immediately inspire in them the most extreme violence, fury and madness, hatred and murder with their train of hideous monsters. Phèdre summarizes them in a synthetic figure of incisive beauty. True, Racine has Christianized the heroine of Euripides, who is simply a passive victim of Venus. He has made more attractive the great adulteress by parading her in all the terrors of remorse and attributing to her a pathetic confession in a tragic death-struggle. The dominant impression, however, left with us by 'the daughter of Minos and Pasiphaë' is that of the Pagan in her bold declaration of love to Hippolytus, instinct with all the insinuating and aggressive guile of woman.

It might be said that Racine, in *Bérénice*, his most touching masterpiece, wished to condense into one his two feminine types, the tender and the passionate, to blend them into something unique. In this drama, with its thrilling and sustained emotion, duty finally overcomes passion, as was the case with Corneille. But upon what painfully quivering lyre was this miracle brought about? When finally the three characters in

THE GENESIS OF TRAGEDY

rivalry of generosity, all sacrifice themselves to inevitable duty, one has the feeling that ephemeral love has now become the great eternal Love which, transcending the sphere of the senses, rises to the spiritual realm and creates its own immortality by the very might of its renunciation. Racine's verbal music, that *interior melody of verse* of which he possessed the secret, reached its highest expression in this exquisite tragedy. Here the melodious words attain to the enchanting power of music, and you come away from such a performance in true psychic harmony, as though you had been listening to a fine symphony. Both in substance and in form, *Bérénice* is a real drama of initiation.

It is well known that Racine, near the end of his life, abandoned the theatre and condemned his own works as immoral and dangerous. It may be that this unjust severity was due to excessive devotion and all kinds of personal disappointments. Still, one wonders whether Racine did not himself feel that which, from the standpoint of spiritual education, was lacking in his work, I mean the purifying power possessed by the dramas of antiquity. However it be, he attempted to write a purely religious tragedy in composing *Athalie*. His success may be doubted. Whatever famous critics may say, notwithstanding its impeccable structure and magnificence of language, this work gives one an ice-cold impression. The action is but a sort of lying in wait contrived by the high priest, and one wonders how Athalie, a cautious queen, allows herself to be caught in the snare.

Impitoyable Dieu, toi seul as tout conduit, she exclaims, on seeing herself surrounded by the drawn

THE INITIATORY THEATRE

swords of the Levites. This God is none other than Joad, the masterful and cunning pontiff. In this play, Jehovah finds expression through him alone, nowhere is one conscious of the speaking mystery, the presence of the Invisible. The choruses which aim at imitating those of old are purely conventional, and the prophecies of Joad, a string of Bible texts, produce no effect whatsoever. We are leagues and leagues away from Isaiah and Ezekiel.

This failure in religious tragedy in no way detracts from the great value of Racine's work as a whole. Summing up its resurrections and conquests, we have a return to the harmonious form of the theatre of antiquity with all its careful gradations, a rigorous distinction between the comic and the tragic *genre*, divers spheres of mind and spirit, a profound study of the passions in a precise condensed form. Illumination, power and rapidity; lack of mystery and of the Beyond. Racine's tragedies are full of lines expressive of the devastating might of passion at its height, such as the cry of Phèdre:

C'est Vénus tout entière à sa proie attachée or of crystal-clear words which depict the innocence of the immaculate soul:

Le ciel n'est pas plus pur que le fond de mon cœur. But we find nothing of those words which seem to have dropped from another sphere and shed light into the darkest places of the soul, such as the interjection of Macbeth after the murder of Duncan: 'Macbeth hath murdered sleep. . . . Macbeth shall sleep no more!' nothing of those phrases which appear to have a celestial origin, such as Juliet's entreaty to Romeo in the balcony scene: 'My bounty is as boundless as the sea, My love as deep, the more I give to thee, The more I have for both are infinite.' Spontaneous cries of an over-burdened heart; unforeseen flashes of light plunging us of a sudden into the immensity around us and into that we bear within ourselves. There is nothing similar in Racine or Corneille, where everything is clear-cut, in well-defined order.

Note had to be taken of this absence of mystery and the Beyond in the seventeenth century drama, because this gap was destined to induce the poets of the nineteenth century to seek a wider horizon, behind the majestic—though somewhat confined—portals of classic tragedy.

The Romantic Theatre in France

Ever since the Renaissance in the sixteenth century, the human mind has gone forth in search of the initiatory theatre. Like a deceptive 'fata morgana', the majestic image of ancient tragedy flickers before the modern imagination. A seductive phantom, fair mirage of the atmosphere, it flees to the horizon before the exploring vessel of Art. The theatre of Shakespeare, the *autos sacramentalès* of Calderon, the tragedy of Corneille and Racine are so many marvellous isles which the beautiful ship has touched one after the other. A new stage of this adventure is the romantic theatre, but before stating in what respects this theatre was alike a godsend and a disappointment, we must say a few words on the subject of romanticism in general.

THE INITIATORY THEATRE

Nowadays it is the fashion to decry romanticism. The acknowledged critics of the expiring nineteenth century and the undeceived positivists of our own generation have been equally severe against it. They assert that romanticism is responsible for over-nourishment of the self, the unrestrained worship of passion, social disorganization, disdain for moral laws, and consequently the widespread anarchy which threatens our civilization with a catastrophe compared with which the invasions of barbarians are no more than child's play. True, the excesses of romanticism have been worse than those of previous movements, but to make it responsible for all the vices of the age, to fail to see how powerful a leaven it introduced into human evolution, is to misjudge one of the most fruitful developments of history, though also one of the most complex and tempestuous. The suppression of romanticism would mean nothing less than the suppression of the very quintessence of art and literature; i.e., of all that is exquisite, profound and inexpressible in the word: poetry.

Had it done nothing more than restore the meaning of history by an understanding of the diversity of periods and local colour, it would, by that alone, have rendered invaluable service to Art. But it did a great deal else. For, behind this variegated façade of history, romanticism made two discoveries of vast import, which none suspected though all profited thereby. *It discovered the significance of the Infinite, i.e., of the Divine, in Nature and in Love.* And these two up-welling springs of inspiration poured into the world two streams of overflowing enthusiasm which have given

THE GENESIS OF TRAGEDY

renewed life to Poetry, Art and the human Soul. A like revolution could not take place without excesses and disturbances. Still, it was necessary, and its effects are incalculable.

The significance of the Divine in Nature! It had existed amongst the Greeks under the collective and anthropomorphized form of the Gods who symbolize its hidden forces. All the same, it had gradually disappeared behind the symbols which represented it. The petrified Gods had become idols and Christianity suppressed them. Through its prolonged contemplations, its studies and its dreams, romanticism regained the direct meaning of—and contact with—the Divine in Nature. As the Gods no longer came between man and nature, this all-pervading and penetrating Divine was limitless. *The Indefinite became the Infinite*; a painful and overwhelming impression. We find indications of this new meaning in Rousseau, Goethe, Chateaubriand, in their numerous emulators and countless successors. Their dreams before the many sights of nature are a blend of profound melancholy and cosmic voluptuousness. Here the Soul faintly guesses what there is in common between it and the Divine Infinite of Nature, though yet unable to unite therewith. Another wonder; this Nature, with its divers forms and fascinating voices, its woods and forests, earths, oceans and heavens, offers the soul a thousand instruments which will help it to harmonize its feelings and sensations, to compose the symphony of its passions which are now about to unfold with all the harmonious amplitude of the elements. . . . Nature and the Soul, finding themselves the one in the other, discover their common

THE INITIATORY THEATRE

divine essence and behold each other in their unfathomable infinitude.

The Infinite in Love! Another spectacle and another emotion. At the time of romanticism, Man and Woman who for thousands of years have been uniting, and who are perpetually giving renewed birth to mankind though knowing each other so little, begin to glimpse each other's nature. The Eternal-Masculine and the Eternal-Feminine, having become aware of themselves, find themselves face to face, like beings who meet for the first time. Their individualities having developed in contrary directions throughout the centuries, it seems as though they discover and oppose each other as strangers, almost as enemies. For all that, the invincible attraction of the sexes, the insatiable curiosity of the mind, and the profound nostalgia of the soul immured in its solitude and in the prison of the body draw the one resistlessly to the other. But what a difference between these two beings! He, with his creative desire and will for domination; She, with her sinuous and capricious passivity and her endless plastic potencies. So long as it was a question only of the love of the senses and of physical procreation, love could be nothing more than a fleeting disturbance and frenzy, followed by disappointment. The only issue was the Child, the rest being nothing but illusion, the skilful play of the Genius of the Species. Now that love of the soul had been added on to the other, an infinity of enigmas to be solved opened out before these two beings who wish to permeate each other in the rivalry of strife or in the fusion of a common action. Now it was a matter of the intellect. Above the Genius of the Species

THE GENESIS OF TRAGEDY

rose the Genius of Individuality, free and creative. And so we may assert that

> Chaque amour est un nouveau monde
> Qui n'avait jamais existé.

From discord between the Couple may spring the most awful catastrophes—from harmony between them, the most sublime creations.

Hence that variety of themes, that gamut of subtle feeling with which Love inspired nineteenth-century romance. In lyric poetry it was to cull its most savoury fruit. We need but consider *Le Lac* of Lamartine, *La Tristesse d'Olympio* of Victor Hugo, *Le Souvenir* of Alfred de Musset, *La Maison du Berger* of Alfred de Vigny, and *Les Femmes Damnées* of Baudelaire, to form an idea of the various keys and accents which Love assumes in our great lyrics. In all the gradations of these supremely emotional poems we find that craving after the Infinite which the Soul gives even more than does Nature, because the Soul comes from the inmost secret of God, and not simply from his expression as Nature.

This sentiment flashes forth in the poem of Alfred de Vigny, 'à Eva':

> Eva, qui donc es-tu? Sais-tu bien ta nature?

For, according to Vigny, God created Woman

> Pour entendre ce chant qui ne vient que de toi,
> L'enthousiasme pur dans une voix suave.

How have these new soul accents reacted on the

THE INITIATORY THEATRE

theatre? Here we touch upon the weakness of romanticism.

We must acknowledge that, notwithstanding its partial beauties and a few striking effects, the romantic theatre culminated only in brilliant failure. To express in drama the sense of the Divine and the Infinite revealed in Nature and the Soul, there would have been needed an organic philosophy capable of synthesizing these two worlds. It is this power of synthesis that was lacking in our romantics. This is particularly apparent in Victor Hugo, the leader of romanticism and its most remarkable dramatist.

Victor Hugo possessed one of the most stupendous imaginations, though it was of a quite special nature. In his *Art Romantique*, Baudelaire makes a striking remark on the personality of Hugo. The author of the *Fleurs du Mal* tells us that whenever he met Hugo walking about Paris or in the country, his eyes greedily devouring all the surrounding objects as though to drink in their very substance, the great poet gave him the impression of being 'contemplation on the march'. Hugo was indeed a mighty 'contemplator'. He possessed in the highest degree the memory of the outer world and the sense of the indwelling Divine, but he had to a far less degree the sense of the inner world, that of the Soul and the Invisible. His psychology halts at the surface of things; his inexhaustible wealth of imagery is not counterbalanced by a like profundity of feeling. Now, it is only by the interior world of the Soul and by the Archetypes of the Spirit that one can attain to a perfect comprehension and synthesis of things.

With an imagination enamoured of the excessive and

THE GENESIS OF TRAGEDY

the vast Victor Hugo must have been struck, on the one hand, by the chaotic substratum of nature, and on the other by the extreme frailty of the human soul. He became obsessed by this contrast, wherein the enigma of life was centred. To solve it, approximately at all events, there would have been needed two ideas which Hugo lacked: that of the Evolution of all beings, and that of the Hierarchy of spiritual powers who rule the world of matter, the key both to the interior world of the soul and to the invisible world. Not having this key, Hugo hypnotizes himself by contrasting the two extremes of Nature, the Ugly and the Beautiful, the Monstrous and the Divine, Evil and Good. The enigma which he cannot solve by a purely physical imagination becomes the obsession of his thought and the object of his poetry. He finally becomes enamoured of the Monstrous which he confuses with the Divine, forgetting the entire scale of values that separates them. This is the main theme of *Notre-Dame de Paris*, that grandiose vision of the Middle Ages in its outer aspect. The monster Quasimodo is enamoured of Esmeralda, the ravishly beautiful gipsy girl, while the priest, Claude Frollo, who has become an atheist and is devoured by a like passion, pines away in impotent longing. Neither monster nor priest can win the love of the woman, who after all is like a frail and fickle dragon-fly. The impossibility of attaining to the Divine in the world of the Soul led Hugo to the cult of the Monstrous. Hence his mania for deducing from the contrast between physical ugliness and moral beauty a forced and artificial pathos as in *Le Roi s'amuse*, where the wicked hunchback is supposed to be transfigured by an unbridled love for his daughter, or as in *Lucrèce Borgia*, where the vicious cynic finds redemption in maternal love. The *jeunes premièrs* of the theatre of Victor Hugo, Hernani, Didier, Ruy-Blas are all just parlour heroes, characters that lack verisimilitude. The *jeunes premières*, Doña Sol, Marion Delorme, Marie de Neubourg are passionate though monotonous *amoureuses*, automatic in their movements. Note that none of these women possess the character and the charm of the real *amantes* evoked by the great poets of the nineteenth century, such as Lucile, the sister of Chateaubriand, the Elvira of Lamartine, the Eva of Vigny. These figures are but exquisite silhouettes standing out from their poems and their souvenirs. But there are worlds in the eyes of each of them. Of these worlds, not a trace is to be found in the theatre of romanticism.

On the whole, in the theatre of Hugo there are admirable lyric pieces and a remarkable understanding of scenic effects. His psychology is always questionable. He has no profound knowledge of the soul, no philosophy of life. The true initiatory theatre is that in which the representation of human passions serves as an instrument for purifying and elevating the soul. The means has been taken for the end. Here we have no longer any other ideal than a deified passion. This takes the place of all else, of morality and philosophy, of religion and the life after death. It is a raging furnace upon which the litter and refuse of life is piled high, to blaze away in a magnificent conflagration. The more awful the catastrophe, the greater the rejoicing of the romantic dramatist. Love has become a phœnix burning upon its own funeral pile. It does not rise again

THE GENESIS OF TRAGEDY

from the flames, however, and leaves behind nothing but ashes.

The two great discoveries not yet exploited—the Divine in Nature and the Divine in Love—were destined to bear their fruit elsewhere.

THIRD EPOCH

THE THEATRE OF THE FUTURE—PSYCHE IN THE THREE WORLDS

Legendary and Philosophical Drama.—The Occult in Goethe and in Richard Wagner

ROMANTICISM, rich in fine discoveries though unaware of their full import, had made one that was destined to give a renewal of life to poetry and restore to the Theatre its transcendent mission. This extremely significant discovery, which our literary historians but little suspect, is the sense of the marvellous in popular legend and mythology.

The marvellous is ubiquitous, though it possesses a high and special savour in certain legends. The people —who live in close contact with nature—are in direct touch with its life-giving powers which cannot be perceived by physical sense and with which our modern scientists are no longer acquainted. Peasants and sailors, workers in fields and on mountains, have always, though intermittently, possessed a sort of inner vision, favoured by their instinctive dreamland kind of life. The spirits of the four elements—gnomes, undines, sylphs and salamanders—are not purely fiction, though folk-lore has made of them a poetic phantasmagoria. These fleeting visions correspond to the living forces of

THE GENESIS OF TRAGEDY

nature, just as demoniacal apparitions larvae and phantoms, ghosts and doubles correspond to real beings that frequent the lower planes of the invisible world which occult science calls the astral. In these popular traditions there is a considerable proportion of subjective imagination and capricious phantasy, though no less certain substrata of real and objective truth. The attraction which these stories exercises upon even the most sceptical is a proof of their importance. Herein they dimly sense the messages of an unknown zone of nature wherein lies hidden the key of the problem.

The Germany of bygone days—so different from present-day Germany—offered in its literature an inexhaustible store-house of the marvellous; such, for instance, as the Fairy Tales collected by the Grimm brothers. On the whole, the romantic Theatre regarded the marvellous simply as a diverting sort of utopia, a disorderly chimera. For the introduction of order and clarity there was needed the mighty genius of Goethe. The greatness and characteristic nature of this genius, unique of his kind, consisted in his being alike a poet, a scholar and a philosopher. The sense of the traditionally marvellous and of the deep symbolism of mythology was intensified in Goethe by his scientific understanding of nature, added to his natural history studies on the essence of light, on the metamorphoses of plants and animals.

At the beginning of his autobiography, *Dichtung und Wahrheit* (Fiction and Truth) Goethe took care that his horoscope should appear. His birth was at noon, with the Sun rising and Jupiter and Venus in

THE INITIATORY THEATRE

favourable aspect. Such men are born for victory and are predestined to great success. The beloved child of a delightful mother belonging to a patrician family of Frankfort, the favourite of a generous prince, this handsome, eloquent and charming poet would doubtless have been nothing more than a selfish *viveur* had not Providence endowed him with a great thirst for knowledge. This thirst was to be the pole-star of his life, the axis of the magnificent work which culminated in *Faust*.

Other German thinkers, such as Hegel, Fichte, Schelling, Schopenhauer have had a like intense desire to pierce down to the essence of things. In Goethe, however, this desire is coloured by two other passions, and so assumes more vivid tints. First of all, he is unable to conceive the True except through the Beautiful; then, in order to find it, he engages in a direct and synthetic contemplation of nature. One might indeed assert that, in a former incarnation, he had been a sculptor of ancient Greece, and even before that time, one of those pre-Socratic philosophers who sought to understand the rhythm of the universal Soul in Nature and in the metamorphoses of the four elements, such as Thales or Herakleitos. Nothing more suggestive from the standpoint of creative evolution—to borrow Bergson's happy expression—than Goethe's studies in natural history. His theory of colours, his ideas upon the metamorphoses of plants and animals, mark the great stages of earth life. One must be alike a great thinker and a great poet to give this definition of the rainbow and of the prism: 'Colours are the actions and the sufferings of Light. They reveal to us its nature, as

THE GENESIS OF TRAGEDY

a man's biography reveals to us his character.' This was the illumination and comprehension, by a stroke of genius, of that which inevitably eludes physics and chemistry, viz., *the spiritual side of Light*. At the same time, it was the discovery of the unity of the human Soul and of the Universe, of the microcosm and the macrocosm, a unity which is the vital centre of ancient revelations.

Such capacity for sympathy and intellectual vibration rendered Goethe capable of expressing, in dramatic form, the impetuous march of the human mind towards its new ideal, and of incarnating this ideal in a type destined to become a rival and a successor of the Prometheus of Aeschylos.

. . . .

Faust is the modern man, issuing from the dry-as-dust scholasticism of the Middle Ages, the man who has escaped from all schools and systems, who aspires after supreme truth through all the fulness of life. 'Where, boundless nature, shall I clutch at thee? Ye breasts, where are ye?' he asks in his introductory monologue, in his musty laboratory filled with retorts and skeletons, with its high and vaulted Gothic chamber. In abstract science he has found nothing but dust and words; now, he intends to plunge into all the torrents of life. To reach its mysterious heart, he has recourse to magic. Nothing could be more moving than his evocation of the Earth Spirit. At the summons of sovereign Desire, the Spirit majestically appears amid the flash of a red light in the alchemist's den and hurls at him the fiery words:

THE INITIATORY THEATRE

In the currents of Life, in Action's storm
      I wander and I wave,
      Everywhere I be!
      Birth and the grave,
      An infinite sea,
      A web ever growing
      A life ever glowing,
Thus at Time's whizzing loom I spin,
And weave the living vesture that God is mantled in!

The evocator thought he had risen to the stature of the Spirit evoked. At the dread vision, however, he steps back in horror and shrivels up like a worm. In vain does he stagger to his feet and exclaim: 'Sublime Spirit, how near akin I feel to thee, I am that Faust, I am thy peer!' Before disappearing, the Spirit dumbfounds him with these words: 'Thou'rt like the Spirit thou dost comprehend, But not like me!'

Unable to associate the Earth Spirit with his own life, Faust evokes the Devil. What is this Mephistopheles? He partakes of the Ahriman of Zoroaster, the master of the elements, the god of Matter. This is not Lucifer, for the fallen Archangel is the Earth Spirit. This is the Satan of the Middle Ages, without either claws or horns, though armed with the most incisive and cutting irony. The popular bogey has become the elegant knight who retains, from his infernal past, nothing but the club-foot hidden in his boot. He has a sword at his side, a black doublet, a red mantle, a fiery plume on his cap, and ever a cynical word on his tongue. He is the incarnation of modern Doubt, 'the spirit that evermore denies . . . the power that still produces Good while still devising Ill', in spite of itself. For Mephisto, apart from representing the factotum of pleasures and the inventor of all artifices, is the indispensable spur to human ambition, the scourge that prevents it from sinking into slumber and spurs it on to action. Mephisto will be Faust's inseparable companion, the one to supply his desires and execute his purposes. At the same time, there will be a deadly struggle between them.

In the popular legend, Doctor Faustus is but a vulgar rake who buys all the earthly pleasures which Satan promises him at the cost of his eternal salvation, and condemns himself to hell. In Goethe's poem, Faust agrees to sign with his blood the pact whereby he delivers up his soul to him for the next life, on condition the devil succeeds in filling up the cup of his desire in this one, and satisfying his soul enamoured of the Infinite. The whole grandeur of the Goethean conception lies in this wager. No longer are we confronted with a wretched libertine and a mean-spirited wizard. The vulgar free-liver of the legend, who has called up the Evil One only for the gratification of his base instincts and who, when being carried off by the devil, trembles and moans in supplication like a silly woman, is here replaced by the virile figure of a great spirit who seeks truth for its own sake and gives his Luciferian soul in pledge of its attainment.

The old Faustus has again become young. The unfrocked doctor has left behind in the laboratory his pedantic science and his weight of years. Thanks to his subtle and froward companion, he has become metamorphosed into a young soldier of fortune and has quaffed the witch's diabolical philtre, a brew of every kind of poison and lust. Faust, who would 'expand

THE INITIATORY THEATRE

his own self to the great human Self', wishes to penetrate more deeply into all things as well as to know the mysteries of evil. He is infallibly allured to commit a grave crime. It is by the touching and simple-minded Margaret that he is to know the greatness of love in its naïve form, unconscious of its greatness and so all the more affecting. Faust savours and contacts this love *intellectually*, whereas Margaret *lives and suffers it* in every fibre of her being, finally dying of it. 'He loves me!' says the innocent girl, picking off the petals from a star-flower, one after the other, before her delighted lover, and she adds: 'This is beyond me!' He now sees Deity in a new light and says: 'Then call it whatsoe'er thou wilt, Bliss! Heart! Love! God! Name for it have I none. Feeling is all in all; Name is but sound and smoke, Shrouding heaven's golden glow!' Faust then receives from Margaret the revelation of the divinity of infinite feeling which dominates contracted reason and of the boundless power of Love. In spite of this, Faust compasses the ruin of the unhappy girl when he allows himself to be led off to the witches' sabbath on Walpurgis Night just at the time when the poor child most needed her friend, after her brother's murder. Such neglect is a crime that merits life-long expiation. Goethe has condensed the horror of remorse in the poignant prison scene. Here we reach the height of suffering, of tenderness and affright. Impotent pity, the delirium of love and madness, extreme distress rend the heart. The spectator is even more moved by what is suggested than by what he sees. The depths of the human heart lie open, gaping and unfathomable. We appear to see, on the one hand, from the stage the whole

THE GENESIS OF TRAGEDY

of hell behind Mephisto and his pawing horses, and on the other the whole of heaven behind Margaret who exclaims: 'Save me! Ye angels! Ministers of light, Compass me round with your protecting might!' One can well understand that Faust, as he turns the lock of the iron door of the prison, says: 'The woe of all mankind possesses me. . . . Oh that I never had been born!'

. . . .

This first part is but the beginning of Faust's evolution. In the second, everything changes: scenery, dramatis personæ, horizon; we are transported to other spheres. The conditions of time and space are no longer the same. Having become more elastic, their scope has singularly widened. Indeed, the second part of this cosmic tragedy carries us out of the material world into that astral sphere where past and present blend to produce the future.

We seem indeed to be taking part in another life of the *ci-devant* doctor, when Faust, lulled by the singing of Ariel and the Sylphs, awakes amid Alpine scenery in front of a cataract which falls from the heights and reflects the sun through countless showers of spray. This sun, whose rising, according to the poet, is proclaimed by dazzling fanfares, is the sun of eternal Truth which cannot look into itself face to face, but may be contemplated through the prism of the universe, flashing with its countless beams.

The legend relates that Faust the magician called up the shade of Helen before a numerous throng of people at the request of Charles the Fifth. Goethe made this

THE INITIATORY THEATRE

motif the pivot of the second part of his poem. The conception is justified by the place this witching figure holds in Greek legend, and by the fascination it still exercises upon the modern mind. This is indeed that woman of most insinuating seductiveness of whom the old men, seated at the gates of Troy, said as they saw her pass: 'One understands why, to possess her, two peoples should engage in mortal combat.' The apple of discord between Europe and Asia and the idol of Greece, this Helen became to Goethe's Faust the unsatiable regret for lost Beauty, a regret and a nostalgia that have settled down upon the world ever since the Renaissance. To restore her, Faust risks all. By means of the phosphorescent key which Mephistopheles procures for him, the fearless investigator of the invisible world enters right into the Unfathomable where the Archetypes of things move silently round the 'Mothers'.

The summoning of Helen before the emperor's court partakes of the majesty of the theatre of antiquity as well as of a quite modern magic.

The hall of the imperial palace is full. The public await the performance in a thrill of impatience. Faust appears on the platform, dressed as a mage. He brings from the world of the Mothers an incandescent tripod, from which rises white and pink smoke. Clouds of incense cover the stage which represents the sanctuary of the temple of Aphrodite. Majestic music ascends from the columns of the Temple and of its triglyphs. All nature is vibrant and thrilling with song before this new parturition of Beauty. And we see Helen come forth, like a human flower, from these clouds of perfumes, beautiful as a goddess. She appears naked, radiantly smiling, on the surface of those caressing and music-laden waves. This and the following scenes are manifestly symbolical. After centuries of separation, Helen, the incarnation of Beauty, and Faust, the incarnation of modern Genius, have met. They are desperately in love, but, notwithstanding the storm of passion that has swept over them, they cannot completely understand each other. Still, the newly-married couple withdraw to an idyllic retreat in Arcadia where they live for a time in the intoxication of happiness in a grotto that possesses all the attractions of a palace. Helen has given birth to a marvellous son, beautiful as Apollo. Euphorion had no childhood. No sooner had he issued from his mother's womb than he stood upright, a proud eager youth. Offspring of the adventurous love of Faust and Helen, he is gifted with an unique power: an amazing elasticity. At a bound, he rises to incredible heights, and when he again touches the ground, he rebounds higher still. Now, Helen is attended by a chorus of Trojan captive women who, in this land of Fauns and Nymphs, have become changed into agile Maenads who dance graceful rounds. Euphorion, armed with a lyre which he has found among the rocks, springs into the midst of the company and, to the entrancing strains of a saraband, lures them away in spite of the angry rebukes of his parents. Then he would become possessed of the wildest and most impetuous of these young Bacchantes. The rebellious maid resists him. Whereupon, he carries her off to the heights, but in his embrace she immediately disappears into flame. This flame fills him with burning exaltation. At that moment, Euphorion, hearing the distant clash of arms, strikes

THE INITIATORY THEATRE

up an enthusiastic song of war and freedom, and dashes off from peak to peak. Soon however, out of breath and with his strength all spent—like another Ikaros—he falls dead at the feet of his terrified parents.*

Might not this audacious episode, fantastic as a dream, be an image of the premature union of the classic and the romantic genius?

Perfect love must produce a perfect creation. This was not the case with Faust and Helen. Their son was the offspring of a love too abrupt and incongruous. Conceived in a blending of mad passion with sublime intellectuality, Euphorion was capricious and violent. He could not live long and had to burn away like a torch in a storm. To the adventurous couple, his tragic end is an irreparable catastrophe: Helen has fulfilled her mission. Deprived of the fruit of her love, she must meet him again in the land of shades. With a cry of pain and grief sumptuous Helen melts like snow in the arms of her dismayed husband. She disappears, leaving in his hands nothing but her silken robe. Fleeting and ever-recurring metamorphoses of the astral! Will the lovers, snatched from one another's arms, meet again in another incarnation?—It may be so. Meanwhile Faust will keep as a precious treasure the robe that clothed those divine limbs, and will oft inhale its voluptuous and shroud-laden perfume. The memory of Beauty, now lost though once possessed, will guard him from all that is common and vulgar.

. . . .

* It is known that Goethe, in this daring phantasy, wished to recall the heroic death of Lord Byron at Missolonghi.

THE GENESIS OF TRAGEDY

On reaching the end of his life, Faust understands that man cannot quench his thirst for truth in individual existence. Science and love, art and politics, have been alike deceptive. Henceforth he will seek appeasement in energetic work, in feverish activity with and for his fellow-beings.

With the help of Mephisto, Faust has won a victory for the emperor who rewards him by giving him a stretch of seacoast with the neighbouring territory. Here, with oars, picks and spades, work a nation of sailors and pioneers, architects and excavators, engineers and labourers. They build innumerable dikes and canals, gradually holding back the encroaching waves. Thus they have snatched from the watery waste a new and verdant land, covered with plants and trees. Faust, who has bid farewell to all life's pleasures and illusions, now takes delight in the spectacle—his creation—which unfolds itself before his eyes. From the balcony of his palace, the old man looks down upon this earthly paradise, the fruit of his own will. There prospers an army of happy workers. Ships with streaming flags return to harbour from the four corners of the globe, laden with the wealth of distant continents. Songs and cries of joy are heard; festivities are in preparation. Surely here is the ultimate truth, the one sole happiness possible, a port to shelter one from every storm, a ground on which to build a refuge. To free oneself by freeing others; on an enfranchised land to create an enfranchised people. . . . In the enthusiasm of his hope and his activity, Faust exclaims: 'He alone merits life and freedom who is obliged to win them anew from day to day!'

THE INITIATORY THEATRE

Suddenly he thrills all over. The predestined hour strikes on the evening silence, echoing throughout the inmost fibres of his being. He feels that he has come to the last page of his life's story. The debt must now be paid. Heavy with the burden of years, Faust has already passed the allotted span. He feels himself a broken man, a cold chill freezes his bones. With tottering steps he advances into the royal garden. And now, once again he is in the grip of that formidable magic which he once used and ever since has wished to banish from his mind. The garden is alive with phantoms. A sinister old witch named Care approaches, and blinds him by breathing upon his eyes. Mephisto, disguised as a foreman overseer, exclaims in jeering irony: 'The great majority of men are blind all life long; only at the end, Faust, is this fate thine.' Behind approach the Lemures, shroud-garbed skeletons who with sinister precautions take his measurement before digging his grave. A black shade approaches afar off. It is Death. Faust, seeing it, gathers up his remaining strength, and affronts all these spectres with the words: 'Why cannot I say to this hour: "Stay, thou art too beautiful!" Centuries will not efface the mark of my days on earth. In the presentiment of such sublime happiness I at this moment taste joy supreme!' whereupon he falls lifeless to the ground and the Lemures seize upon his body to bury it.

In his pact with Mephisto, Faust had promised him his soul when the devil should succeed in satisfying his desire and Faust declare himself to be happy. By the letter of the contract, the soul of the seeker after truth should then belong to the perfidious tempter. As things

THE GENESIS OF TRAGEDY

happen, however, the contrary takes place; in reality, it is not Mephisto who has satisfied Faust with a frivolous pleasure; rather is it Faust who has found satisfaction in a divine joy. He has found supreme bliss in the accomplishment of his task. This is nothing personal, since it has for its object thousands of other souls. Consequently he has greatly transcended the physical and the lower astral planes with their passion-darkened emanations and has already won his heaven world in a free forward effort.

And so Mephisto's deception is on a par with his cunning. In vain has he summoned to his aid all the demons of Hell to seize Faust's soul which is about to rise from his corpse as does the butterfly from the chrysalis. A shower of roses scattered by a group of angels removes the infernal spirits and carries off to higher realms the immortal essence of Faust. In these lofty regions, noble anchorites sit enthroned in forest and grotto sheltered by celestial peaks. The ascension takes place to the accompaniment of mystic choruses admirably composed by Schumann. Even apart from the music, the reading of the words is inspiringly beautiful. Their majestic soothing rhythm gives one the feeling of an expansion of soul as the light increases. We ascend higher and higher, hovering about in flight from the cell of the *Pater Profondus* to that of the *Pater Seraphicus* on to that of the *Pater Marianus*, near the highest peak. Above, appears the sublime figure of the Virgin-Mother, the *Mater Gloriosa*. At her feet, like a silvery cloud, stands a group of humble penitents, one of them being the gentle Margaret. She it is who will henceforth be appointed to instruct and guide the newcomer in the

THE INITIATORY THEATRE

heavenly spheres: She and not Helen, for Helen is only physical Beauty, whereas Margaret is the Beauty of the Soul purified by sacrifice and divine Love. To her prayer the *Mater Gloriosa* responds in the encouraging words: 'Come! Rise to higher spheres. If he feels thee near him, he will follow thee.' And the invisible Chorus strikes up the mystic incantation to the Queen of Heaven:

> All of mere transient date
> As symbol showeth;
> Here the inadequate
> To fulness groweth;
> Here the ineffable
> Wrought us in love;
> The ever-womanly
> Draws us above.

Though one part of Goethe's *Faust* may be too audacious to be performed on the stage, its world-wide popularity is a striking proof of the return of the modern soul to the mystical and transcendent drama. We should have to go back to the glorious days of Athens and of the Mysteries of Eleusis to find so magnificent a conception. In the whole history of the theatre it is the most grandiose attempt to blend Hellenism with Christianity.

Ever since the Renaissance, the Theatre had strictly confined itself to the things of earth. *Faust* is an expression of the passionate desire to include also the astral and the divine worlds.

. . . .

THE GENESIS OF TRAGEDY

The Occult in the Life and Work of Wagner

In the poetical effervescence of the nineteenth century, no work expressed so brilliantly as did Goethe's *Faust* the aspirations of the modern man towards a new ideal, where Hellenic naturalism and Christian spiritualism blended in one ardent life, one clear translucent beauty. The vast scope and import of this work was apparent in its European success. It was like a wide breach that had been made in the sombre rampart which materialistic Science and a dogmatic Church have raised around the human mind. Through this luminous outlet of the legendary drama, contemporary man, bound down to brute matter by his machines and confined in arid theological forms, escaped as in days long past into the world of the *marvellous*, where the soul can freely expand and feel its wings grow anew.

By the word marvellous, I mean the occult of both visible and invisible nature, to wit, the ascending powers of the astral and spiritual worlds. An army of commentators, poets and philosophers poured out through this breach into the open spaces, wherein the mind that has no guide or compass is too easily led astray, though a boundless field lies open to the intuition and the imagination.

One of these men, a creator and innovator of the highest order was destined to make extraordinary discoveries even more surprising than those of Goethe. This man was a poet, a musician and a dramatist. In concentrating these three powers upon the theatre, Richard Wagner is perhaps the most perfect and amazing artist that ever lived. After the opposition which it at first

THE INITIATORY THEATRE

encountered, his work has had a triumphant vogue throughout the world. In spite of the new and remarkable attempts made since his day, he has remained king of the idealist theatre. The violent antipathy which he still arouses in a few who are hopelessly behind the times, has but increased the volcanic enthusiasm for his music felt by artistic natures. And yet, in spite of his worldwide success and the glowing pages written about him, especially the two studies by Baudelaire and Nietzsche and the recent book of Louis Barthou,* the enigma of his mission has not yet been solved. There is such a gulf between this work and the time at which it appeared, and there is also such a contrast between the character of the man and his genius, that one wonders, in a sort of anguish, what is the meaning of this destiny, the import of his work.†

In attempting to solve the puzzle, perhaps I may be permitted to advance an hypothesis.

By physical descent, Wagner is a German of pure Saxon race; this is not so in the case of his spiritual descent. If we consider his genius throughout his life, it appears before us as one of the most striking models of the Scandinavian type, the main aspects being fierce energy and indomitable self-will. In his moral attitude —which from the beginning to the end of his career

---

* Baudelaire's volume on *L'Art romantique*; Nietzsche's study on Wagner at Bayreuth; *La Vie amoureuse de Wagner*, by Louis Barthou (Flammarion, 1925).

† I have dealt with this matter in *Richard Wagner, son œuvre et son idée*, but I now see that in this book I had not penetrated to the heart of the question. In the present work, I make an attempt to read its esoteric centre.

THE GENESIS OF TRAGEDY

was one of bold challenge to his age—he indeed resembles one of those sea kings of old Norway, those bold rovers who coasted along the Atlantic and the Mediterranean in their ships with red dragon-headed prows, which spread terror throughout Europe and intimidated Charlemagne himself. Such were the conquerors of Normandy and of the kingdom of the two Sicilies. Wagner really seems to have been the reincarnation of one of those ancient Vikings who, gazing upon the ocean from the peak of a high mountain, swept with a glance the distant spaces he was about to traverse. Passionate and unbounded was their pride. They looked upon themselves as demi-gods, descendants of Odin, the envoys of old Saga, of the great Seeress of the Gods, the Voluspa; the protégés of the Walküre, those warrior maidens of Odin who rode the clouds and gathered the souls of slain heroes on the battle field, to bear them away to Valhalla.

In the case of Wagner, the Viking ambition was transferred from the material world to the world of art. Nietzsche compares his nature to 'an insatiable demon, athirst for power and splendour, ready to overthrow the world and ravage the earth like a raging torrent. This demon, however, is dominated by a sublime genius, gentle and mild, who has sworn that he will never forsake his terrible companion.' This image is a veritable key to the psychology of Wagner and the understanding of his work. Be it added that Providence gave to this rebel soul for guide the Angel of Music, that powerful Genius of Light and Love who was to lead the mighty Daimon to the inmost secrets of the Divine.

THE INITIATORY THEATRE

In the following short sketch of Wagner's work, we shall fix our mind on the providential thought that governs it. We shall then see that this creative Luciferian soul was all the time controlled and guided by its celestial Double towards a mysterious end culminating in deliverance and redemption.

Speaking generally, poet and musician form but one in Wagner the artist. Did not he himself say: 'When I write my poem, I am already intoxicated with the musical perfume of my work.' Here the poet represents the creative male element; the musician, on the other hand, is the female element, the plastic receptive force. The types invented by the poet: Tannhaüser, the lover of Venus and of a saint; Lohengrin, the initiate from a higher world; Tristan and Isolde, the inseparable lovers, united by the philtre of love and death; Wotan, the God in quest of man; Siegfried, the simple-minded and spontaneous hero; Parcifal, the champion of the Holy Grail; Kundry, the woman with two alternate souls and lives, the sinning lover of Christ throughout her many incarnations—these are doubtless figures that existed vaguely in legend and mythology, but it was Wagner who gave them new life, and whose genius made of them immortal types. Thus he introduced into the nineteenth century and the centuries to follow, that element of grandiose poetry which they lacked.

Let us now see how he became aware of his own mission.

At twenty-six years of age, Wagner was conductor of the orchestra at Riga. Even then he had a premonition of his powers. Devoured by ambition and disgusted with his narrow environment, he determined to seek his fortune in Paris and embarked upon a merchantman sailing for London. A violent squall drove the ship on to the coast of Norway, compelling it to seek refuge in a small harbour. What distant echoes, what marvellous memories did this stormy crossing, the shouts of the sailors mingling with the howling tempest and that fantastic entrance into the Norwegian fiord, arouse in the turbulent soul of the traveller? It may be that even then he had a faint glimmering that this Scandinavian land was that of his Gods of long ago. In a lightning flash, he had seen rising above the heaving billows his own Daimon. The sailors had told him the legend of *The Flying Dutchman*. This ill-fated captain seemed to be the image of his own destiny. Listen to the Dutchman's monologue at the beginning of the opera which Wagner composed, two years later, on this very legend: 'The term is past, and once again behind me lie seven long years. The weary sea throws me once more on land. Ha! Ocean proud and strong! A little while and thou again shalt bear me! Thou e'er art changing, but endless is my pain! The grace that on the land I seek for, never shall I find it! True, thou sullen ocean, am I to thee, until thy last broad billow shall roll, and thou thyself be swallowed up.'

But simultaneously with the vision of his fateful Daimon, Wagner had the vision of his saving Genius on that memorable night when he was almost shipwrecked. This Genius shone before his eyes, like the dazzling star which shines through the stormy opening of *The Flying Dutchman*, and whose consoling beams point out the harbour of refuge to the hapless wanderer. At the end of his age-long torture, because of the sacri-

THE INITIATORY THEATRE

fice of a loving and beloved woman, he is to find redemptive Woman, the Woman of the future!

This Senta, who appears in the second act, is no less novel and impressive a creation than the ill-fated Dutchman. The simple daughter of the people, seated in the ancestral armchair amid a roomful of spinning maidens, her eyes fixed upon the portrait of the legendary Dutchman, has attained to Seership along the path of love and compassion. In her broods the entire visionary power of the human soul directed upon the vast empire of the Beyond. This power shows itself when Senta, at the request of her companions, breaks into the famous ballad:

> Yo ho ho! Yo ho ho! Ho ho ho! Yo ho!
> Saw ye the ship that rides the storm,
> Blood red the sails and black the mast?
> Upon the deck a ghostly form
> By day and night defies the blast.
> Hui! The whistling wind! Yo ho ho! Yo ho he!
> Hui! The whistling wind! Yo ho he ho!
> Hui! Like an arrow he flies,
> Without aim, without end, without rest!

After this strophe, reminding one of the shreds of a tempest-torn sail, the singer suddenly stops, and then begins a song telling of sweet and angelic assurance:

> Yet may the spectral seaman be saved,
> Find he a maiden faithful to death, an angel supernal.
> Ah when, poor seaman, this maid wilt thou find her?

After murmuring these words in trembling accents, Senta falls back exhausted into her armchair. But when

THE GENESIS OF TRAGEDY

her pitying companions take up the refrain: 'Ah when, poor seaman, this maid wilt thou find her?' Senta springs to her feet and in a sudden transport of enthusiastic rapture, exclaims:

> 'Mine be the glory by my love to save thee!
> O may God's angel hither speed thee,
> My love to grace again shall lead thee.'

In this scene a psychic miracle is effected by the violence of desire and its power of magnetic attraction. One is conscious that the predestined mariner is at hand. The door is about to open; soon he will enter. At a bound, the space that separates the past from the present, the dream from the reality, the invisible from the visible, has been crossed. The roomful of spinning girls and the crowd of listeners are alike aware of a spiritual presence.

Thus, from the very beginning of his operatic work, Wagner came into the occult—never to leave it. The whole of his work, instinct with life, unfolds in the material world, though at the same time it is permeated throughout by the inflow of the spiritual powers governing it,—powers which his music expresses with a force never previously known. So that while other musicians place us in rapport with the various powers of nature and the soul, Wagner alone brings us into communion with the universe, because this master magician alone holds equal sway over the three worlds of Nature, Soul and Spirit; in other terms, over the terrestrial, the astral, and the divine worlds.

Let us take a brief survey of the combat between the Daimon and the Angel which develops in constant

THE INITIATORY THEATRE

progression on to the ultimate victory of the latter over the former.

. . . .

After two years of cruel disillusionment—though fruitful experience—in Paris, Wagner returned to Germany. A popular chronicle on the legend of *Tannhäuser* supplied him with a subject wherein the two opposing forces of his nature met with free and unchecked expression.

Here we find, though in another form, the Daimon and the Angel mentioned in dealing with *The Flying Dutchman*: the great *leit-motiv* of Wagner's life and work. The rôle of the Daimon is played by the pagan goddess, the Germanic Holda of antiquity, popularly mistaken for the Greek goddess, and who, as the legend goes, dwells in the deep caverns of the Venusberg with her cortège of Fauns and Bacchantes, Nymphs and Sirens, alluring Christian knights to the mountain of perdition. The Angel is represented by Princess Elisabeth, daughter of the margrave of the Wartburg. Her exquisite nature blends the passion of a virgin with the heroism of a saint. The culminating scene of their struggle is the singing contest in the second act. It is worthy of note that this dramatic stage representation of the mediaeval 'courts of love' is the only one that has met with success in the theatre. Though his rivals all sang to depreciate the love of the senses and in favour of the chaste love of the soul, Tannhäuser himself boldly chants the praise of that love without reserve which demands complete possession of the beloved. Without the slightest prudery, Elisabeth, the arbiter of the

THE GENESIS OF TRAGEDY

contest, gives the singer a nod of approval. The noble princess, who loves Tannhäuser with entire candour though unrestrainedly, also regards true love as that which gives itself in its entirety. Now, by a fateful concatenation of memories and thoughts, the voluptuous images and delights of the Venusberg crowd upon Tannhäuser's soul as the contest increases in animation. Throughout the impassioned singing of the poet may be heard in the orchestra the soft murmurings and the degrading accents expressive of the grotto of Venus along with the alluring appeals of sirens and bacchantes, until his frenzy is unleashed in a tempest of desire and the poet breaks into a hymn to the pagan goddess:

> Ever I'll sing thy beauty sweet and tender,
> In accents bold to thee I'll ever sing!
> Thy gracious charm is source of all earth's splendour,
> And all its fairest marvels from thee spring!
> Oh blest is he who in thy arms unfolded
> Has learnt what love is, heard thy tender sigh!
> Poor mortals who that love have never tasted,
> Away! Swift to the hill of Venus fly!

All present spring to their feet, with a cry of horror and indignation. The women depart, with fans raised to their faces, though not without casting a stolen glance of envy and longing upon the audacious singer, who is straightaway surrounded by a group of lords ready to fall upon the blasphemer with drawn swords. Tannhäuser, in the rapture of his pagan ecstasy, stands erect in an attitude of defiance. Thus does the curse of Venus assert itself on the desertion of her lover and his promise ever to sing her praise.

THE INITIATORY THEATRE

Here we reach the climax of the interior drama externalized by the playwright, and here Wagner exhibits all Elisabeth's greatness of soul. With queenly gesture she flings herself between the drawn swords and her faithless lover, as she utters the words:

Stand back! From death with him I do not shrink!
What is the wound your souls can deal me, match'd
With the deadly wound that he hath given my heart?
    At me, a maiden young and tender,
    He dealt one swift and cruel stroke.
    I who did love him, oh! so deeply,
    Exultantly my heart he broke.
I plead for him, oh spare him, I implore you.
Let him repent him of his sinful pride.
Let him again, this heart with new faith burning,
Know that for him too our Redeemer died!

And Tannhäuser, brought back to the reality of things by this sublime voice, sinks from his Venusian ecstasy into a state of terrible remorse and deep prostration. All that now remains for him is to undertake a pilgrimage to Rome to obtain pardon at the hands of the Pope.

Such psychology is neither classic nor romantic, in both of which, suicide or insanity were *de rigueur* after a like catastrophe. Elisabeth is aware that the one she loves is lost to her: he is branded and condemned alike by social convention and by ecclesiastical law. Her own happiness is crushed and her life broken; nevertheless, she does not yield to passive resignation. She is determined to restore to the guilty Tannhäuser, who is still her heart's beloved, *the courage of faith* through

THE GENESIS OF TRAGEDY

her power of loving. This is the object of the third act.

On a sad autumn evening, as the leaves are falling, we once more find ourselves in the smiling valley of the Wartburg, beneath the rays of a setting sun which seems the kiss of a last farewell. This valley, once resounding with lively fanfares and preparations for the hunt, is now silent as the tomb. On the wayside, near the statue of a madonna, Elisabeth watches the pilgrims as they pass, on their return from Rome: she seeks Tannhäuser, to discover if he has found pardon. In vain, he is not there. When the last pilgrim has passed, Elisabeth sinks to the ground. Her prayer reveals the final convulsive aspirations of a soul offering itself as a sacrifice for the loved one. During this supremely pathetic prayer, the passion-rent woman, once ready to expand and give herself in all the fulness of life, now lies there in mortal anguish; she has wrapped a hair-cloth over her heart and is enveloped in a shroud of death. When she rises and returns to the castle, after waving farewell to Wolfram who watches her from a distance, we receive the impression of a saint ascending her calvary to die the death of the cross.

A sinister twilight has fallen upon the valley. A man with tottering steps and torn garments approaches Wolfram. It is Tannhäuser returning from Rome. Notwithstanding all his mortifications, he has not been able to obtain his pardon from the Pope. The story of his pilgrimage to the Eternal City and of the condemnation pronounced upon him because he has guiltily shared in the infernal joys of the Venusberg, forms a drama within the drama and one of the most touching episodes

THE INITIATORY THEATRE

the theatre has ever produced. Without the music it is impossible to express the reprobate's despair amid the joy and gladness of the sinners who have found grace, his cries of impotent rage and his sardonic laughter ended by the shattering blow of eternal condemnation which falls upon the wretched man. Not from dread of hell but to spare 'the tears of his angel' had the pilgrim wished for pardon. Ruined in body and soul, he will not expose his infamy before his Beloved. He has now but one desire: to return to the cave of Venus—not for enjoyment, but for self-forgetfulness. . . . And now in the night we hear the calls of the Sirens. The mountain of perdition opens once again; in rosy mist the Bacchantes dance around; the goddess herself appears in a phosphorescent light and her gentle voice throbs with desire. . . . Tannhäuser endeavours to free himself from the grasp of Wolfram who tries to hold him back. With a violent effort, he is about to fling himself into the outstretched arms of the eternal Enchantress—when Wolfram utters the name of Elisabeth. The effect upon Tannhäuser is that of a magic charm—and Venus disappears with the words: 'Woe! I have lost him!'

Pale dawn appears and the frosty morn beholds a cortège of pilgrims carrying on a stretcher the body of Elisabeth found dead by the roadside. On seeing it, Tannhäuser falls prostrate in death. The impression is given that the soul of Tannhäuser has been saved by the intercession of Elisabeth whose martyrdom has won for her the sainthood. Two sacrifices have been effected and interblended, as it were: that of the woman who has loved unto death and that of the guilty Tannhäuser purified by divine love. When the strains of the

THE GENESIS OF TRAGEDY

Pilgrims' March, again taking up the first *motif* of the overture, are heard above the bodies of the lovers, the two worlds meet in one. The stream of a transfigured pagan joy mingles with the stream of Christian grace. Both combined compose a foam-clad ocean, with billows welling up before the rising sun of Truth, which proclaims the victory of Spirit over Matter.

The dramas of Wagner are formidable epitomes of life. In them, the dream of the Soul finds its fulfilment.

.   .   .   .

The transition from *Tannhäuser* to *Lohengrin* marks in the life of Wagner a radical transformation, the central stage of his evolution. Having become Kapellmeister at Dresden and being momentarily freed from material cares and at the very height of his genius, he could now retire into the inmost recesses of his thought and freely pursue his ideals. He himself has confessed in his *Communication to my Friends* (Mit-teilung an meine Freunde), that when he wrote *Tannhäuser*, he had liberated himself from the grosser elements of his nature and risen to higher spheres. He was conscious of a marvellous expansion of his being: almost that of one suddenly transported from a burning plain to the topmost peaks of the Alps, where one sees only snowy peaks piercing the azure sky, one's lungs meanwhile breathing in the purest ether. Far from human society and separated from the outer world by an invisible though impenetrable barrier, Wagner felt himself in close touch with the soul of the universe. It was in this lofty spiritual realm, this rarefied luminous atmosphere that he conceived and worked out his *Lohengrin*.

THE INITIATORY THEATRE

This mental condition must have been akin to mystical ecstasy for him to have said, when recalling it after an interval of thirty years: 'No sooner was *Tannhäuser* completed than I journeyed to Bohemia. I was then in such exaltation of spirit that I was able to conceive *Lohengrin* and *The Meistersinger* simultaneously. At that moment, a mother gave birth to my guardian angel.' The event to which Wagner here alludes is the birth of Ludwig II, King of Bavaria, born at that very time (October, 1845), and who, eighteen years afterwards, was to make it materially possible for the artist to produce his works, in accordance with his own ideas, on the stage of Bayreuth. By mentioning this curious coincidence, the reformer of the modern theatre appears to imagine that the birth of his protector was the answer of Providence to the intensity of his own enthusiasm, to the call and summons of his Genius.

Is this equivalent to saying that Wagner was a believing mystic like the monk Tauler, the cobbler Jacob Boehme, the Rosicrucian Angelus Silesius? By no means, though there is one striking peculiarity about his case. In him there was a clear line of demarcation between the thinker and the artist, between the everyday man and the inspired poet. In the realm of speculative thought, he asserted himself to be a sturdy disciple of the pessimistic Schopenhauer, who believed neither in God nor in the immortality of the soul. If conversation drifted to this subject, Wagner made no mystery of his opinions, confessing his incredulity with his wonted frank impetuosity. No sooner, however, did the poet-musician come into action than he proclaimed the faith of transcendental spiritualism, of a sublime Seer. Then

THE GENESIS OF TRAGEDY

it was that his true nature asserted itself. In his writings, this super-consciousness is found here and there, showing itself in familiar discourse by involuntary flashes, such as that in which he speaks of the coincidence between the conception of *Lohengrin* and the birth of Ludwig II.

I insist on this striking dualism and on this contradiction in Wagner's personality because it is indispensable to the full understanding of his genius and casts a flood of light upon his work as a whole.

Most of the traditions—whether ancient or modern, Oriental or Occidental—that relate to occult initiation, speak of a disturbing and dangerous phenomenon which befalls the initiate at a given moment: the momentary disassociation of sensibility, intellect and will. Normally, these are inseparable, but at this particular moment they become disjoined and act separately. While this phase lasts, the initiate obtains, either in the dream or in the waking state, the vision of his INFERIOR DOUBLE which summarizes and personifies his former incarnations and is frequently of a repulsive and terrible character. This vision is called the GUARDIAN OF THE THRESHOLD because it guards the portal of the Beyond which cannot be passed until this guardian has been encountered and overcome. Exceptionally however, this sort of vision comes about apart from any traditional initiation, by a spontaneous release of interior clairvoyance. In the great man—especially the great poet or artist—the Guardian of the Threshold is always an imaginative phenomenon of profound significance.

Now, the INFERIOR DOUBLE appeared to Wagner under

the form of *Tannhäuser*. In writing this glowing drama of sensual passion, the poet-musician overcame the Guardian of the Threshold and entered through the open door of the mystery into the splendours of a new world. Then there appeared before him his SUPERIOR DOUBLE, the Archangel of genius, who clears the path to divine secrets. To the artist he showed himself under the resplendent form of *Lohengrin*.

The Flemish legend on which this masterpiece is based is that of the Swan Knight. A princess, falsely accused of the murder of her brother, is defended by a mysterious knight who has come from over the seas on a barque drawn by a swan. After slaying her traducer in single combat, he marries the young princess but forbids her to ask him either for his name or for his origin. She promises, but after a short time, impelled by curiosity, she asks the fateful question. Immediately the knight returns in his miraculous barque, never to come back. Of this legendary tale Wagner made a drama which might well have for its title: The Mission of the Initiate or the Conflict between Doubt and Faith.

Symbolically, this drama, which possesses all the movement and colour of an historical event, but which is also of an initiatory character, expresses the call of the Soul to its unknown saviour and the triumphant arrival of the heavenly messenger. The oppressive anguish of expectant waiting is followed by the delirium of rapturous joy. In the second act, we see the full power of Evil about to envelop with its poisonous breath and darksome pinions the dreamy timid soul of the feeble Elsa. This power is concentrated in Ortrude, the black

THE GENESIS OF TRAGEDY

magician of Envy and Hatred. Here, the tortuous *motif*, generally confined to the double-basses, calls forth the image of a monstrous serpent crawling about in the lowest depths of the soul and preparing to inject into its victim the deadly venom of doubt. And when in the Third Act, the work of evil is being done, when, on that thrilling bridal night when the still virgin bride, maddened by a thousand sinister fears, asks her mysterious spouse the forbidden question—we witness the lack of Faith in Elsa's soul, full of the sweetest tenderness though too lacking in intuitive belief, too feeble to withstand the doubts that beset her.

The final scene when Lohengrin, in the presence of the king, the armed vassals and the assembled people, reveals his true nature and his divine mission, is of superhuman beauty. It possesses the majesty of a sublime revelation. Elsa's mistrust and the question she asks, force him to give her satisfaction. This he does in the full light of day and before all the people. But at the same time the law of his order compels him to leave his wife and withdraw from the world after proclaiming his name and origin. Consequently, the public proof of his greatness condemns him to a heart-rending farewell. I know nothing more solemn or imposing than his declaration, standing in the centre of the vast circle shining with lances and shields:

> On distant shores which you will visit never,
> Rises Mount Monsalvat as on a throne,
> There stands a temple which is bright for ever;
> So glorious nought on earth was ever known!

. . . .

THE INITIATORY THEATRE

Now hear, the chosen one suspicion scorneth;
Sent hither by the Holy Grail I came!
Its knight, my father its crown now adorneth,
Great Percival, and Lohengrin's my name.

Lohengrin has not explained the mystery of the Holy Grail, but his words and attitude express its creative radiance. The orchestra, which now resumes the *motif* of the prelude, splendidly sustains the entire narrative. There forms around the initiate a circle of flashing light, isolating him from all else and connecting him with his divine origin. The messenger of the Grail departs heart-broken, though leaving in the souls of men an ineffaceable trace of his sojourn on earth. The world will never forget that in him it has looked upon a radiant beam of the divine Word.

It is no ordinary moral that we learn from the drama of *Lohengrin*, rather is it a truly esoteric moral, dealing with the most intimate mystery of the life of the soul. This mystery may be formulated as follows: Faith is a direct intuition of Truth by Feeling, an impulse of the soul to which responds an influx of spiritual life. Faith is proved by its communicative vibratory power. No sooner does it insist on another proof, anything material whatsoever, than it ceases to be Faith and becomes Doubt. Whilst entire and complete, it is all-powerful; it transports mountains and creates its own object. The sound of its expression is as piercing and pure as that of a bell whose thrilling tones fill the surrounding spaces. At the slightest crack, however, it breaks and falls to pieces.

Thus did Wagner succeed in showing, through the

THE GENESIS OF TRAGEDY

medium of the drama, *the influx of spiritual powers into human life*, a sovereign and regenerating influx without which the Ideal would be but a vain word, Love a snare and the Divine an illusion.

.   .   .   .

While *Lohengrin* with lofty serenity glorifies the culminating point of spiritual life in the person of an initiate hero, *Tristan and Isolde* plunges us irresistibly into the ocean of passionate love. We shall find that here also Wagner shows himself transcendentally esoteric, for he reveals the fact that love has extraordinary and unexpected perspectives, totally unknown to literature and the theatre before his time. It is well known that this drama, incomparable in depth of emotion and power of expression, was the outcome of the poet-musician's love—reciprocated though unassuaged—for Mathilde Wesendonck, his great inspirer and protectress during his prolonged exile at Zurich. The Celtic romance is too well known to be related here: I wish simply to point out the esoteric import of this immortal work. After listening to a performance of Tristan, I once wrote to the author: 'You have done what no poet or musician has ever hitherto done; you have shown the genesis of love.' I might also have added: 'In addition, you have proved both poetically and musically the possibility of a complete fusion between man and woman through a mutual permeation of soul in the passion of love.' But how did Wagner perform this miracle of psychic alchemy? The answer to this question takes us into the depths of the subconscious.

THE INITIATORY THEATRE

In truth, this drama expresses in succession three modes of the life of the soul, corresponding to three very different spheres of its cosmic life. It functions therein without departing from everyday life.

At the beginning, we are in the material earth life, on the deck of a ship. Tristan is conducting to his uncle, King Mark, the King of Ireland's daughter whom he has won for him in victorious warfare. Isolde secretly loves Tristan whom she has healed of a serious wound when he was her country's enemy, and whose life she saved when she might have slain him. She is indignant with him for not having understood her love, for having asked her hand for King Mark instead of claiming it for himself. Tristan also loves Isolde but respectfully holds himself in check, from fidelity to his king. In the psychic struggle on which this first act is based, the love of Isolde assumes the mask of hatred and that of Tristan the mask of honour. Isolde, in furious exasperation, wishes to kill both herself and the man she loves and whom she regards as a traitor. She constrains him to drink, along with herself, the contents of an expiatory goblet into which she has ordered her attendant to pour a deadly poison. Without uttering a word, Tristan grasps her intention and accepts the death she offers him. At a draught he empties half the contents of the goblet, whereupon she snatches it from his hand and drinks the rest. Then a marvellous thing takes place: the servant has not poured into the goblet the philtre of death, but instead the philtre of love. Now, this is but a symbol. The mighty love hidden away in the depths of the heart and now so clearly shown in words and looks, these burning thrills which fill them with mingled

THE GENESIS OF TRAGEDY

delight and dread, are only the upwelling of the passion that has been lurking within them ever since they first met, and which now—at last—breaks through and submerges all the barriers of silence. Silently and heroically they have together braved death . . . and now they awake in another world, liberated, transfigured and rejuvenated, as though they had indeed crossed the dreaded portals of death. Here the orchestra shows itself supremely eloquent. The insinuating *motif* of the love philtre had at first appeared only as a faint magnetic influence during the poignant silence which follows the tragic chord of the death philtre. Now it rolls along in mighty billows, in a foaming sea of sound. We hear the nuptial song of passion raising to heaven its shouts of victory, its siren melody of infinite tenderness. There is nothing conventional in this stupendous duo. Already, the lovers form but one; their thoughts and voices—so long hostile—unite and blend in a wondrous transport:

> Bliss unforeseen;
> Unconceived of,
> So unknown!
> Joy overflowing;
> Lifted to heaven,
> Shouting for joy;
> Lost in high heaven,
> Forgotten the world!
> My Tristan!
> Isolde!
> Tristan!
> Isolde!
> Mine and thine!

THE INITIATORY THEATRE

> Thine only!
> Mine only!
> One are we two
> For ever and ever!

By their rash pact in defiance of all social conventions and obstacles, the lovers have really dedicated themselves to death, but they have made conquest of a new world: that of the soul. The nocturnal delights of the Second Act bring us into that 'Kingdom of Night' entered only by those who have been initiated into a mighty love. A torch is burning in front of the royal tent. In spite of Brangwaine's entreaties, Isolde extinguishes the torch in front of the threshold: the signal of meeting. The delirious encounter of the lovers can be compared only to two torrents dashing into an abyss and blending their waves in whirling pools until they finally expand in one vast calm which reflects the starry heavens. In this unique duo, where man and maid, sheltered by overhanging branches, finally sink upon a flowery bank in a dream of ecstasy, we completely forget that earthly love contains any element of bodily caress. In their frenzy, we see and feel—as they themselves see and feel—only the workings of the soul. To them, the glorious Night opening out its boundless splendours, is the only truth. It contrasts with the false deceptive light of Day, the world of empty appearance and illusion. In reality, this august world of Night, where Love, the origin and the end of all things, reigns alone as sovereign lord, is the higher astral world which man enters only after physical death, but of which he may have a foretaste when in a state of ineffable ecstasy.

THE GENESIS OF TRAGEDY

There the stars, larger than ever, flame forth like suns.

>Oh fall, sweet night,
>Upon us both,
>Thou night of love;
>Give us oblivion,
>Make us forget
>That we are living.

Ah, take us to thy breast! From the world free us!

This state of exaltation, expressed in majestic symphony by the harmonious chords of the harps, rises until it becomes a veritable renaissance. The lovers rise from their flowery bank and gaze upon each other in amaze. In their eyes glows the inextinguishable flame of resurrection. Their souls have reached a condition of complete fusion. . . . They are on the point of flinging themselves into each other's arms when suddenly the piercing cry of Brangwaine, watching on the turret, brings them back to a sense of reality and the arrival of King Mark hurls the enraptured couple into the abyss of their destiny.

The curtain falls suddenly upon the scene in which the adulterous pair is surprised, *en flagrant délit*, by the king. When it rises, we find ourselves on the terrace of the castle in which Tristan was born. The hero, grievously wounded in a duel by the traitor Melot, lies in mortal agony on an improvised couch beneath the shade of an old lime tree. He is in a profound lethargy from which he returns only to await impatiently the arrival of Isolde who has been brought to the spot by the faithful Kurvenal with the aid of a trusty seaman.

THE INITIATORY THEATRE

Such is the situation after the curtain rises on the last act of *Tristan*.

The ruined castle, desolate sea and measureless solitude correspond to the mental state of the sleeping hero. After the supreme transports of mutual love come the torments of a separation which seems nothing less than death to true lovers. Dreary is the awakening of Tristan in his inferno. Through torture and distress, he proceeds to all the exasperation of grief, until he hears the frightful curse uttered by the king. The marvellous art of the poet-musician consists in persuading us that it is Tristan's unquenchable desire that constitutes the magnetic force, the sovereign power which brings Isolde from beyond the sea. This is the telepathy of sound; such desire is really stronger than all distances and obstacles. From the very first bar, the orchestra sounds forth a kind of colossal sob mingled with the groaning of the counter-basses twice repeated and with those ascending notes which painfully linger over the immensity of the sea, vainly scanning the horizon for the white sail which is to bring back Isolde.

This tyrannical sob seems to say: 'She must come! She will come!' And afterwards, what lassitude and despair in Tristan's plaints, in his confession to Kurvenal of a life-long unassuaged desire, a desire interpreted by the melancholy *cantilena* on the shepherd's pipe, behind the stage. For this dreamy monotone melody contains all the atavism of his race dedicated to the fatality of love. But when, of a sudden, the melancholy strains change into a joyous fanfare, we know that the sail is visible! . . . A trembling joyousness fills the orchestra. The dying man rises from his couch. In

THE GENESIS OF TRAGEDY

this final meeting, he would shed the last drops of his blood, as in the great battles of his life. He tears the bandage from his wound, and, at that moment, hearing the voice of Isolde calling him from afar, he exclaims: 'I hear the light!' She enters panting, opening her arms to receive her staggering friend who falls back on to his couch. Their mouths murmur the two words which are the world to them: 'Tristan! Isolde!' It is the same ecstasy as on the day of the love philtre. Their eyes and breaths drink in one another, though on this occasion Isolde has only time to receive on her lips Tristan's expiring sigh.

Wagner, the great artist and inspired poet, could not end on so funereal a note his favourite drama depicting the triumph of Love. Consequently, the transfiguration of Isolde and the apotheosis of her lover follow Tristan's death. Standing before the body of the Beloved, she repeats the resurrection song of the Second Act. Her wings have expanded; their beating now fills the heavens. She imagines that she sees Tristan's soul free itself from his body and rise in an ocean of sonorous light. With his she ascends, lulled by the waves of the glorious symphony.

> In the billows,
> In the music,
> In the world's great whirlwind—lost;
> Sinking, drowning;
> Dreamless, blest.

It has been asserted that there is a pessimistic meaning, a tinge of negative Buddhism, about this ending. Such is not the case: the entire work, words and music,

THE INITIATORY THEATRE

proclaims the contrary. The swoon of Isolde expresses but the supreme bliss of complete union after the torments of separation. Here there is no dispersion into the elements, but rather a resurrection into a fluid diaphanous atmosphere.

.   .   .   .   .   .

In this dazzlingly splendid and amazingly profound drama, married to music which penetrates into the inmost essence of the soul, Wagner has made a bold incursion into the three worlds—the material, the astral and the divine. It may truly be said that, in his case, the subconscious is the main spring of action. Through it he conducts us, and his dramatis personae, into the invisible spheres which influence and govern us. The two forces we have indicated at opposite poles of the Wagnerian soul, and which strive and strain in his other dramas, are completely fused together in *Tristan*, metamorphosed into new power by the magic of Love.

There would be a great deal more to say, were we to follow this study of the Occult in Wagner right through the *Nibelungen Ring* and *Parsifal*. The former is a pagan cosmogony magnificently reared upon Scandinavian mythology; the latter is a splendid *mise en scène* of the Celto-Christian mystery of the Holy Grail. Enough, however, has been said to illustrate the predominant rôle of Wagner in the history of the initiatory Theatre. It marks a return to his transcendent symbolism through the most intense living.

There is also one striking fact worth noting, both from

THE GENESIS OF TRAGEDY

the philosophical and from the religious point of view, that, whereas Goethe concluded his *Faust* by paying homage to the Eternal Feminine under the image of the *Mater Gloriosa*, Wagner ended his career by glorifying the esoteric Christ in the tradition of the Holy Grail.

The Theatre of the Future

In his *Récits Mérovingiens*, Augustin Thierry relates a luminous story of a darksome pediod. As we are aware, the barbaric chiefs of those days were wont to give their feasts in large rustic rooms made of wood, the upper part of which had wide openings on to forest and plain, through which the air freely passed. At one of these nocturnal feasts, when hydromel and wine were being quaffed from aurochs' horns, an old Gaul happened to speak about the life after death to these barbarians somewhat as follows: 'Did you see that swallow which has just crossed the room? It came in at one window and flew out at the other the next moment. It came out of the night and returned into the night. Well, the present life of the soul resembles the swallow's flight. It too enters the light for an instant, but comes out of black night only to return thereto. . . .' The listeners were silent for a moment; through their wine-steeped brains flashed a glimpse of the Infinite. But soon the Bacchic songs and shouts continued louder than ever.

This anecdote gives a fairly good idea of the attitude of the modern mind to the poignant problem of the soul's past and future. For though the aspect of the world has changed since the days of Chilperich, king of

THE INITIATORY THEATRE

the Franks, the soul remains in the same distressing situation regarding its past and future. Not so was it in the great civilizations preceding the Christian era. Then the Beyond was present, more or less visible to man. It spoke to him through the symbols of religion, through a certain gift of seership at that time widely spread throughout the collective soul. Christianity, however, which has intensified the inner life of man and his longing after the mysteries of the Infinite, has separated him from his Beyond by closing the door of initiation. True, in the mysteries celebrated in front of the churches—mysteries which constituted the entire theatre of the Middle Ages—the three worlds were represented by the *Inferno*, the *Purgatorio* and the *Paradiso*, purgatory corresponding more or less to man's life on earth, in addition to its special signification. These artless representations, however, offered but the most childish and coarse ideas of the Beyond. In the sixteenth and seventeenth centuries, when the art theatre again flourished in England, France and Spain, its external reconstruction was after the style of the theatre of antiquity, though without its esoteric inspiration, without the initiatory drama of Eleusis.

The Gods were no longer there; a mask was flung over the Beyond; the divine horizon had disappeared. But as the invisible forces governing the world are irresistibly imperative upon men of genius, the divine symbols reappeared *in toto* in the *Faust* of Goethe and in the work of Richard Wagner. The stupendous power of the latter is due to the fact that he harnessed into his service the sovereign magic of music which, in him, became the manipulator of the three worlds, the

THE GENESIS OF TRAGEDY

marvellous interpreter of the Beyond. It will never be possible to surpass the power of expression displayed in his musical drama, where all three worlds seem blended into one homogeneous organism.

Nevertheless, this drama possesses one drawback: here music transcends all else. Feeling and thought are submerged by sensation. The three worlds combined into one frequently find themselves in a state of confusion. The root differences between these worlds, which persist in the life of nature as in that of mankind, despite their interpenetration and incessant co-operation, converting them into diverse though superimposed spheres, these differences are not clearly outlined in the sung drama, their hierarchy is not sufficiently emphasized. Consequently, the objective reality of the divine world, its independence as regards the other two, its sovereignty and absolute dominance are not distinctly marked in *musical drama with continuous symphony*.

It is possible to conceive of another kind of drama, in which this hierarchy would be respected and these differences recognized: *spoken drama with intermittent music*. Here, the music would no longer be the sovereign motive of the action, but rather the mediator between the three worlds. It would not be grand orchestral music, but quiet stage music, appearing only at climaxes of suggestion or inspiration, when the influx of the spiritual into the human world reaches its greatest intensity and power, when the infernal and the supernal become perceptible. Then, the stage music would be its intelligent and conscious interpreter. This spoken drama would resemble the melodrama of old, though with this difference that the latter sinned only at producing external effects

THE INITIATORY THEATRE

which shattered the spectator's nerves, whereas the stage music of the initiatory drama would strive to express the most delicate gradations, the most profound and sublime phenomena of the interior life. Music allied to thought would then be the interpreter of self-conscient inspiration. Along with these striking and incisive effects the spoken words of the characters, with the verbal melody entrusted to the actor's free inspiration, assumes its full importance in a well studied psychological drama.*

The musical drama, in the form of the sung drama with full orchestra, will doubtless still survive as the most perfect and complete form of art. But its younger brother, the initiatory drama spoken with stage music, will develop untrammelled by its side as an intrepid pioneer. It has an unlimited field of action.

. . . .

But as we have entered upon the domain of hypothesis, we may inquire what will be the conditions of a theatre which has at its disposal all the treasures of the past,—history, legend, and poetry,—vivid reality and winged dreams, and which illumines this moving panorama with the light of the new Psyche.

The first condition for the existence of such a theatre would be to find and bring together its founders.

* The annals of dramatic art afford rare though striking instances of these lucky finds. I was particularly impressed, long years ago, when listening at Munich to a performance of Byron's *Manfred*, with stage music by Schumann. The effect of the evocation of the phantom of Astarte in the Hall of Arimanes, was most striking. Never have I seen anything on the stage of a more moving character.

THE GENESIS OF TRAGEDY

In former ages, during the few privileged periods when there flourished the idealist theatre which we have called the initiatory theatre, there came automatically into being, as it were, political and social circumstances which favoured its birth. In India, it was founded by the rajahs, guided by the brahmans; in Greece, by the Areopagus of Athens aided by the Eumolpides of Eleusis; in England, during the Renaissance, by the aristocracy under the reign of Elisabeth; in France, by the court of Louis the Fourteenth; in Spain, by the absolute monarchy; at the time of romanticism, by a literary *élite* consisting both of the *Ancien régime* and of the Revolution. These examples—the lesson of the centuries—prove that the initiatory theatre was ever the product of a wisely selected intellectual aristocracy. In the very heart of this levelling democracy in which we are living, it is possible to say that the initiatory theatre will be aristocratic or it will not exist. The ancient aristocracies having crumbled away, however, it can find rebirth only in an intellectual and spiritual aristocracy selected from every class. This self-electing *élite* must consist of scholars and thinkers, artists and poets, producers and creators of every kind who have recognized the social necessity of such a theatre and will consciously join forces with a firm determination to create it. It can be based on nothing else than the Aristocracy of the Soul, the Supremacy of the Spirit.

The second condition will be a religious atmosphere and a certain philosophical discipline, not a rigid detailed catechism nor an arid doctrine based on abstract dogmas, but broad spiritual convictions dominated by

THE INITIATORY THEATRE

a number of vital principles, such as belief in God the Spirit, conscious Creator of the world; in the World Soul, shaper and conserver of Nature; in the survival of the individual Soul and its progressive evolution in freedom; and finally, in the ultimate redemption of all men, whatever be their crimes and backslidings. Materialism is destructive of all fruitful work, as of all poetry and art. Only a sincere and profound faith in spirituality can set up, between the poet and his interpreters, between artists and public, the magnetic chain, the intelligent collaboration, and the enthusiasm needed for the production of serious work. By faith in his ideal has the poet created his poem, by that same faith must the artist express it and the public understand it. And this faith makes them all creators, each after his own fashion.

. . . .

But how are we to inspire the unbelieving masses, enslaved to blind instincts, with this faith? How can we create this free religious atmosphere in the mentality of our intellectual leaders, our governors who are almost entirely dominated by secret or open materialism, or by bigoted traditionalism? Where hides this divine Psyche of yours with her subtle receptivity, her latent seership, her marvellous powers? The most famous thinkers of these latter days do not believe in her. Some reject her with pitying scorn, others say with indulgent smile: this is a delightful creature of the imagination which we must keep because it amuses us and incites us to well-doing, but do not let us forget that it is pure fancy. Are we to believe these disdainful masters? If

THE GENESIS OF TRAGEDY

your divine Psyche really exists, produce her and make her speak to us.

These sceptical questioners and unsatisfied investigators are right. The invisible forces of Nature and Spirit can be proved only by their effects. Divine Psyche, whose presence is now manifested only by feeble gleams, has long been dumb, and apparently dead to the majority of people. Pale Persephone, gentle Psyche, passionate Eurydice, immortal Daughters of increate Light, where are they who long ago adorned your flowing and perfumed locks with the starry narcissus, with myrtle and rose? In truth, the story of divine Psyche is one alike of glory and of sorrow.

Glorious indeed, at the beginning of our Mediterranean civilization, when the Orphics and the Eumolpides of ancient Greece imaged her as Persephone rescued from Hades by Pluto and restored to life by Triptolemos so that she might return to her divine Dionysos. This naïve Persephone was scarce aware of her divinity, though full of impulse and fire. Her soul and senses formed but one. Overflowing with repressed passion, once restored to her God in Olympos, she shone with celestial beauty. This Persephone did but catch a glimpse of Eros (Love) under the form of a crafty youth, but already she is wholly his.

After more than a thousand years of history, after Plato and the Nea-Platonists, Persephone has become the poor human Psyche—a kind of Cinderella tormented by her jealous sisters. She is beloved of Eros, who becomes her husband and visits her at night-time, though he will never allow her to see him. Overcome by curiosity, she approaches her sleeping husband with

THE INITIATORY THEATRE

lighted lamp, gazing upon him in amaze. A burning drop of oil, however, falls upon the white skin of Eros. The enraged God awakes, and flies away, to return no more.—This Psyche is the human Soul that has become awake to Love and would like to grasp him mentally, but she has not the necessary strength; she cannot keep him.

Now, after numberless adventures, after the promise of perfect bliss on earth and in heaven, unhappy Psyche is imprisoned within a vast and gloomy cavern that has no exit into the world of light, and is illumined only by balls of fire, imitations of the sun and the stars. In a state of stupefaction, she looks with terror on the machines controlled by demons, moving and roaring with infernal din throughout the subterranean regions like some vast factory. The friends of the disconsolate one bestow on her every attention, assure her that these machines are far more beautiful than anything in the world without, that the soughing of the leaves and the singing of the birds are nothing in comparison, and that balls of fire and electric lamps are infinitely superior to the sun and the stars before which the humans up above, so lacking in invention, fall into ecstasies.

Nevertheless, unhappy Psyche dimly remembers the marvellous worlds in which she once lived. In the inmost fibres of her being, she feels that she has powers that would expand therein, wings that would grow and fly. She rolls over her couch, like a caterpillar imprisoned in its chrysalis, mindful of having been a libellula though without the strength to become a butterfly. In her dumbness she is unable to express her pain and longings except by starts and exclamations. Thereupon

THE GENESIS OF TRAGEDY

faithful friends, watching over her with boundless devotion have tied her down to prevent these spasms of fury and madness. Will she recover from her malady? The doctors, who have expended on her behalf their learned elixirs, shake their heads and mutter among themselves, whereas the majestic pontiffs of Negation, fed and fattened on the wealth of the patient, heirs presumptive of her property, smile with triumph. For they have already drawn up and signed, on the finest parchment, a solemn attestation of the decease of Psyche. And indeed she will die, of weariness and despair—unless someone delivers her. . . .

But who will set her free? Ah, indeed, to rescue the modern Psyche from her cavern calls for an Orpheus more powerful than he who, according to legend, brought back Eurydice from her Inferno. In addition to the wisdom of Hermes and the flame of Eros, one would need the might of Herakles to snatch the martyr of silence from the cruel clasp of her jailors. These are more formidable than the fabled monsters, than Cerberus, the Gorgons and the Furies who attempted to prevent the poet of Thrace from approaching his dear departed and whom he so easily overcame by the sweet strains of his lyre. For these present-day masters, these crafty exploiters, these tormentors under the guise of seducers, have succeeded in persuading their victim that she can be saved by none but themselves. All the same, the sorrowing Psyche, now mute, will unhesitatingly follow the bold rescuer who succeeds in breaking through the circle of these dangerous witcheries. Reaching the light of day, the couple would look upon each other, nor would the new Psyche disappear, as did

THE INITIATORY THEATRE

Eurydice of old, in the embrace of her deliverer. He would show her a gleam of light on the horizon, an arcade of yellow, violet and crimson flames within a conflagration of clouds: the entrance into the three worlds. Above the firmament glowing with myriads of suns, she would see the flaming Archetypes in the twelve constellations of the zodiac; higher still, towards the zenith, the Thrones, Dominions and Powers coming from the glowing circle wherein shines the creative Word! . . .

Then,—divine Psyche, having regained speech, in a transport of enthusiasm will say to her deliverer:

> Enfin!—de l'air . . . de l'espace . . . et le ciel!
> Voilà ma vraie patrie! Elançons-nous!
> Un coup d'aile—et derrière nous les mondes!

But, let the happy jailors of the modern Psyche be reassured. The Orpheus who is to rescue her from them and bring their dominion to an end is yet unborn; his hour has not yet come. But it assuredly will come, because of the urge of the past and by the irresistible attraction of the future.

Meanwhile humanity, driven into a tempestuous sea on its rolling vessel that has neither chart nor compass, will do well to keep a lookout for the beacons capable of preventing shipwreck, and for the heavenly lights which should guide it safely into harbour.

SECOND PART

THE GENESIS OF TRAGEDY AND THE DRAMA OF ELEUSIS

CHAPTER I

THE SACRED DANCE IN THE HINDU THEATRE

Psychology of the Contemporary Theatre

THERE is no more striking antithesis than the contrast between the materialistic anarchy of the contemporary theatre and the ardent aspirations of a select few towards a theatre of sublime and lofty initiation. We may try to discover the reason of this.

The causes may be found when we consider, on the one hand, the stupendous intellectual development that has come about in the few (*élite*) during the past half-century, and on the other hand the democratic rush for enjoyment and power on the part of the ill-educated and organically ungrouped masses. The requirements of the thinking and refined *élite*, which include all the conquests of science and thought, increase daily, whilst the coarse and chaotic tastes of the invading masses govern and tyrannize over our theatre, which has become a purely commercial enterprise whose value and importance are measured by financial standards. The astute business man is nowadays the judge of aesthetics. It is terrifying to note how during the past fifty years the standard of theatrical aesthetics has deteriorated.

THE GENESIS OF TRAGEDY

Though there was no philosophy in the romantic theatre, it was not without a certain grandeur, a sincere aspiration after heroism. From 1870 onwards, its reign was a thing of the past. The bourgeois play which succeeded had retained a certain moral sense, notwithstanding its mediocrity. The plays dealing with satire and licentious living which almost exclusively fill our theatres have replaced traditional morality with a craving after pleasure in the form of worldly morality which safeguards appearances. In many of these *pièces à succès*, there is an infinity of talent and ingenuity, and wonderful technical ability is shown, but there is no trace of the ideal, no profound study of the human soul, no concern for its eternal needs. In the last analysis, what is needed to rescue the theatre from a commonplace vulgarity and raise it to a higher level—is the hero. Here I must quote from the *Revue d'art dramatique* a noteworthy passage of an article by M. Suarès on the public of the contemporary theatre. 'Heroism,' he says, 'is ever more or less the soul of the drama. There are heroes both in ideas and in actions, and their thoughts form a matter no less heroic than the deeds of fable. A drama without a hero is a painting without light. The only beauty is the heroic. This is why it is possible to have an endless number of playwriters as is the case nowadays; the tragic poet, however, will always be the rarest of men. For how can you create heroes without first being one yourself?'

And so we may assert that the contemporary theatre gives us only men and women, passions, virtues and vices on the small scale. Its great virtuosity consists in extracting from the most trifling subjects the greatest profit.

THE GENESIS OF TRAGEDY

Still, it must be acknowledged that certain of these dramatic attempts have been generous impulses towards the heroic theatre. I will quote two noteworthy instances; *La Fille de Roland* of Henri de Bornier, first played in 1875 at the Théâtre Français, and *Cyrano de Bergerac* of Edmond Rostand, which, played thirty years later by the elder Coquelin at the Porte Saint-Martin, obtained the most dazzling success on the stage ever since *Le Cid* of Corneille. These two triumphs—though they had no successors—have left behind imperishable memories and given us two masterpieces. They also show how easy it is, given noble enthusiasm and genuine talent, to raise the public to higher realms, though criticism too complaisant and managers too worldly-wise speedily bring them down to earth again.

These individual attempts have not been the only ones that point to the incessant and indefatigable efforts made by the Occidental soul in the direction of an idealistic theatre. We have had Wagner's operas at Bayreuth and the dramas of antiquity given at Orange in South-Eastern France. Though these two phenomena seem to be dissimilar, they spring from the same need and are related in their effects. On the one hand, we have the extraordinary genius of a man who was alike a dramatist, a poet, and a musician of the highest order, who, by the dual magic of music and legend, produced a theatre on strictly aesthetic lines and solely dedicated to a lofty human ideal. On the other hand, we have in the Græco-Latin theatre of Orange a superb resurrection of ancient Greek tragedy in all its religious majesty, through the inspiration of an actor of genius.

THE GENESIS OF TRAGEDY

At Bayreuth, when the mystic chords of the invisible orchestra evoked the great scenes of the *Rheingold*, the *Walküre* and the *Götterdämmerung* between the Corinthian columns of a sort of temple dimly outlined, there presented itself the vision of a superhuman world, glowing with life and beauty, far superior to the drab realities of our everyday life. At Orange, when Mounet-Sully revived the *Œdipus Tyrannus* of Sophokles, in a kind of poetic frenzy and sublime rapture, when this stupendous tragedy, interrupted only by the melodious declamations of the choruses, was given in the open air, by torchlight, in a huge amphitheatre packed with three thousand spectators breathless with emotion, one had the irresistible sensation of the mysterious presence of the Gods in the ancient drama. At last one grasped the deep meaning of Aristotle's definition of tragedy: a Purification Κάθαρσις of the Soul by Terror and Pity.

These two events were the sure precursors of a new art. In the soul of all present they left a glowing and ineffaceable mark, though, of themselves alone, they were unable to change the character of the theatre. That would have implied a previous change in contemporary mentality and morals. Despite praiseworthy efforts, they have not had the power to create a new theatrical institution on a firm basis. Harassed by industrial art and the democratic onset, we have continued to stagnate, to wallow in the bog of scepticism, pessimism and anarchy. To the many advocates of an idealism present in every class of society, though powerless because isolated and without any organic grouping, the two exceptional happenings just mentioned now

THE GENESIS OF TRAGEDY

appear only as two strips of azure sky seen from the black depths of an abyss.

Yes, we are indeed sunk in the mire. Call to mind the circus of Gavarny, in the Pyrenees. Along a narrow valley, we come upon a chaotic mass of rocks that have crashed to the bottom of a vast funnel created by overtowering mountains. Giant walls rise on every side; glaciers and cascades fall around from inaccessible peaks. How are we again to reach those dazzling summits, the open sky, space and the horizon? It seems impossible. For all that, there exist perceptible footpaths, steep ascents known to the goat-herd and the hunter. Such is our position with regard to the idealistic drama.

If we should attempt this ascent, we must study the abyss from top to bottom and from bottom to top, descend to its lowest depths in order to learn how to escape from them.

Outline of the Evolution of the Theatre in Three Thousand Years.

Let us look at the problem a little more closely. There would seem to be one practical means of considering a possible restoration of the idealistic theatre in the future, and that is to examine the theatre of the Soul and of 'initiation' drama by studying the great historical epochs during which it flourished, and discerning the real causes which produced its successive revivals. This will be undoubtedly a modest—though not ineffective—way of preparing its future advent for

THE GENESIS OF TRAGEDY

a generation more fortunate than our own, which will have the joy of realizing it both in the verbal creations of its poets and in the plastic beauty and the vocal melody of their interpreters.

The great periods during which the theatre of the Soul flourished have been few—for good reasons. Indeed, they presuppose a stupendous concentration of force and an exceptional combination of favourable circumstances which it is not easy to obtain. We may say that, when the theatre carries out the whole of its mission, it is the synthesis of all the arts, the quintessence of a civilization. Hitherto, however, these glorious periods have been separated by long centuries—oases in the desert, tiny islands in the vast ocean. They extend from primitive India and ancient Greece, passing through Hellenism, Christianity and the Renaissance, on to the modern chaos in which we now find ourselves. We shall see that, in its divers and ever new manifestations, the institution of the theatre of the Soul and its instrument, the 'initiation' drama, obey immutable laws which condition their birth and growth. The disappearance of a single one of these conditions inevitably brings about the decline of the drama, the downfall of the institution. These conditions are reproduced, and these laws operate, at all times and in every nation whenever the idealistic theatre reappears in history after prolonged intervals of stagnation. We shall formulate the laws only at the end of this work. There is, however, at the same time, a higher law which embraces the entire evolution of theatrical and dramatic art during the last three thousand years.

Glancing at the history of the theatre from its begin-

THE GENESIS OF TRAGEDY

nings in the sacred dances of India, continuing along the various phases of Athenian tragedy on to the theatre of Shakespeare—who may be called the father of all modern drama—we find that this history closely resembles a rapid descent from the heights of a transcendental Ideal into the fundamentals of reality and life. Then follows dramatic art along the many experiments of the French classic theatre in the seventeenth century and the romantic theatre in the nineteenth, on to Goethe's *Faust* and the work of Richard Wagner. It will be seen that this second part of the story resembles a return to the heights of the ideal, to the lost paradise,—a scaling effort no less formidable, and far more difficult, than was the descent into the depths of the pit. For it leads us, along a labyrinth of peaks and ravines, to giddy heights and a new aspect of the earth, to a reconquest of the lost heaven over an extended horizon.

Involution into life—evolution towards the ideal: here in a phrase we have the whole history of the theatre.

We shall attempt this journey in short stages and over long intervals of time, beginning with an attempt to form a concise idea of what this theatre was among the Aryans and to witness its birth in the mysterious art of sacred dance.

The Dance in Primitive India

We are in India, at the height of the Brahmanic civilization, i.e., at least a thousand years before the Christian era. The white race of the Aryans, warlike

THE GENESIS OF TRAGEDY

and chivalrous, which has come down from the plains of Iran through a breach of the Hindu Kush, has brought into subjection the black race, along with the remnants of the yellow and red races, the most ancient in the world, scattered over tropical India, between the Himalayas and the Indian Ocean and extending to Ceylon. The one cult of the primitive Aryans, was that of Fire. This fire, lit at sunrise on an altar of turf, sending up its flames to the Sun-king, they called Agni, the sacred Fire, hidden in all things, that gives life to the universe. During this sacrifice, the patriarch or priest recites Vedic hymns invoking all the cosmic powers, visible and invisible: Varuna the Sky, Indra the Sun, the Pitris or ancestors, the Asuras who correspond to our Archangels, and the Devas or Heavenly Powers. This cult, however, is meant rather for learned rulers and warriors than for the masses. Another is needed for the lower castes, one that will give joy to Kshatriyas and Kings.

And here we see the first appearance of that marvellous art of sacred dance, that lost art which an endeavour is now being made to recover under the name of *Eurhythmy*, and which played so important a rôle in primitive India. In the *Vishnupurana*, the God Krishna teaches shepherd maidens the sacred dances; he shows them how to express, in rhythmic gesture and movement, the grandeur of the heroes and the beauty of the Gods. This dance was an harmonious blend of pantomime and rhythmic dance. It might be given the name of lyrical eurhythmy, or plastic ecstasy under the incantation of poetry. It translated feelings rather than passions, thoughts rather than deeds. It was not an art of

THE GENESIS OF TRAGEDY

imitation, it was one of expression and exaltation belonging to the interior world.

The Brahmans, then, in their temples, maintained veritable colleges of young maidens, entrusted to the charge of aged women instructed in the art of religious dances. Living in strictest chastity, these graceful dancing girls appeared only at certain public festivals. Their skilled choreography accompanied the recitation of sacred poems before the people: it was their sole occupation.

We should, however, form but an imperfect idea of these dancing girls and of the respect they inspired in the people, did we not remember the mystical atmosphere with which religion invested them. In the religion of the Vedas, the Apsaras are celestial nymphs, the *danseuses* of Indra. They symbolize the shining spirits that live with the Devas, serve as their messengers to men, and sometimes incarnate in a woman. Thus the sacred temple dancer assumed, so to speak, in the official cult, the mystic rôle of the Apsara or the celestial nymph in mythology. She was the mediator between heaven and earth, between Gods and men. In the public festivals, she expressed the profound symbols of religion by the beauty of her attitudes, giving eloquent mime interpretations of the sacred poems which the Hindu bards, the *Bharatas*, recited to the people. Hence the high rank of the dancing girl in the temple; hence, too, her name of *Devadasi*—handmaid of the Gods.

Imagine, at the entrance to one of the capitals of ancient India, the great pagoda with its pyramidal roof and the sacred ponds around. The oppressive noonday heat has given place to the delightful cool of evening.

THE GENESIS OF TRAGEDY

The vault of heaven is spangled with stars, and the moon appears on the scene, reminding one of a swan asleep upon a lake. The vast enclosure is lit by streams of light. The king appears, with his courtiers, on a raised dais. Around are crowds of people of every caste, and including the pariahs. All listen in silence to the voice of the rhapsodist who, standing on the terrace of the temple, recites epics of past times and heroic exploits.

Through the brightly illumined porch of the pagoda comes the cortège of sacred dancers, with tiny bells fastened to their ankles and helmets and tiaras on their heads. Their supple limbs are enveloped in the silky *langouti*, while their shoulders are adorned with golden flames and sprouting wings. The superb coryphœus wears the royal diadem, and a breast-plate sparkling with precious stones. The string instruments begin to play, the bamboos mark time, and the sacred dancers entwine themselves into wreaths or trip after one another—a veritable pearl necklace—on the terrace. Then, beating time to the music and interpreting the melody of the rhapsodist, they fall prostrate in adoration before the sublime coryphœus, who at that moment represents Rama, Sita, or the God Krishna. They form expressive groups, flexible as a grape-vine, with their undulating hands and sensitive fingers. At that moment, the light-wrapped *devadasis*, with their amber and opal-tinted faces and dilated pupils, have really become the messengers of the Devas, the Apsaras themselves. For they appear to bring to men the souls of heroes in their tender virgin arms, to incarnate them in their quivering bodies as in a pure and perfumed chalice.

THE GENESIS OF TRAGEDY

As may easily be imagined, in becoming imbued with such spectacles, even the pariah had a far-off though glorious glimmering of the secrets of the Vedic religion, of a divine world.

As we see, this art is not yet drama; though it is drama in potency under the aspect of two combined arts. For we have, on the one hand, an epic tale recited by a rhapsodist, and on the other a group of dancers who express the dominant ideas of the poem by their attitudes and movements. Only at a considerably later period, during the early centuries of the Christian era, do we find dialogued drama at the court of contemporary Rajahs. Certain scholars claim that the original idea of representing an action in dialogue on the stage was suggested to Hindu poets by the introduction of the Greek drama into Bactriana, after the conquest by Alexander the Great. The most recent Indianists—including Sylvain Lévy who has written the most complete and profound work published on the Indian drama—dispute this opinion. What is certain is that the Hindu drama resembles the Greek tragedy neither in spirit nor in form. It brings on to the stage the heroes and heroines of the ancient epics, and,—a characteristic proof of its national origin,—the sacred dancer therein plays an important rôle, as we shall see, that of the celestial nymph, the Apsara. This drama possesses an idyllic, almost paradisiacal, character, in striking contrast with the sombre colours of Greek tragedy. There are no violent passions, no tragic denouements. Challenge, blasphemy and murder have no place in the Hindu theatre. The poetry imposed by the Brahmans is opposed to that of Aristotle who looked upon terror and pity as purifying elements in the human soul. The Brahmans regard these elements as dangerous stimulation of slumbering passions; it is for this reason that they banish them from the drama, assigning to it as its sole end such gentle emotions as tenderness and admiration.

The various scenes were presented in a spacious enclosure, covered with cloth supported by richly decorated pillars wreathed with flowers and festoons. On his throne in the centre sat the king, surrounded by his officers and courtiers and by a few of the people. A simple platform, supplied with side rooms, formed the stage. The dramatis personæ made their exits and entrances by the curtain at the back. This curtain—a thing that would have delighted our symbolists twenty years ago—had to suggest by its colour the dominant emotion of the play. It was white for a love drama, yellow for an heroic one, red for a drama containing some element of passion, and black for a mystical drama. On this uniform background the imagination of the spectators found play in creating mountains, snowy peaks, cloudy skies, interiors of palaces, royal gardens and public squares. This sumptuous and ever-changing scenery was called into being only by the gestures and movements of the actors and such detailed description as Oriental poetry delights in.

The Hindu theatre, it must be acknowledged, scarcely offers us anything but unequal plays, full of partial beauties though devoid of clarity and proportion. *The Chariot of the Child*, by Sudraka, with the exception of one or two delightful scenes, is nothing more than common melodrama. *The Sequel of the Story of Rama*, by

THE GENESIS OF TRAGEDY

Bavabuti, is a lyrical and insipid diluting of a grandiose theme. And these are two dramas which the Hindus regarded as models of the *genre*. Nevertheless, this theatre has given us two exquisite pearls, marvellously depicting the divine dream of a dying India, and reminding one of the dazzling daylight which becomes blurred and softened in the sumptuous purple of a tropical sunset. These two charming works are by Kalidasa: *Sakuntala* and *The Hero and the Nymph*. Considered from the purely human standpoint, these dramas set forth the relations between the hero and the woman under different aspects. In their religious and philosophical meaning they represent, the latter, the incarnation of the soul, and the former, its earthly trials up to the stage of purification when it catches sight of the possibility of a return to its heavenly home. Thus do celestial bliss and an heroic idyll, in the open air and at the foot of the Himalayas, dimly outline the entire poem of the soul, consisting of its descent into matter and its ascent to Spirit.

I say nothing of *The Hero and the Nymph*, a most interesting subject though faulty in execution, but will examine *Sakuntala* which tells of the loves of a daughter of an Apsara with a king of the lunar dynasty. Here we find all the variegated interplay of the dominant feelings and thoughts of the Hindu soul.

The Heroic Idyll. Sakuntala
Sacontalá; or the Fatal Ring

Sakuntala is justly regarded as the masterpiece of the Hindu theatre. Goethe was the first to welcome it as a

THE GENESIS OF TRAGEDY

revelation when* *William Jones* translated it into English, a hundred years ago. Lamartine and Paul de Saint-Victor wrote of the exquisite idyll in glowing language. The famous stanza of the author of *Faust* to Kalidasa is the exuberant homage paid by Occidental thought to the marvellous poetry of the Orient. 'Dost thou wish for spring flowers and autumn fruits?' says Goethe. 'Dost thou desire that which charms and delights? That which assuages both hunger and thirst? Wouldst thou embrace earth and heaven in a single name? That name is *Sakuntala*, and there is nothing more to say.'

The *décor* of the drama is delightful and sumptuous, a tropical paradise through which are wafted the light breezes of the Himalayas. The hermitage of Kanwa lies hidden away in the depths of a dense forest through which slowly winds a limpid stream, whose surface is dotted with aquatic plants and birds. Following the custom of certain hermits, the old anchorite lives here with Gautami, his aged wife, who has become the venerable companion of his solitude. Young disciples are around Kanwa, whilst three charming maidens engage in pastoral and religious duties under the direction of Gautami. There is no constraint in this happy Thebaid, which is no cloister but rather a peaceful glade in a virgin forest. Here in one sweet mysterious bond of fraternity all beings are united; men, animals and flowers. Here all that breathes is sacred to the name of Brahma, for everything that lives possesses a soul akin to his own. The forest guests appear to know this, for

* Sir William Jones, the eminent judge and orientalist and poet, 1746-1794. Published 1799 in 6 vols. Vol. VI.—Ed.

THE GENESIS OF TRAGEDY

the birds peck at the grains of rice on the rush-mats of the hermits, and the gazelles take grass from the hands of the maidens.

Sakuntala, the daughter of an Apsara, who has been brought up by Kanwa and Gautami, is the human flower, the virgin Eve of this sylvan paradise. She is thrillingly sensitive. One must see 'the glow and languor of her eyes, to which antimony has given added volume', to divine the tormenting passions that lurk in their silent depths. Sympathy for all beings is her dominant characteristic; with the result that all creatures love her and feel drawn to her. Her name means: 'She whom birds protect.' No less charming, though less passionate and more prudent, are her two companions. The name of Anusuya means 'skilful in blending shades', that of Priyamvada 'the honey-tongued beauty'.

Pursuing a gazelle in the hunt, King Dushyanta comes upon the hermitage of Kanwa. Just as the king is about to let fly a deadly shaft at the graceful animal, a hermit stops him with these noble words: 'This gazelle, O king, belongs to the hermitage, it must not be killed! Replace the arrow which thou hast aimed. Thy weapons are for the defence of the oppressed, not for the injury of the innocent.' Immediately the king puts back the arrow into its quiver and respectfully salutes the pupil of the solitary sage. A gentler prey awaits him; soon he will be both huntsman and victim, victor and vanquished. Hiding behind a thicket, he watches the three maidens who have come to water their favourite plants. They wear garments made of cork, a costume obligatory for the penitents of the hermitage. The bodice, however, leaves exposed their bare arms and fair bosoms. The naïve coquetry of these virgins makes one liken them to dryads whose faces peer above the silvery bark of the birch trees. The king takes pleasure in their graceful ways, their harmless prattle. But he stands there, fascinated by Sakuntala, who treats all the plants as friends and gives a sisterly kiss to a vine-creeper. A bee having begun to pursue the maiden who cries out and darts to and fro to escape the menacing sting, the king leaves his hiding-place and drives away the audacious insect. He pretends to be a pilgrim and conversation at once begins between the unexpected guest—whose incognito will speedily be discovered—and the comely gardeners.

It is a case of love at first sight between Dushyanta and Sakuntala, though the effects produced are different. The king's love is exuberant and lyrical, finding expression in a torrent of words; that of the maiden is deep and concentrated, making her silent at first. And yet it is love that has entered her heart, like wick smouldering in a wisp of cotton. Kalidasa has delicately shaded the gradations of feeling in his heroine with penetrating observation and delicate artistry. At first we have the timid grace, the instinctive coquetry of the virgin who has become a woman at the first sight of the beloved. In his presence she utters not a word, but leaves her friends to speak. Before going away, she turns her head, under the pretext that her dress has caught in a bush, and the prolonged look she fixes upon the retiring king forms an eloquent comment upon her fierce silence. When he has gone, she falls into a passionate all-devouring languor. Her friends are compelled to fan back to consciousness the lovelorn maid, sighing on a flowery

THE GENESIS OF TRAGEDY

couch. Finally, when the royal lover returns, we witness the thrilling modesty, the sensuous and childlike innocence of the first avowals of love, occasionally starting in sudden fright, with all the nervous outpouring of a soul that will be proud and passionate once it comes to know itself.

The seduction, discreetly veiled by the poet, takes place between the third and fourth acts. Everything favours the lovers: the complicity of the two girl friends, the very innocence of Sakuntala, the prestige of her royal betrothed, the service he has rendered the monks by protecting them against dangerous enemies, and even the law of Manu which tolerates this kind of free love, when confirmed by marriage. There is general unanimity. Before his departure, the king has given the wedding ring to his betrothed. Kanwa who, in his clairvoyance, foresees the painful trials and final happiness of his foster daughter, promises to send her within a few months to the capital under an escort.

Soon a cloud appears in the radiant sky. In her amorous frenzy, Sakuntala has forgotten to pay due respect to Durvasa, the most austere and irascible of the ascetes. The enraged monk utters a dreadful curse upon the distraught maiden: 'no sooner has he left her presence than the king will forget her.' Priyamvada, interceding on her friend's behalf, obtains from the powerful ascete the favour that Dushyanta shall remember his betrothed once he sees the wedding ring.

It is the king's forgetfulness and the slow return of memory that form the climax, the psychic knot of the drama.

The Fourth Act deals with Sakuntala's farewell to the

THE GENESIS OF TRAGEDY

forest in which she was born; at the moment she is preparing to rejoin her husband. This forms a description unique in the world's literature, an adorable elegy, impregnated with that brotherly feeling for all creatures which distinguishes Hindu poetry from all other verse.

In the Fifth Act, Sakuntala is presented by her escort to the king, sitting in solemn state in his palace, with all the crown dignitaries around him. This glorious prince, whom the unhappy Sakuntala sees on his throne, is no longer the lover in the forest glade; he is a stranger, almost a god surrounded with regal pomp and the terror born of absolute power. This scene is the most dramatic in the whole work, the one that approaches nearest to the modern theatre. It must be given in its entirety. [M. Edouard Schuré, unfortunately, does not give the scene in full.—ED.]

The king (Dushyanta, Emperor of India), is seated on a raised throne, between two gigantic columns. Warriors and courtiers stand in rows on the stage.

. . . .

Enter Sakuntala, led by her adoptive mother Gautami and two disciples of Kanwa the ascete. The King's betrothed is deeply veiled.

SARNGARAVA. (*Brahmin disciple of Kanwa.*) What do I hear? Dost thou, then, hesitate? Monarch, thou art well acquainted with the ways of the world and knowest that

> A wife, however virtuous and discreet,
> If she live separate from her wedded lord,
> Though under shelter of her parent's roof,

THE GENESIS OF TRAGEDY

Is mark for vile suspicion. Let her dwell
Beside her husband, though he hold her not
In his affection. So her kinsmen will it.

THE KING. Do you really mean to assert that I ever married this lady?

SAKUNTALA. (*Aside despondingly.*) O my heart, thy worst misgivings are confirmed.

SARNGARAVA. Is it becoming in a monarch and magnificent prince to depart from the rules of religion and honour and justice, merely because he repents of his engagements?

THE KING. I cannot answer a question based on a mere fabrication.

SARNGARAVA. Such inconstancy is fortunately not common except in men intoxicated by power.

THE KING. Is that remark aimed at me? I am reproved with too great severity.

GAUTAMI. Be not ashamed, my daughter. Let me remove thy veil for a little space. Thy husband the King will then recognize thee.
(*Removes her veil.*)

THE KING. (*Gazing at Sakuntala. Aside.*)

What charms are here revealed before mine eyes!
Truly no blemish mars the symmetry
Of that fair form; yet can I ne'er believe
She is my wedded wife; and like a bee
That circles round the flower whose nectared cup
Teems with the dew of morning, I must pause
Ere eagerly I taste the proffered sweetness.

(*Remains wrapped in thought.*)

WARDER. How admirably does our royal master's

behaviour prove his regard for justice! Who else would hesitate for a moment when good fortune offered for his acceptance a form of such rare beauty?

SARNGARAVA. Great King, why art thou silent?

THE KING. Holy man, I have resolved the matter in my mind. The more I think of it, the less able am I to recollect my marriage with this lady. What answer, then, can I possibly give you when I do believe myself to be her husband, and I plainly see that she is soon to become a mother? But how then can I lay aside all consideration of my military tribes and admit into my palace a young woman who is pregnant by another husband.

SAKUNTALA. (*Aside.*) Woe! Woe! Is our very marriage to be called in question by my own husband? Ah me! Is this to be the end of all my bright visions of wedded happiness?

SARNGARAVA. Beware!

> Beware how thou insult the holy Sage!
> Remember how he generously allowed
> Thy secret union with his foster-child:
> And how when thou didst rob him of his treasure,
> He sought to furnish thee excuse, when rather
> He should have cursed thee for a ravisher.

SARADWATA. (*Another disciple of Kanwa.*) Sarngarava, speak to him no more. Sakuntala, our part is performed; we have said all we had to say and the King has replied in the manner thou hast heard. It is now thy turn to give him convincing evidence of thy marriage.

THE GENESIS OF TRAGEDY

SAKUNTALA. (*Aside.*) Since his feeling towards me has undergone a complete revolution, what will it avail to revive old recollections? One thing is clear, I shall soon have to mourn my own widowhood. (*Aloud.*) My revered husband—— (*Stops short.*) But no, I dare not address thee by this title, since thou hast refused to acknowledge our union. Noble descendant of Puru! It is not worthy of thee to betray an innocent-minded girl, and disown her in such terms, after having so lately and so solemnly plighted thy vows to her in the hermitage, and shown the excess of thy passion in the consecrated forest.

THE KING. (*Stopping his ears.*) I will hear no more. Be such a crime far from my thoughts.

SAKUNTALA. If then thou really believest me to be the wife of another, I will easily convince thee by this token.

THE KING. An excellent idea!

SAKUNTALA. (*Feeling for the ring.*) Alas! Alas! Woe is me! There is no ring on my finger.
(*Looks with anguish at Gautami.*)

GAUTAMI. The ring must have slipped off when thou wert in the act of offering homage to the holy water of Sachi's sacred pool.

THE KING. People may well talk of the readiness of woman's invention! How skilful in finding excuses!

SAKUNTALA. (*Angrily.*) Dishonourable man, thou judgest of others by thine own evil heart. Thou, at least, art unrivalled in perfidy and standest alone, a base deceiver in the garb of virtue and religion—

THE GENESIS OF TRAGEDY

like a deep pit whose yawning mouth is concealed by smiling flowers.

THE KING. (*Aside.*) Her anger, at any rate, appears genuine, and makes me almost doubt whether I am in the right. For indeed,

When I had vainly searched my memory,
And so with stern severity denied
The fabled story of our secret loves,
Her brows, that met before in graceful curves,
Like the arched weapon of the god of love,
Seemed by her frown dissevered; while a fire
Of sudden anger kindled in her eyes.

(*Aloud.*) My good lady, Dushyanta's character is well known to all. I comprehend not your meaning.

SAKUNTALA. Well do I deserve to be thought a harlot for having, in the innocence of my heart, and out of the confidence I reposed in a Prince of Puru's race, entrusted my honour to a man whose mouth distils honey, while his heart is full of poison.

(*Covers her face with her mantle and bursts into tears.*)

As Iphigeneia is saved by Artemis when on the point of being sacrificed, so Sakuntala is carried away by her mother the Apsara, on leaving the royal palace, and transported to the retreat of the asceti Marachi, in the Himalayas, where she gives birth to her child and awaits the return of the faithless spouse. The news of the sudden disappearance of Sakuntala confounds the king.

THE GENESIS OF TRAGEDY

The final glance of the rejected bride has entered his heart, piercing it like a fiery dart, and now this heart burns with a grief for which he can find no cause. A fisherman brings to the palace a gold ring bearing the king's initials, which he has found in the belly of a fish. This is the wedding ring given by Dushyanta to Sakuntala, and which she has lost when bathing. On seeing it, the king's memory returns; there comes back the remembrance of his love; too late is he stricken with keen remorse.

Here we have the emotional symbolism of the Hindu drama appearing in the guise of a marvellous fairy tale. The ring is but the outward sign of the deep spiritual love uniting both. Sakuntala, who loves the more deeply of the two, has lost by accident the ring, though not the intimate consciousness of her love. The king, enslaved by sense and blinded by his power, has need of the outer sign of fidelity in order to believe in his wife. Still, the sight of the recovered ring, by affording him material proof of Sakuntala's innocence, stirs him to the very depths of his nature.

The Sixth Act depicts the torture of impotent regret and tardy remorse, which alike constitute for the king an expiation and an initiation into true love. The wise Rishis and their gods, who wonderfully combine to further as well as possible the destinies of their protégés, speedily bring together the unhappy lovers once more. Nevertheless, before witnessing the reconciliation of the couple, the poet has insisted on showing us the king performing a superhuman act, as though expiation did not suffice to enable him to merit final happiness, and some heroic effort were needed.

THE GENESIS OF TRAGEDY

Dushyanta has been summoned to the help of Indra to resist an army of demons; we see him only after this exploit has been performed, crossing from heaven to earth in the chariot of the god, and relating his victory.

The description of the scenery—between the king and his guide Mátali, Indra's charioteer, during this headlong course, is one of the most glorious visions in all poetry. The vast dwellings of Indra have disappeared. As they pass, the travellers see the loftiest source of the Ganges which pours down like a white cataract from celestial lakes on to the snow-clad dome of a mountain. The chariot traverses the cloudy space with the speed of lightning. At first, there is seen nothing but the undulating outline of the peaks of the Himalayas, the labyrinth of valleys, then the clear shining silvery thread of the streams through a mist of dew. We have a bird's-eye view of the whole of India. Strange to relate, Kalidasa's description recalls the accounts given by our airmen when they effect a dive *vol plané* from considerable heights. Delightful is the sensation: whilst the king approaches the earth, it appears as though the earth is rising to meet him. He exults as one intoxicated by an unexpected conquest and exclaims: 'Would not one say that an unknown hand is bringing me the earth as a gift?' And Mátali, Indra's charioteer, answers: 'Yea, the earth too is fair. . . .'

At their feet, on Mount Hemacuta, Marichi the saint is seated in a state of ecstasy before his hermitage. The King, his whole being filled with unknown bliss, exclaims: 'Ah! this abode of peace is sweeter than heaven itself! I feel as though I were bathing in a lake of nectar!' The snow-white horses, dripping with a

THE GENESIS OF TRAGEDY

foam of light, and the chariot wheels, aflame with the furious speed, come to a halt. The king descends, and enters the groves of the lonely Ascetics who have attained to perfection. They live in the ether of the holy forest 'where crystal streams shine with the golden pollen of the flowers'. The king sees a beautiful child playing with a lion's cub which he teases with the utmost audacity, opening its jaws with the full strength of his tiny hands. 'Ah! This can be no one but a son of Puru!' exclaims the king. The father's heart beats tumultuously. He would clasp the child in his arms, but the little Bharata resists vigorously. Sakuntala now appears, dressed like a nun, in sombre mourning, her locks bound in a single tress, her cheeks pale and thin.

The King recognizing her murmurs: 'Ah, what means it that my heart inclines to this boy, as if he were my own son?' Then comes the following dialogue between child, father and mother:

THE BOY. (*Going hastily to Sakuntala*.) Mother, here is a stranger who calls me son.

THE KING. (*To Sakuntala*.) Oh! my best beloved. I have treated thee cruelly, but my cruelty is succeeded by the warmest affection and I implore forgiveness.

SAKUNTALA. (*Aside*.) Be confident, O my heart!—— (*Aloud*.) I shall be most happy when the king's anger has passed away. (*Aside*.) This must be, son of my lord.

THE KING. O my only beloved, banish from thy mind my cruel desertion of thee. A violent frenzy

THE GENESIS OF TRAGEDY

overpowered my soul. Such, when the darkness of illusion prevails, are the actions of the best intentioned, as a blind man, when a friend binds his head with a wreath of flowers, mistakes it for a snake, and foolishly rejects it.
(She falls at his feet.)

SAKUNTALA. Rise, my husband. Joy now succeeds affliction, since the son of my lord still loves me. *(Drying her tears and seeing the ring on his finger.)* Ah! Is that the fatal ring?

THE KING. Yes, by the surprising recovery of it, my memory was restored.

SAKUNTALA. Its influence indeed has been great, since it has brought back the lost confidence of my husband.

THE KING. Take it, then, as a beautiful plant receives a flower from the returning season of joy.

As the pair take hands and gaze upon each other with feeling wherein the flame of desire melts away in the pure light of love, we see, coming from the cedar forest, Marichi, king of the anchorites. His long white beard is tossed by the wind like a lichen of a snow-covered fir tree. Motionless eyes flash in his wrinkled face. His outstretched hands are so thin as to be transparent, while his feet seem scarcely to touch the ground. The majestic old man is scarce more than a human form, his soul having almost become re-absorbed in Brahma. Nevertheless, he turns benevolently towards the royal couple bending before him, and blesses them with the words: 'Thy wife is living faith, thy child is thy wealth, in thee power is incarnate.' To such a sage, time and space no longer exist. Eternity alone is present; through it, all becomes crystal-clear. Oblivion of the lover by the beloved, what was it? 'A breath that dims the surface of a mirror, but the veil is dispersed and the image appears again.' Are the appearance and disappearance of a world aught else? The soul, however, of the great emancipated breathes in unison with all beings. He would give of his might to help the royal couple to lead men aright. To a seer who fathoms Spirit, a king worthy of the name is a 'son of heaven', a true queen is a 'sister of earth'. And so the great Ascetic crowns his blessing by this wish whereby he identifies the pair with their royal task: 'May friendship endure between earth and heaven for the world's happiness.'

Thus the heroic idyll of Sakuntala ends in a higher world wherein perish the storms of the passions, and the soul perceives the concert of the worlds within its own harmony.

The Essence of Dramatic Emotion

The drama just analyzed has shown us the abyss that separates the Hindu theatre from Greek tragedy and from the whole of our modern theatre, setting it aloft, as it were, upon a summit apart. This abyss consists of the almost total absence of strong passions, of the violent clash of wills. Here, there is scarcely any struggling, and just sufficient suffering to intensify the charm of life and break the monotony of cloudless bliss. In

THE GENESIS OF TRAGEDY

Sakuntala and the other Hindu dramas, there are comic characters, mostly brahmans or the common people, though only three main dramatis personæ: the King, his wife, and the Rishi or Ascete. The royal hero is of weak and hesitant nature; this is explained by the fact that the Hindu drama appeared during a late stage of decline. Here, however, the woman, the passionate wife exhibits a graciousness that is alike heroic and tender. Nowhere has been extolled the beauty of the Eternal-Feminine, the power of a single faithful love, as in Hindu poetry in the persons of its royal spouses: Sita, Damayanti, Sakuntala. The ascete or rishi appears as a demi-god, dominating the hero. The action takes place in a sort of earthly paradise, where man freely inhales the atmosphere of the divine world that envelopes him. These hermitages, of which Hindu poetry is so fond, represent a region midway between heaven and earth. The kings hold familiar converse with the gods. The Apsaras spend their time equally between the heaven of Indra and the royal couch: a strange blend of mankind and the heaven world, a kind of foretaste of Devachan on whose threshold expire the sights and sounds of human suffering.

This deliberate optimism may, at first sight, evoke a smile in the modern world of the West. It is explained by the philosophy and the morality of the brahmans. One might set forth a number of most interesting historical and psychological ideas. I wish, however, simply to deduce an aesthetic conclusion of supreme importance as regards the origin and the essential aim of dramatic art. The product in India of the sacred dance —as subsequently we shall see that it is the product, in

THE GENESIS OF TRAGEDY

Greece, of the Mysteries of Dionysos—the theatre, in its origin, was no mere imitation of real life, rather was it an aspiration towards the loftiest ideal, a raising of the human to the divine life. Now, it is an universal law, infallible both in human and in natural history, that the origin of a thing reveals to us its goal. The golden ear of corn is contained in the grain, the gnarled oak in the acorn, the winged bird in the egg, although neither human eye nor microscope can detect them. It is the same with the theatre. Born of a transcendental idealism, it will always have an invincible tendency to return thereto, whatever catastrophes and vicissitudes it may encounter.

The theatre of an India of dreamy meditation has held us in a kind of earthly paradise, wherein man is sheltered from crime and death. In Greece, we shall see the tragic Muse, the grave-visaged Melpomene, dip her white robe in the blood of the blackest crimes. Shakespeare takes us down into yawning gulfs of grief and madness, into the torture chambers of history. But inevitably, if its interpreters are true poets, the theatre retains an ineffaceable memory of, a supreme aspiration towards, its lost heaven. Aeschylos, Sophokles and Euripides, in their sombre tragedies, bring before us the whole of Olympos, and the sacred drama of Eleusis appears before us as the glorious theophany of a future world. Into the abysses of human suffering to which Shakespeare takes us, the Beyond casts but phantasmal gleams, but these blasting flashes from a vanished heaven are only the more poignant on that account. And lastly, over beyond the romantic wanderings and the orgies of realism, we find, in the new legendary

THE GENESIS OF TRAGEDY

drama of Goethe and Wagner, that the theatre has suddenly risen to unexpected heights, where vision stretches over a wider horizon. Only when all this is realized shall we attempt to formulate the laws and conditions of the theatre of the Soul in its entirety, and of what I call the 'initiation' drama—or *Psyche in the three worlds*.

Before entering upon this rash adventure, I should like to ask, and to solve a preliminary question.

In this journey or voyage through the history of the theatre, what is to be our ruling principle, our directing instrument, our compass? In other words, what is the true formula of dramatic emotion, and what should be its object? Here is the answer of Emile Faguet, who is even in these days regarded as an authority. Taking for granted, in his *Philosophie du Théâtre*, that human suffering is the main object and the essential spring of all dramatic effort, he reaches the conclusion that the reason why we take so keen a delight in such suffering is that it gives us pleasure to contemplate ills from which we ourselves are exempt. Consequently, we should inscribe on the front of our theatres the famous couplet of Lucretius:

> Suave mari magno, turbantibus acquora ventis,
> E terra magnum alterius spectare laborem.

'When a mighty storm is lashing the ocean, it is pleasant from the land to gaze upon a ship in distress.' So this is the upshot, the ultimate secret, of theatrical pleasure: to see others suffer without suffering oneself! I confess that, were such the case, this pleasure would

THE GENESIS OF TRAGEDY

appear to me very mediocre, although slightly 'sadic'. With all due respect to the scholarship and the subtle logic of Faguet, I affirm that there has never been given a more superficial reason for a profound reality. Such an opinion is more than an error, it is an insult to the human soul, a blasphemy against Art itself.

A thousand times no! Dramatic emotion, the pleasure afforded by the theatre, is quite another thing; it is the very opposite of what Faguet imagined. It corresponds to the deep necessity experienced by a human being to share and understand the suffering of another. *Human sympathy is the secret of the pleasure afforded by the theatre.* The desire to feel all the joys, as well as the sorrows, of mankind, to thrill in sympathy with the most diverse beings, to identify ourselves with them and thus bear witness to our kinship with the World Soul: such is the basis of dramatic delight. True sympathy is alike emotion and understanding: it is creative of love. As a poet has said 'les hommes aiment à frissoner'. One might also say: *men love to change soul. The theatre affords them the joy of metamorphosis and resurrection.* In identifying ourselves with another soul, we change personality, but this is in order that we may return to our own enhanced and strengthened individuality. Apart from that sympathy, Aristotle could not have said that tragedy is a soul-purification through terror and pity.

Not, then, with the dark lantern of scepticism, with its flickering gleam, shall we descend into the arcana of tragedy, into the cruel depths of human suffering. We shall take with us the wings of sympathy, and it is the

THE GENESIS OF TRAGEDY

torch of intuition that will help us to return to the luminous heights of initiatory and redemptive drama where —behind the ephemeral Soul—we shall find immortal Psyche.

CHAPTER II

THE GENESIS OF TRAGEDY

The Mystery of Dionysos and the Dithyramb

THERE is no more wonderful phenomenon in the history of poetry than Greek tragedy; its genesis is as glorious as it is astounding. Like some shining meteor, it sprang from the naïve enthusiasm of a people of artists. It came into being, as though by chance, on the day that Thespis left for Athens, with a band of peasants disguised as satyrs, to play the rôle of Bacchus on an improvised stage. No one then suspected that the throbbing womb of Dithyramb, that masquerade of grape-gatherers, was about to give birth to a most synthetic and living artistic form, wherein all the arts —architecture, painting, music and poetry—were to find sovereign expression through that living sculpture whose other name is the plastic dance. Such, however, was the case: a miracle of aesthetic alchemy came about unconsciously and spontaneously through the sheer force of things. Tragedy and comedy had simultaneous birth. They leapt into flame like two wood piles, kindled by the same lightning flash. In a brief space, through the instrumentality of Aeschylos, Sophokles and Euripides, tragedy illumined the world, like a

THE GENESIS OF TRAGEDY

lighthouse with its revolving flashes. And we have been steering our course by its light for the last two thousand five hundred years. Greek tragedy has revealed to us the eternal laws of the theatre. Notwithstanding all the new ideas introduced by civilized peoples, heirs of the Graeco-Latin tradition, they have changed neither its scheme, nor its technique, nor its controlling principles.

Still, in spite of these undoubted facts, I assert that both the genesis of tragedy and its transcendent signification—by which I mean its ethical meaning and educational power—are still for us a psychological enigma, a profound mystery. This is because tragedy has its roots deep in the esotericism of Greek religion, because the mysteries of this religion have so far been unknown alike to official science and to men of letters. It is along the line of these mysteries that we shall try to understand Greek dramaturgy in all its bearings.

But there is one preliminary fact upon which light must be thrown and a clear explanation given.

At the end of last century appeared a man of ardent genius, independent of science though gifted with flashes of dazzling intuition. Unwittingly he penetrated to one of the secrets of the Hellenic religion. He made a discovery which sheds a totally new light upon the entire Hellenic civilization. I refer to Frederick Nietzsche and his first book—the most remarkable of all his writings—*The Birth of Tragedy by the Genius of Music*. Nietzsche's discovery consists in the fundamental distinction he makes between the cult of Apollo and that of Dionysos. These represent two contrasting

THE GENESIS OF TRAGEDY

forces of Greek genius. Apollo personifies the dream, serene contemplation; Dionysos extols the frenzy and intoxication of enthusiasm. Their struggles and reconciliations form the subject of the inner story of Greek art. Tragedy is the expression of their crowning interpenetration, their perfect fusion. This heaven-born vision throws a flood of intense and revealing light upon the whole of Hellenism.

Had Nietzsche taken a further step, he would have penetrated into the profound arcana of the Orphic mystery and into those of the mystery of Eleusis. His materialistic philosophy, in contradiction to his aesthetic idealism, prevented him from taking this decisive step. And so he halted half-way on the path of truth. None the less is his discovery a precious one. We shall now take this further step.

Whence comes the wondrous magic of these two deities, Apollo and Dionysos? Whence spring the formidable powers they use, unleashing them one after another along the course of history. What is the origin of the commanding clarity of the sanctuary of Delphi, and of the orgiastic contagion of the mysteries of Dionysos in Asia Minor, Thebes and Athens? What do these gods really mean to Greece? What do they mean to us? Is the Apollonian religion simply a moral doctrine? Are the Dionysiac rites only the intoxication of the soul by immersion into the Great All, the voluptuousness of a return to the unity of oblivion and nothingness after the dispersion of life? No, this would not explain their amazing regenerative potency. The phenomena of dream and frenzy inspired by these gods are but the physical consequences of psychic and

THE GENESIS OF TRAGEDY

metaphysical phenomena which take place in the invisible world, the world of eternal causes.

Apollo and Dionysos are two divergent manifestations, in reality two words or expressions of deity who act simultaneously and concurrently in the world. Apollo is the divine light and word previous to the descent of deity and its manifestation in matter. He soars above earth life, a coryphæus of the spiritual world. This is why he presides over the oracle of Delphi and inspires the Pythia. Not sexually, like the other gods, does Apollo impregnate women. In his embrace, the nymph Daphne changes into a laurel. He is the god, not of voluptuousness, but of inspiration and poetry. A whole hierarchy of rescuing heroes advances in his wake; and so the legend states that he came from the land of the Hyperboreans with his cortège of singing swans. The Christ is not the Apollo; all the same, previous to His incarnation in the Master Jesus, it may be asserted that the Christ shed his radiance upon all Apollonian appearances and manifestations, as the sun shines through the purple and gold of glass ornaments. Apollo is indeed that solar god whose flaming centre dwells in the unapproachable frigidity of space, though his beneficent warmth is manifested on earth by his glowing radiance.

Dionysos, on the other hand, represents the desire of deity for self-manifestation in the world of matter and life. His name signifies deity moving in all beings. He symbolizes the might of Spirit incarnating in Nature, delighting alike in the ivy and the vine, the bull and the panther, the hind and the bacchante. He corresponds to Lucifer, the genius of unbridled Desire and of Indi-

THE GENESIS OF TRAGEDY

viduality, of human Liberty and of that vital energy of which we become aware by voluptuousness and by suffering through the terrors of death and the transports of resurrection. In him burns the frenzied madness of endless metamorphoses. Dionysos is the Greek Lucifer —Lucifer who sacrifices himself, allows himself to be torn to pieces by the Titans so that he may be born again.

Nietzsche perceived acutely and felt intensely the human faculties corresponding to the cult of Apollo and Dionysos. He divined that Homer's majestic poetry, soaring above mankind in the calmness of contemplation, corresponds to the Apollonian genius, whereas tragedy, identifying itself with human passion and flinging itself recklessly into the whirlpool of life and death, corresponds to Dionysiac enthusiasm. His mentality, however, steeped in the pessimism of Schopenhauer, did not permit him to deduce from his psychic perceptions all the consequences of which they admit. Nietzsche did not see that Apollo and Dionysos are even more than human faculties personified in gods. He did not see the expanding spheres of spiritual worlds, of Powers and Archetypes, whereof Apollo and Dionysos are the centres. Behind Apollo stretches a long line of creative entities who never incarnate, with occasional exceptions when they became Messiahs, Sons of God, Messengers of the Eternal. Behind Dionysos is an innumerable throng of spirits aspiring after physical life and athirst for incarnation, those who, in Hebraic-Christian esotericism are called the Regions of Lucifer. Not only does Nietzsche not understand pre-natal and posthumous life—and consequently the incarnation of souls—he is

THE GENESIS OF TRAGEDY

even far from suspecting what the Orphics meant by the resurrection of Dionysos. When a tragic hero succumbs to his fate or voluntarily immolates himself in a sublime sacrifice, Nietzsche thinks that this soul is dissolved into the Great All and disappears without a trace. He has no suspicion that, from out of the thousands of spectators who filled the theatre of Bacchus, there is an *élite* of initiates that placed a vastly different interpretation on what was being depicted. They did not regard all things as ending with the death of the hero. These initiates never uttered the cold and cynical words of the Latin sceptic: *post funera nihil*; they knew that the drama was being continued on another stage.

Now, this mystical and divine drama, this complement of the tragedy, which showed what was before and what comes after life, was the drama of Eleusis which Nietzsche does not mention, and of which he wishes to know nothing because he does not understand it. This drama was a symbolic representation of the history of the human Soul, the daughter of Heaven and of increate Light, come down to earth in the form of Persephone, carried off by Pluton into the blackness of matter, though destined to return to her divine homeland where again she will find Dionysos, her celestial spouse.

Modern criticism has not hitherto been willing to take into consideration an important fact which these studies, I hope, will prove. Once we grasp the full meaning of the Eleusinian mystery, we see how impossible it is, without the drama of Eleusis, to understand the profound significance of tragedy and its emotional aesthetics. The secret of these mysteries supplied the

THE GENESIS OF TRAGEDY

explanation to the initiates of old. This illuminating key introduces us moderns both into the genesis of tragedy by the mystery of Dionysos and into its sublime fulfilment by the sacred drama of Eleusis and the mystery of the two Great Goddesses. And so the solemn brow of Melpomene shines with a wreath of narcissus, like that of a new Persephone. It is the torch of the mysteries that is to throw light on the evolution of the Greek theatre through the work of Aeschylos, Sophokles and Euripides. After this, we shall attempt to form some idea of what really was the drama of Eleusis, according to ancient testimony, corroborated by modern archaeology.

But we must first recall the origin of Greek tragedy in its outer aspect. Here, we see it first as a sort of profanation of the mysteries of Dionysos, a profanation refined and corrected by the Areiopagos of Athens. Strange to relate, the great Muse Melpomene, that matron bitterly weeping over human suffering, whose majestic statue in the Louvre we admire even now, first appears in history as one who had escaped from the temple, who became an intoxicated Bacchante and, so to speak, an intruder in the city-state.

Simultaneously with the mysteries of Demeter, Persephone and Dionysos, which go back into the night of time, the popular cult of Bacchus continued to delight and trouble Greece. Delirious Corybantes in Phrygia, Maenads with streaming locks in Thebes, joyous Satyrs in Attica—all these were so many irresistible manifestations of enthusiasm for the hidden powers of Nature, through which were frequently made known certain secrets of the sanctuaries. Everything possible was done

THE GENESIS OF TRAGEDY

to prevent excesses, but Dionysiac forces, once unchained, are not easily mastered. Peasants of Megara were told that the God Bacchus had long ago been torn to pieces by the Titans and that he had come to life again, just as the grape issues each year from the vine stalk and the sparkling wine from the foamy vat. They were delighted not only with the mystery and tragedy of the story but also with its keen piquancy. Did they dimly suspect that this fable contained the secret of the worlds? And they had been told that Bacchus, when living on earth, had had Satyrs for his companions. Being alike cunning and devout, they had the idea of disguising themselves as these hybrid creatures, cloven-footed and horned Fauns, and, thus accoutred, to fête the God in enthusiastic songs, to the sound of flutes and drums. This was the beginning of the dithyramb which quickly spread throughout Greece. There was no great harm in this, but soon a rival poet Thespis, a bold impressario, conceived the idea of going on to the stage, and in person representing the God amid a chorus of Satyrs, who responded to his sorrowful or lively stories by laments of cries of joy—all in rhymed strophes. The innovation was wonderfully successful. The example of Thespis was immediately followed by another poet named Susarion, a sprightly jester who, instead of setting forth the serious aspect of the fable, drew from it all the laughable details possible, and referred them to everyday happenings. This interplay saw the simultaneous birth of tragedy and comedy.

The psychic essence of this phenomenon—the most amazing in the history of art—deserves to be fathomed. In Greek mythology, the Satyr represents primitive

THE GENESIS OF TRAGEDY

man, alike nearer both to the beast and to the Gods because he is still in direct and instinctive communion with the divine forces of Nature. In him, sexual energy runs riot, for which the Greeks had a sort of religious respect as a creative power, but in him there also shows itself a quality of spontaneous divination, accompanied by flashes of wisdom and prophecy. In a word, the Satyr is a remembrance, a reminiscence, of Atlantis, where a dim sort of clairvoyance existed as a natural state.

Such is the profound logic which affirms that tragedy owes its birth to a chorus of Satyrs. In their Dionysiac exaltation, the troup of Bacchanalians, disguised as Fauns, bewail and celebrate in turn the dead or resurrected god, summon him with their shouts, and finally end in a state of hallucination. This constitutes the acme of the dithyramb. When the skilful stage-manager presents himself under the aspect of Bacchus, speaks in his name, relates his adventures and holds converse with the chorus, who receive the story of his martyrdom with funereal chants and that of his resurrection with delirious joy, he simply fulfils the desires of the over-excited crowd. This sudden duplication of the self, this projection of the inner vision into vital action, gave birth to tragedy. Dionysos sprang forth living because of enthusiasm for the dithyramb. He has now but to split himself into the multitude of gods and men—and the result is the drama, human and divine. The theatre is in living action for all time. It might have been imagined *a priori* that the drama originated in an imitation of real life. Nothing of the kind. The most potent of the arts was born of the longing of a god and the desire of man to return to his origin. Only after having seen his god did man laugh at all he had lost, that is, at himself.

One may imagine the success of such a spectacle, with its many violent and contradictory emotions, upon a spontaneous audience. Out in the open country, the Dionysiac festivals became choreographic and dramatic representations, to the accompaniment of dancing and the drinking of innumerable skins of wine. When Thespis brought his troop to Athens, the whole city became delirious with excitement: men and women, scholars and illiterates. The magistrates rightly grew concerned. In his *Life of Solon*, Plutarch relates that Solon sent for Thespis and asked him: 'if he were not ashamed to tell so many lies before so great an assembly.' The sage who then ruled over Athens must have dreaded the harmless scenic illusion less than the profanation of the Mysteries owing to the coarse travesties of them that were given by the early writers of tragedy. The torrent having burst the dike, it could not be checked: still, the attempt to canalize it was successful. Here was shown the wisdom of the Areiopagos, enlightened by the science of the Eumolpides. Dramatic authors were allowed to find material for their plays in the mythological traditions, which all sprang from the Mysteries, but it was forbidden, under penalty of death, to divulge their hidden meanings or to pollute them by unworthy jests. The first citizens of Athens, appointed by the Archon and the Areiopagos, made a choice of plays at the annual competitions. The performances became solemn fêtes in honour of Dionysos. Tragedy ceased to be a country diversion for tipsy

THE GENESIS OF TRAGEDY

peasants and became a public cult of the queen city. By this master stroke, a dangerous profanation was transmuted into a beneficent revelation. Under the aegis of Pallas Athene and aided by the Eumolpides of Eleusis was born that Melpomene who was destined to draw streams of divine tears from the human heart.

But to bring out of the night of the Mysteries the Muse of tragedy, an evoker was needed. This proved to be Aeschylos, an Initiate with the heart of a Titan.

The Adolescence of Aeschylos at Eleusis

The traveller who journeys from Athens to Eleusis along the ancient Sacred Way, once lined with mausoleums and cenotaphs and now planted with fine olive trees, leaves behind him the Akropolis and the Parthenon. After crossing the fertile plain of Attica, a gentle ascent brings him to the summit of Daphni, where he finds himself in a wood of pines and myrtles containing the ruins of a small temple of Aphrodite. On the other side of the hill, one suddenly sees the marvellous bay of Eleusis, in dazzling light, like a sapphire triangle, shut off by the island of Salamis glowing like an amethyst on the horizon.

Here Aeschylos was born. His youth was wholly steeped in the religious atmosphere of this Eleusinian bay where once rose the temple of the two Great Goddesses and where their sacred Mysteries were celebrated. Let us halt for a moment at this sanctuary, before following the creator of tragedy along his stormy career.

THE GENESIS OF TRAGEDY

Aeschylos was the son of Euphorion, one of the Eupatridae of Athens who lived in the deme country district of Eleusis. Euphorion was a friend of the Eumolpides and his son was their disciple. The name of Eumolpides, the family of which for over a thousand years retained control of the mysteries of Eleusis, comes from a word signifying 'healing melody'. The Eumolpides claimed to be healers of sadness, magicians of the soul. 'They are priests,' said the initiates in their symbolic language, 'who came from the Moon, the sphere where is found the bridge between heaven and the soul, along which souls descend and ascend. There they are united by the Daimons to material bodies; from there also they take their flight to loftier spheres.' The Eumolpides, by virtue of their origin and their functions in the Mysteries, are placed, as it were, upon this limit between heaven and earth, as mediators and natural initiators. They are also, as their name implies, skilful singers who, from the depth of this abyss of sorrows, chant the delights of heavenly mansions and the way to reach them.*

From childhood, every year during the month of Boedromion (September), Aeschylos had seen going down from Daphni, along the Sacred Way, a long procession of mystae in single file, clad in white linen and bearing the thyrsus. In his curiosity, he had watched them carry out their ablutions near the salt lakes and then enter the temple court of Demeter and Persephone, built of Eleusinian black marble. While yet a child, he had heard it said that these mystae were about to descend, by the temple of Hekate, to the other world, there

* G. F. Creuzer: *Symbolik und Mythologie der alten Völker, besonders der Griechen.*

THE GENESIS OF TRAGEDY

to behold the terrible sights of the infernal regions before rising to the heavenly fields. Subsequently, by reason of the intimate relations between his father and the Eumolpides, Aeschylos had early received instruction from them. He had taken part in the Lesser and the Greater Mysteries, in their complicated ceremonies and symbolic performances. The sacred drama of Demeter and Persephone had made a deep impression upon him. The part of Demeter was generally taken by the wife of the High Priest of Eleusis. One of her daughters or one of the Prophantides played the part of Persephone. The Lesser Mysteries were celebrated at Agrae in the spring. Here the mystae had seen performed the seduction of the daughter of Demeter who, following the suggestion of Eros, plucked the narcissus of desire in the field of the nymphs, a scene related in Homer's famous hymn to Demeter. It ended with the abduction of Persephone, who is carried off by Pluto, the god of the infernal regions, in his chariot. This scene symbolized the descent of the Soul, leaving the celestial abode of her Mother, the region of increate Light (Demeter), to incarnate in a material body in the elementary world. The Torch-Bearer $\delta\alpha\delta$-$o\hat{v}\chi os$ and interpreter of the Mysteries $\dot{\iota}\epsilon\rho o\kappa\hat{\eta}\rho v\xi$ explained to the mystae the meaning of this myth. That which in the official religion represented life beyond the grave, i.e., Tartaros or the Infernal Regions, also signified, in the secret religion of Eleusis, the earth life of the human soul, with all its passions and torments.

The second and third acts of the Sacred Drama, which were given at Eleusis itself at the Great Dionysia, depicted the sojourn of Persephone in the Infernal Regions and her return to the divine kingdom of her mother. Now, it was the second act, representing Persephone in Tartaros, which had left on the soul of the youthful Aeschylos its ineffaceable stamp. To the end of his life he retained in his memory the image of the young seeress who that day represented Persephone in the temple of Hekate. In a state of indescribable emotion, he saw her seated on the throne of Hades by Pluton's side, the king of the dead. Overhead the Tree of Dreams spread its shady branches, through whose tangled foliage crawled fantastic monsters: larvae, vampires and harpies. Pallid Persephone was clad in black, a violet nimbus hovered about her head, and a moonbeam seemed to come from her dark blue eyes, whilst a wreath of narcissus adorned her dark hair. Sombre Aidoneus, Pluton, offered his sorrowing spouse a split pomegranate, showing a pink savoury pulp. Immediately, a chorus of demons, crowding round the foot of the throne, exclaimed: 'Persephone! Persephone! Eat and taste of the red fruit of life. Forget the past, and thou shalt know a bliss supreme! . . .' At the same time, a band of shades murmured softly: 'Persephone! Persephone! Taste not of Pluton's treacherous fruit. Save us from this pit of torment! . . .' The beguiled Persephone, however, extends her hand for the pomegranate; gazing upon it, she appears to hesitate. The monsters of the Tree of Dreams gaze complacently upon her with shining red eyes. A prolonged thrill swells through her heart. The robe of Persephone becomes diaphanous. From her eyes stream tears of mingled pain and longing. She is on the point of yielding to the temptation, when a dazzling light rends the caverns of Hell and a terrible thunder-clap shakes its vaults. The voice of the invisible Hierophant is heard: 'Behold the Liberator!' and Triptolemos, the founder of the Mysteries, appears in the chariot of Hekate, drawn by fiery serpents.

'Persephone! Persephone!' he exclaims. 'In the name of thy Mother, in the name of all those heroes who have fought for thee, remember Heaven and Him who awaits thee! . . .' At these words, Aidoneus in his fury attempts to clasp his wife to himself, when Persephone springs to her feet and, throwing all her soul into her voice, exclaims: 'Come to my aid, Dionysos!' Then, after another lightning flash and thunder-clap, everything disappears in darkness and the mystae continue their wanderings amid disturbing apparitions and fearsome spectres, until they stumble upon the door of light which opened out, at the end of a narrow passage, on to the temple of Demeter.

This scene worked upon the mystae, sensitive as they were to the magic of symbols, like a dazzling revelation. Persephone, being interpreted as personifying the human Soul, her captivity in Tartaros and her deliverance therefrom, evoked a dramatic vision of the disincarnation of souls and of their many alternate existences. But initiates were forbidden, under penalty of death, to reveal these truths or any other secrets of Eleusis, outside the temples. One may imagine the enraptured though awesome delight which this spectacle must have roused in the ardent soul of the youthful Aeschylos. What a rent in the mythological ranks of the official gods! What a formidable gap in the thick wall that conceals the Beyond from the masses of humanity! What an immersion into the abyss of the Infinite! An image of the queen of the dead, in all the profundity of her sadness and the immensity of her hope, entered the heart of the youth, never more to leave it. At the tragic hours of his life, it must have presented itself to him, grave and fascinating, forewarning him of the great crises he would have to pass through, of the crowning decisions he would have to make.

And so it was Persephone who initiated Aeschylos into the secrets of the inner world. For a time, however, world-shattering events removed him from her sway.

In the year 494 B.C., began the Persian wars.

The Persian Wars—The Persae of Aeschylos

The few details of the life of Aeschylos given by ancient writers show that his dramatic vocation was both precocious and all-absorbing. They relate that, in the poet's early youth, Dionysos, the sovereign god of the Mysteries, appeared before his disciple, and said to him: 'Aeschylos, write tragedies.' Whether an occult happening or a symbolic legend, the tradition is important and significant for the man whom the Athenians subsequently called 'the father of tragedy'. During his long dramatic career of over half a century, he wrote about seventy plays, though only seven have come down to us. In his eloquent work, *Les Deux Masques*, Paul de Saint-Victor justly calls this loss 'le plus désastreux naufrage littéraire de l'antiquité'. What wonderful masterpieces, what imaginative works of genius were for ever destroyed in the burning of the library of Alexandria! Still, it is credible that the seven tragedies of Aeschylos which we possess in their entirety were his most characteristic plays, since they survived the fanaticism of Christian monk and of Mussulman, barbaric invasions and the devastating flight of time. There was no Plutarch for Aeschylos, any more than for Sophokles or Euripides. In default of a biographer so richly informed, however, the outstanding events of his life as a dramatist have been recorded by the scholar. His work itself enables us to follow the trend of his creative thought. It gives us the stages of that powerful inner life which the Titan of tragedy repressed within himself, though it involuntarily found expression in the language of his heroes. Nevertheless, some light must be thrown upon it by external political events which exercised a predominant influence, now exciting, now overwhelming, upon the soul of this mighty combatant.

The Athenians espoused the cause of the allied cities of Ionia against Darius, king of the Persians. For the first time, the whole of Greece rose in defence of its independence in the year 494 B.C. The Asiatic menace upon Europe united the hitherto divided city-states of Hellas and the Peloponnesos into various rival democracies and petty tyrannies. Exaltation was at its height; for this was to be the greatest crisis of Greek history. How could Aeschylos avoid sharing in this delirium of courage and hope? His combative nature responded to his country's enthusiasm for war. He was among those who, at the command of Miltiades, rushed out from the wood of Marathon upon the Persians who had scarce set foot on land, and awaited them with bent knee and stretched bow. In spite of their heavy lances

THE GENESIS OF TRAGEDY

and great shields, the Greeks were at first driven back, but at the second assault, they pierced the battalions of the invaders and slaughtered them like sheep. No more than one-third of the Persians succeeded in re-embarking and reaching the open sea. Kuneigeiros, the brother of Aeschylos, attempting to hold back a boat that was carrying off the fugitives, had an arm cut off by the stroke of an axe. The huge mounds covering the bones of the vanquished even now testify to the slaughter on that memorable day. They remind us of Lord Byron's words, after an interval of two thousand years:

> For, standing on the Persian's grave,
> I could not think myself a slave.

Far more glorious still, ten years afterwards, was the battle of Salamis, in which Aeschylos again took part. He gives a wonderful description of it in his tragedy *The Persians*. In very truth, this was the greatest triumph of Greece. The situation was apparently desperate for the Greeks. The vast hostile army, consisting of the whole of mobilized Asia, had invaded Attica at Thermopylae, massacring the people and burning the towns, destroying the temples and breaking to pieces the statues of the gods. The Pythia of Delphi, on being consulted, had uttered this gloomy message: 'In vain does Pallas seek to turn aside the implacable decrees of Zeus. The temple roofs are dripping with blood; the statues of the immortal gods shed tears. Athenians, flee from your homes, take refuge behind wooden shelters.' The Spartans claimed that these shelters referred to the ancient walls of the Akropolis, but Themistokles, interpreting the oracle to suit his designs, had persuaded

THE GENESIS OF TRAGEDY

the Athenians to emigrate to Salamis and all the Allies to bring together their fleet to oppose that of the Persians collected in a creek of the bay. Deceived by a false message from Themistokles, Xerxes imagined that the Greek fleet was anxious to take to flight during the night. He had set guards at all the exits of the gulf and was quietly waiting for sunset in order to crush and overwhelm the tiny fleet in its escape. 'So night was advancing and assuredly the Greek army was in no wise concerting any stealthy exit. When, however, day with white steeds had overspread the whole earth, gloriously bright to behold, first with a loud ring a shout sounded forth cheerily from the Greeks like a burst of music, and the echo of the island rocks sent back the stirring strain the while; and terror came on all the Persians who were deceived in their expectations; for the Greeks were not singing their great Paean then as for flight, but as pressing onward to the battle with resolute valour. And the trumpet with its blast fired all their hearts, and forthwith at the word of command, they smote the deep brine with the measured stroke of the plashing oar, and quickly all were full in view.'

There was an impetuous and formidable clash. Mind prevailed over brute force, the chosen few over the masses. The light barques of the agile Greeks attacked with their brazen prows the heavy Phoenician galleys of the Persians, which dashed against one another, and were crushed and destroyed in helpless confusion. 'And no longer could the sea be seen, being filled with wreckage and slaughtered men, while the shores and reefs were full of corpses. And every ship, all that there were in the Persian armament, rowed off in disorderly

THE GENESIS OF TRAGEDY

flight. But they smote, they hacked and hewed our men like tunnies or any draught of fish. . . . And all the while, wailing filled the sea far and wide with shrieks till the eye of black night put an end to the carnage.'*

Aeschylos, who took part in this fight on one of the conquering ships, must have had his soul filled with the grandeur of the spectacle. A new Greece was born in the sun of Salamis; she was already thrilling with life in that unforgettable dawn. Now may arise in shapely marble the Propylaea, the Parthenon, the theatre of Dionysos. Like a new Aphrodite, the fighting poet saw arise from the azure waves this Greece, mother of art and science and poetry, this Hellas, proudly conscious of human dignity and triumphant beauty. In a kind of superstitious wonderment, the Greeks took delight in bearing witness that their three great tragic poets, each in his own way, had had a part in the glorious happenings of that epoch-making day. Aeschylos, at the age of thirty, had fought with the fleet; Sophokles, aged only fifteen, had been chosen for his youthful beauty and harmonious voice to dance and sing the paean of victory in honour of Apollo; while Euripides, so tradition relates, was born at Salamis on the very day of the fight! And so the radiant sun of Salamis was like a smile of Apollo; sending to his brother Dionysos on the wings of Victory three of his greatest poets.

The battle of Salamis inspired Aeschylos to write his tragedy of *The Persians*. This play does not represent the height of his genius. His predecessor, Phrynikos, had had the idea of producing on the stage a contem-

* *The Persians*. The story of the Messenger, at the court of Queen Atossa.

porary event, but this had been a failure. He had chosen for his subject the capture of Miletus—a town allied to Athens—by the Persians, and had been condemned by the Areiopagos to a fine of a thousand drachmae for having revived the memory of a national disaster. It was the good fortune of Aeschylos to deal with the most brilliant of Greek victories, and he used the opportunity in masterly fashion. He depicted the consequence and reaction of the Greek victory in the soul of the conquered foe. The action takes place at Susa, in the palace of Xerxes, the main characters being a chorus of old men and queen Atossa, widow of Darius and mother of the vanquished king. From the very beginning of the play, an atmosphere of dread seems to hang over everything. Tidings of fleet and army are expected. Though a fervent Athenian, there is nothing of the biassed patriot in Aeschylos. A true initiate, to whom nothing human is alien, he treats his enemies with respect. The aged queen, trembling for her son, is depicted in a noble dignified attitude, calculated to awaken the spectator's sympathy. And lastly, the law of progression—the one essential law of theatrical technique—is duly observed. When the Messenger runs up panting, and exclaims with a groan: 'The whole army of the Persians is crushed,' we see the glory of a mighty nation crumble away in a second. There is a long and doleful recital of the flight of Mardonius, with his army defeated at Plataea, cut to pieces in the defiles of Thrace, or drowned in the icy waters of the Strymon. Then, in solemn libations, performed with due religious ceremonial, queen Atossa evokes the shade of Darius. In sombre accents, the phantom of the great king

THE GENESIS OF TRAGEDY

pronounces the conclusion of the tragedy. When the haggard queen asks how the utter loss of the empire is henceforth to be avoided, the sorrowing phantom responds: 'Attack the Athenians no more!' The joy of the spectators must have been at its height when at the end of the tragedy, king Xerxes, in wretched garments all ragged and torn, appeared as a beggar before the crowd. The moral decline of the enemy constituted a complete revenge and sealed the victory once for all.

The technical genius of Aeschylos is very evident in this work. In condensed and graded form, it represents the external tragedy of life, though not yet that inner tragedy of the soul which alone makes possible its purification and ascent to higher spheres. This was to be revealed in the subsequent works of the great dramatist. But it is easy to understand why, after such a success, the government of Athens, represented by the Areiopagos, regarded Aeschylos as the master of tragedy and entrusted him with the material establishment of the theatre of Bacchus. Up to this time, this theatre had existed in only a rudimentary form; now Aeschylos became its organizer. To give it its full artistic importance, he had to make himself simultaneously architect, costumier, choreographer, scene-shifter, actor and musician. It was he who was appointed to construct by the side of the Akropolis the first wooden theatre, which was afterwards burnt down and rebuilt in stone. It was doubtless Aeschylos who invented the Kothornos, intended to increase the height of the actors in stage perspective, who invented the masks which gave fixed expression to the types of heroes and gods, and who had the ingenious idea of supplying these magnified faces with a mouth of sounding brass which carried the rhythmic vibrations of the human voice to every corner of the amphitheatre. And finally it was Aeschylos who arranged in affecting groups the choruses as they evolved around the $θύμέλη$, the altar set up in the middle of the orchestra. Aided by the best workmen of Attica, he must have performed prodigies of ingenuity to imitate sirens and monsters and dragons, as well as flying chariots that brought the gods down to earth. For these gods were no vain phantasmagoria in the mind of the tragic Demiurgos; they were an impressive image of the most powerful forces in the cosmos. Besides, as we shall see, the intestine struggle between these gods and the struggle of men against them was to become one of the main subjects of his drama.

All this, however, called for new political happenings and a revolution in his inner life.

CHAPTER III

THE LIFE AND WORK OF AESCHYLOS

The 'Prometheus' of Aeschylos and the Promethean Idea

WE have now to rise to a loftier sphere, to the topmost peak of the thought of Aeschylos culminating in *Prometheus Bound* and the Promethean idea. This work proceeds from the arcana of the poet's inner life. On the other hand, it also was a repercussion of the tragic consequences of the great national war of the Greek world.

The Persian wars had ended in the dual victory of Plataea and Mykale: the one on land, the other on sea. The former freed Hellas and Thrace from Persian invasion and preserved Europe from the hordes of Asia. The latter added Ionia to Greece, i.e., the islands and coastal towns of Asia Minor. This decisive victory, due to the vigilance and energy of Athens, momentarily conferred on her the hegemony over her Allies and the exclusive control of the Aegean Sea. During a hundred years there followed the most splendid development of art and literature that the world has ever seen. All the same, this civilization already bore within itself the poisoned germs of its decline and coming dissolution. So profound a thinker, so prophetic a seer as Aeschylos, could not fail to notice this.

THE GENESIS OF TRAGEDY

Though momentarily unified by the common peril, Greece was honeycombed with bitter envy and deadly hatred. The treachery of Thebes and Megara had been followed by frightful massacres. The various towns, infuriated with one another, dreamt only of mutual destruction. Above all private hatreds, Sparta's implacable jealousy of Athens—from which was to arise the disastrous Peloponnesian War—raged like a blazing torch. In Sparta, the constitution of Lykurgos had created a brutal heroism, based on the slavery of the helots and the domination of a bigoted aristocracy. Athens had the advantage of freedom; she also had the overflow of an impatient democracy. The saviours of the homeland, Themistokles, Aristides, Kimon, were all ostracized in succession. The wise, the intelligent and the powerful were speedily confronted with the yelping of the populace. Undoubtedly Athens shone in all her glory. Her trophied temples, her bronze and marble statues raised to the blue vaults of heaven their harmonious columns in rhythmic grace. But in these never-ending wars, for one trireme which returned to the Piraeus with purple sails and flower-wreathed victors, how many black-sailed ships filled with corpses and funeral urns were awaited by wailing families on shore! For one triumphal hymn at the Akropolis, how many funeral piles shot forth their flame and smoke! Hideous pestilence, wan haggard-eyed fever and tattered misery crowded the harbours. Base and frenzied envy seemed the one ruling influence at the people's assemblies. Perikles, with gentle hand and golden speech, had not yet appeared for the taming of the savage beast let loose. In the Pnyx, the precursors of Kleon exhibited

THE GENESIS OF TRAGEDY

their grotesque royalty in rough and brutal fashion. Reality set idealism at defiance. Sometimes it appeared as though the larvae and the loathsome monsters of Tartaros, had invaded the city, in order to mock and rail at the Olympians.

Before such spectacles, the great soul of Aeschylos assumed a garb of mourning and disdain. He felt himself a demi-god in a world of pigmies. Simultaneously he felt a sullen anger against the sovereign god who permitted such happenings, against that Jupiter Zeus who, in the pride of his omnipotence, left the human ant-heap to swarm about in this abject slime. Taking up his *Iliad*, he read the words of old unhappy Priam, kneeling before Achilles and beseeching him to give back the body of his son Hektor. 'The gods have destined wretched mortals to spend their lives in sorrow; the gods alone are free from care. Two casks stand at the threshold of the abode of Zeus, one contains evils and the other blessings. The Thunderer, mingling together that which he gives, now sends evil and now good.' Such arbitrariness filled the tragic poet with indignation. He wondered if it were worth while to chant the praises of such gods, to bow before the impassive Olympian and compose dull tragedies for this poor humanity which the son of Saturn spurned. There came over him a vast longing for the days of his adolescence which had been passed in Eleusis. There at all events, in the mystery of the two great goddesses, he had glimpsed a radiant Beyond that would bring consolation for the troubles of this life. He remembered the seeress who played the part of Persephone in the sacred drama, and her piercing cry as she tears herself from the arms of Pluton:

THE GENESIS OF TRAGEDY

'Aid me, Dionysos!' And the poet, wrathful with human destiny, determined to return to Eleusis and ask the Eumolpides to complete his initiation. For it had only been commenced, having been interrupted by the Persian wars.

I have already said how we are told Aeschylos as a youth had had a vision of Dionysos ordering him to write tragedies. Since then, he had not again seen the occult god who held sovereign sway over his life. At this sombre hour, in profound sleep, the same figure now returns and speaks to him. No longer, however, is it the hilarious Bacchus of former days, bearing the thyrsus and wreathed with vine-leaves. Now his hair streams like a halo about his head. He carries a ferule from which issues a great flame. In his glowing eyes shine the creative fire, for it is now Dionysos who says to Aeschylos: 'Evoke Prometheus, the ravisher of celestial Fire. By him shalt thou overcome Destiny and prevail even over Zeus himself! . . .' At these words, Aeschylos steps back in affright. What! Brave the lord of gods and men! To which Dionysos smilingly: 'Read thy Hesiod once again. . . .' And, with a gentle wave of his torch, disappears.

Aeschylos awakes, his brain aflame. His heart burns with superhuman joy. Not then did he understand the cause of this, though he did after he had read the following passage from Hesiod's *Theogony*: 'Prometheus stole from Zeus the fire of heaven and brought it to men in a hollow tube or ferule. And Zeus, who thunders in high heaven, was grievously angered when he saw the flash of fire shine among mortals. To punish the Titan, the lord of gods and men inflicted on him the cruellest

THE GENESIS OF TRAGEDY

of all penalties: that of being bound to a column whilst a vulture preys upon his liver which eternally grows anew as the fierce bird devours it. Prometheus shall be delivered by none but a son of Zeus, Herakles, who shall slay the vulture with his arrows.' From this myth, Aeschylos produced the most grandiose of his trilogies: 1° *Prometheus the Fire-Bearer*; 2° *Prometheus Bound*; 3° *Prometheus Unbound*. *Prometheus Bound* is the only one that has survived, though it enables us to divine the other two and to reconstruct the idea of the trilogy. The genius of Aeschylos consists in having made fire the symbol of civilization and the origin of all the arts, and, what is even more, in regarding the compassion of Prometheus for men as the motive which impelled him to steal fire from heaven. Long before this, Zoroaster and the Rishis of India had looked upon Agni, the Fire-Principle, as the origin of physical life. But no one had yet dreamt of opposing to this awesome fire which splits the clouds, sends oaks crashing to earth, and kills men, the invisible and trembling flame which pity rouses in the human heart. Now, the torch of Dionysos had kindled this flame in the heart of Aeschylos. The divine spark, which audaciously responded to the zig-zag flash of the Jovian bolt, was omnipotent human sympathy, the creator of a new world. Thus, on reading Hesiod, the figure of the Titan Prometheus appeared before Aeschylos as a gigantic incarnation of mankind struggling with the gods.

And so the brain of Aeschylos conceived the Promethean idea, the torch of his genius and the motive dominating all his work. This idea is both the contrary of the Eleusinian idea and its inevitable complement.

THE GENESIS OF TRAGEDY

The latter lays stress upon the deliverance of the soul and its ascension to a divine Beyond through a divinely-aided understanding of the cosmic mysteries. The former asserts the search after earthly happiness and its realization by the human will. These two ideas meet in an indissoluble combination. For struggle on earth is possible only by the help of the spiritual powers that created it, and the conquest of heaven presupposes effort on earth. These are the two scales of the balance controlling the evolution of the worlds.

We shall now see how Aeschylos expressed the Promethean idea in his *Prometheus Bound*. Plot, characters, action: all are on a colossal, a superhuman scale. One's thought, however, is concentrated on figures impossible to forget, on mighty deeds and commanding words. It is as though one were witnessing the birth of a human race in the midst of a dialogue of cosmic powers.

The scene represents the top of a mountain in Scythia. The wild barren rocks are far from the haunts of men. Power and Strength, ministers of the high decrees of Zeus, lead the bound Titan. Behind these monstrous women comes the lame God Hephaestos (Vulcan), the blacksmith of Olympos. He drags along a train of chains, iron collars and nails, intended to fasten down the victim to the place of torture. Strength and Power stretch Prometheus on the rock, with arms and legs outspread. What takes place afterwards is almost a crucifixion. It is with regret that Hephaestos performs his task, for, in spite of everything, he feels himself a brother of the Titan who has constituted himself the ingenious defender of men. Still, he must obey the implacable command of an all-powerful master. Strength urges on

THE GENESIS OF TRAGEDY

the servant of the gods to his stern task: 'Here are rings for his arms; pass his hands through them; squeeze and strike hard. Hoop round his legs with force. . . .' One hears the grating of chains, of screws and iron implements. At each hammer stroke, Strength redoubles her cries: 'Rivet! Strike! Finish the work!' Hephaestos obeys with many a groan. 'He now has the toils about his limbs,' he finally exclaims, turning aside in horror. Strength flings a parting insult at her victim: 'Now defy the gods, steal their possessions, share their honours with the children of a day!' The tormentors now disappear, leaving the accursed Titan nailed to the mountain, in the open glare of heaven.

Not a word has escaped his lips during the dreadful torture. Now that he is alone, however, he raises his mighty frame with superhuman effort, and his arms are flung to heaven in a gesture of protest. A loud and vibrant cry issues from the depths of his being, a cry which will shake all nature and resound throughout the world: 'O Ether divine, swift-winged breezes and founts of rivers and countless smiles of ocean waves, and thou Earth, mother of all! you and the all-seeing orb of the Sun I call upon, behold what I suffer, a god, at the hands of gods! . . .'

Thus summoned, all these powers of the Cosmos appear in succession to give advice to the chained Titan. First of all, through a side passage of the orchestra, appears the winged chariot of the daughters of Okeanos. Clad in light filmy garments, they form a graceful group. These maidens, personifying the springs of streams and rivers, form the chorus of the tragedy. They represent the passive and compassionate souls of elementary

THE GENESIS OF TRAGEDY

nature. The winged chariot, which carries them gently along, emphasizes their aereal and fluidic character: the primitive Eternal-Feminine in all its weakness, but also in all its grace and *naïveté*. The sound of flutes and lyres played by skilful musicians assembled round the θὔμελη,* accompanies this entrance of the chorus of Okeanos' daughters. They have come to console the great Sufferer. Their tender words and affectionate tears fall like refreshing dew on to the tortured limbs of the Titan. How sweet, too, is the melody: 'The noise of the sound of steel pierced the hollow of the caves and chased away my sedate modesty; yea, I set forth without sandals on my winged chariot.' And now they come down from their chariot and, one by one, approach the Titan: 'I see thee, Prometheus, and a fearful mist comes over my eyes full of horror as I behold thy form withering against the rock in these tortures from thine adamantine chains.' Thus the Eternal-Feminine, which is to be man's consolation throughout his numberless sufferings, is already present at the birth of heroism, sustaining it by pity and compassion.

At the earnest prayer of the daughters of Okeanos, Prometheus relates his quarrel with the ruler of Olympos. At first, he had sided with Zeus against the Titans and had helped him to overcome them. Zeus, however was determined to crush the still feeble and wretched race of mortals, fearing their progress as a menace to his own power. Prometheus prevented

* In Athenian theatres, an altar-shaped platform in the middle of the orchestra, on the steps of which stood the leader of the chorus (anciently the poet himself), to direct its movements.

Zeus from annihilating men and gave them Fire. 'I had pity on mortals, but he (Zeus) had no pity on me!'

In the account he gives to the daughters of Okeanos of the arts and sciences into which he has successively initiated men, the Titan shows himself full of the most understanding compassion, and righteous indignation. This is the active pity of all true and strong heroes. He gave to men 'hope and illusion' which help them to live and prevent them from knowing 'the hour of death'. Consequently, they approach more gently the goal of their existence, whereas he himself, who has become the protecting genius of progressive humanity, who foresees the future, as his name indicates, knows that he is destined to suffer for century after century until he has compelled Zeus to become just or until Zeus has been replaced by another God who will establish the rule of justice among mankind.*

And now, from the other side of the orchestra, accompanied by a strange snorting sound, comes a wild-looking and grotesque mythological character. This is Okeanos (Ocean), riding astride a winged dragon, a sea monster that is rather ludicrous than startling. Here we do not see the majestic Poseidon (Neptune) with his Tritons and his Nereids. He is the master of the primeval waters who has been dethroned by the Olympians, and now he appears, a decrepit and drivelling prattler, dripping with foam and shells. He is the Géronte of the play, and represents interested medio-

* Hesiod states that Prometheus is the son of one of Okeanos' daughters. Aeschylos says that his mother is Themis, Justice. This example, along with a hundred others, proves how independently the poet-thinker dealt with myths.

THE GENESIS OF TRAGEDY

crity, shameful and calculating cowardice. With a protecting air, in emphatic and diffuse language, he advises prudence to the rebellious Titan, i.e., humble submission to the present ruler, though he may resist and avenge himself by any underhand means possible. Prometheus answers such sermonizing with scornful irony: 'As useless to speak to the waves as to attempt to win me over to your counsels of prudence.' And Okeanos goes away grumbling on his dragon.

The daughters of Okeanos become alarmed and again lament the fate of the Titan, abandoned in this cowardly fashion. 'O Prometheus,' they exclaim, 'We bewail with streaming eyes your deadly fate.' Then they hang on to the crag and weep at the feet of the victim, caressing his tortured arms. Their laments are heard afar off. 'The whole land cries with groans. The gods once powerful bewail the glory of thy brothers, all those mortals who dwell on the sacred soil of Asia, the virgins of the Kolchian land (the Amazons), and the throng of Scythians who inhabit the Lake Maeotis.' Listening to the strains, we seem to see the entire universe sympathize with the grief of the Titan whose wish it was to save mankind. Another group of Okeanos's daughters again come down into the orchestra by way of the proscenion stairs and arrange themselves as suppliants around the altar, bewailing the fate of Atlas in supporting the heavens. And now trumpets blend with the flutes and cymbals of the $\theta \breve{v} \mu \acute{\epsilon} \lambda \eta$ to emphasize the evocation of the chorus: 'The billow of the sea roars in cadence; the abyss groans and the black realm of Hades rumbles beneath the earth, and the stream of pure flowing rivers bewails the pitiable woe of Atlas.'

THE GENESIS OF TRAGEDY

But while the chorus are weeping over the lot of Atlas and the Titans, Prometheus, far from dwelling upon his own misfortunes, explains to the simple-minded and compassionate daughters of Life all the good that has come to mankind through his so-called crime of high treason against deity: the theft of Fire. His work is wholly civilizing. Before Prometheus awakened their soul, men were like shades. For centuries they lived like the beasts, confusing all things—as ants do—in sunless caverns. He taught them the rising and setting of the heavenly bodies and the science of numbers; by combining letters with one another he taught them memory, that instrument of the Muses, and then the art of taming horses, and building chariots and ships propelled by canvas wings, capable of carrying sailors over the vast seas. And behold, we have man, a mere worm, who has become king of the earth and brother of the gods through his knowledge of the laws governing the universe.—Here we have the entire history of civilization spread before us at a glance, and the Fire-stealer adds, coming back to his own situation and as though anxious to twist the steel in his wound: 'It is my industry that has created everything for mortals, and yet I cannot free myself from my own anguish!'

The daughters of Okeanos do not understand. Why cannot he who heals others heal himself? Again they utter a wail of sorrow. But Prometheus, who ever finds consolation for his own misfortunes in the good that he has wrought for others, continues to defend his work for mankind. He points to the discoveries he has made for curing men of their ills: medicine, divination, sacri-

THE GENESIS OF TRAGEDY

fices, all that can be made from brass and iron, silver and gold, the bestowers of power. He concludes: Prometheus is the inventor of all the arts.

Thereupon, a feeling of exaltation comes over the chorus. Like a huge foaming billow dashing upon a reef, the maidens fling themselves upon the crag. Then, forming a kind of pyramid with their bodies and arms, they exclaim: 'I have stout hopes that, loosed from these chains, you will yet be no less powerful than Zeus.' Bitter is the answer of Prometheus: 'Art is of very feeble might compared with Necessity which governs the world by the Fates and the Furies, so that even Zeus cannot escape from his own destiny.' 'And what is the destiny of Zeus, save to rule for ever?' ask the eager maidens. But Prometheus refuses to reveal the great and awful secret.

The chorus, grouping themselves again near the altar, sadly call to mind the hymeneal chant they sang when their sister Hesione married the Titan. It is, as it were, the plaintive recollection of an idyll for ever lost. . . .

Suddenly, a woman with streaming locks rushes on to the stage in a frenzy of delirium. This is Io, daughter of Inachos, from whose proud head spring a pair of heifer's horns.

Greek mythology states that Io was a priestess of Hera (Juno). Zeus falls in love with her, and Hermes is ordered to lull the maiden to sleep with the music of his flute so that the god may take her by surprise. Jealous Hera, however, prevents her husband from attaining the object of his desires. She causes Io to be watched by Argos of a hundred-eyes, and whenever the lord of heaven would approach the sleeping beauty, the latter starts up, stung by an angry ox-fly. Then the wretched Io dashes from field to field, wanders from town to town and from country to country, nowhere finding rest. Often does the sweet-sounding flute of Hermes lull her with dreams of love, but Hera's ox-fly torments her with his sting, Argos watches her from every side; the very firmament itself seems to her one vast Argos threatening her with innumerable fiery glances.—Prometheus and Io, the chained Titan, image of genius, and woman, the victim of a desire for superhuman love: Aeschylos wished to set these two tormenting elements over against each other. This genius will finally save mankind, but in the meantime he suffers martyrdom; this woman will give birth to a hero, though only after what an Odyssey of suffering!

Two unfortunate beings: Prometheus and Io, martyrs of Eternal Desire, look upon and understand each other. . . . Io would like to tear from Prometheus the great secret which he alone knows, to learn what will be the end of Zeus. Prometheus contents himself with foretelling all the misfortunes which still await her, her journeyings across Europe, Asia and Africa, and finally her deliverance on the banks of the Nile where Zeus will finally overtake her, and, touching her from hand to head, will plunge her into profound sleep. This will make her the mother of a race of heroes from which will spring Herakles, the mighty liberator and the avenger of Prometheus himself. This fleeting vision of her ultimate deliverance affords a moment's respite to the unhappy Io, a prey alike to unassuaged desire and to poignant anguish. The respite, however, is not a lasting

THE GENESIS OF TRAGEDY

one. Once more she is caught up by ardent frenzy and rushes off the stage, in perpetual quest of the lover she cannot find.

On seeing her disappear, the daughters of Okeanos raise a cry of terror, and their leader, in accents of dismay, exclaims: 'May Destiny preserve me from the love of Zeus!' Thereupon Prometheus, straining upwards as well as his chains will permit, and raising his arms to heaven, utters in resounding accents these proud and ironical words: 'And yet, spite of the pride which now fills his soul, he shall some day be humbled. The marriage for which he is preparing will fling him from his throne: he shall have no empire left . . . so terrible is the adversary he is now creating! A giant unconquerable who will discover more powerful fire than the lightning flash, more resounding peals than thunderclaps, and who will break asunder the trident in the hands of Poseidon (Neptune), that fateful weapon, the ocean plague and shaker of the earth. Having stumbled against this misfortune, he shall learn how wide apart are sovereignty and slavery!'

This represents the Titan's supreme defiance; he has reached the limits of endurance. Zeus has heard the challenge. Thunder rolls along the sky. A gigantic bird crosses the stage, the fiery eagle of Zeus. Hermes, his messenger, follows, and, with awful threats calls upon Prometheus to reveal the great secret. The rebel scornfully refuses. At once the threat is carried into action, and catastrophe follows. Another roll of thunder is answered by a subterranean quaking. The daughters of Okeanos flee in terror. The rock splits in twain, the pit yawns open, darkness falls around, and

THE GENESIS OF TRAGEDY

Prometheus majestically descends to Tartaros where awaits him the insatiable vulture.

Such is a brief summary of this drama of *Prometheus Bound*, which far transcended the religious and moral consciousness of the times.

Its essential idea dwells in its plastic force, its dramatic power. Neither Homer nor any other Greek poet ever conceived anything on such a scale. All their heroes are humble servants of the gods, docile instruments of their wills and the sport of their caprice. Here we see a demi-god waging war upon the Immortals, a superhuman hero creating himself. His physical defeat was changed into moral victory, the punishment of his rebellion became an apotheosis. Doubtless in the third part, *Prometheus Unbound*, there was effected a reconciliation between the rebellious Titan and the sovereign of Olympos, but this understanding was only a compromise based on mutual concessions. Already we catch a faint glimmer of that idea which is clearly to manifest itself only in the future: the collaboration of Man with Deity in the Cosmic Task. This idea was known to the Eumolpides who taught it under the seal of secrecy. Such dangerous mysteries were not meant for the masses. The oath of silence was imposed on initiates. In agreement with the Eumolpides, the Areopagos inflicted the penalty of death on those who violated it. Naturally, Aeschylos was protected by his past, his renown and his title as one of the Eupatridae. All the same, his play was a far more serious insult to the supreme national god than were, at a subsequent period,

THE GENESIS OF TRAGEDY

the timid doubts of Sokrates who nevertheless, for simple reasonings, was condemned to drink the hemlock. The *Prometheus Bound* of Aeschylos was bound to cause a scandal. It was probably because of national *amour-propre* and a kind of patriotic modesty that contemporary authors refrained from mentioning the extraordinary episode which marked the first performance of the work. The scholiast however alludes to it.

At that period, Aeschylos was very famous. Frequently had he shown himself superior to his rivals in competing for the tragedy prize awarded by the magistrates and confirmed by popular acclaim. But jealousy had been roused, intrigues were quietly being hatched.

As Eupatrid, he belonged by birth to the aristocratic party. He was hated by the opposite party. The demagogues took advantage of the discontent caused by certain of the poet's audacious fancies, to weave against him a cunningly organized conspiracy. The performance of *Prometheus Bound* was an excellent opportunity for a determined attack. As had always been the custom—though it speedily fell into disuse—the author, after himself instructing the choruses, personally played an important rôle in the drama. Aeschylos, whose calm courage did not shrink before anything, however audacious, was determined himself to take the part of the rebellious Titan. From the first accusations of the Titan against the Olympian, a murmur ran through the vast amphitheatre; soon the shouts and cries became universal. When the Titan finally announced the fall of Zeus, a dozen hired youths rushed on to the stage and surrounded the hero. Brandishing their daggers,

THE GENESIS OF TRAGEDY

they shouted: 'Death to the blasphemer!' The public, taken by surprise, hesitated, women shrieked with terror; the magistrates, seated in the front rows, uttered not a word. Was the tragedy about to end with a murder? Aeschylos, however, removed his mask and boldly faced his nonplussed aggressors who did not dare to touch him; then, majestically descending the orchestra stairs, he went up to the altar placed in the centre of the space given up to the evolutions of the chorus. In Graeco-Roman antiquity, no one dared approach any guilty person who had taken refuge at the foot of an altar. Now, the amphitheatre of Dionysos was a temple, and the poet had placed himself under the protection of his God. By this action, alike dignified and eloquent, the prevailing atmosphere of tense anguish changed in an instant. Applause broke forth on every side, and the play concluded by the enthusiastic triumph of the poet who, with arms raised as he stood on the altar steps, appealed to Dionysos!

All the same, after this scandal, the position in which Aeschylos now found himself was not the same as before. The Areiopagos accused him of holding subversive ideas on religion that were dangerous to the security of the State. The Eumolpides were indignant with him for betraying one of the profoundest secrets of Eleusinian initiation—namely, that the nature of the gods may to some extent be modified by human will and that it might be possible for Zeus himself to be replaced by another god or constrained to undergo transformation. The poet was summoned before the chief judges of Athens and severely reprimanded. The scholiast even goes so far as to claim that he would have been forced, as was Sokrates, to drink the hemlock, had not the Eumolpides, in order to save him, resorted to lying, and asserted that he was not an initiate. However it be, from that day onward the author of *Prometheus Bound* was stamped with an indelible sign, alike glorious and formidable. He had become the Titan-hearted Initiate.

The 'Oresteia'. The Poet's Exile in Sicily

As one discovers an unsuspected horizon of mountains and plains, lakes and rivers, from the top of a peak scaled for the first time, so Aeschylos perceived a new heaven and a new earth from the summit of his *Prometheus*. He then saw how deep was the gulf separating his hero from the heroes of Homer and of all his contemporaries. He faintly glimpsed the dramas he was to write on the heroes of the Argonautic legend, on Jason, conqueror of the Golden Fleece, on Perseus, liberator of Andromeda, and also on Semele that audacious woman who, beloved of Zeus and visited by him under the form of a haughty youth, wished to behold her lover in all his divine splendour, and was struck down by lightning as she gave birth to the divine Dionysos. All these tragedies, now lost, were daughters of *Prometheus*, propagators of the Promethean idea.

All the same, we may conjecture that the poet's joy was considerably lessened by the bitterness he must have felt at the accusation of the Areiopagos and the blame he received from the Eumolpides. To this must be added the diminished personal glory to himself caused by the success of the youthful Sophokles, with

THE GENESIS OF TRAGEDY

his more human and more seductive tragedies. Nevertheless, he must have surpassed his fortunate rival on his own territory, i.e., in a subject where the study of human passions replaces the great cosmic and divine problem. The trilogy of the Oresteia is justly regarded as the masterpiece of Aeschylos. It would appear to merit a plastic and psychical exposition similar to that here attempted in the case of the *Prometheus Bound*. It is however, sufficiently well known and understood for me simply to bring forward its essential elements. The *Prometheus Bound* far surpassed the mentality of the contemporaries of Aeschylos and of the whole of antiquity. Only in modern times has it been truly understood and appreciated. The *Oresteia*, on the other hand, is the highest expression of the tragic ideal as the Greeks conceived it. Two royal figures stand prominent, that of Agamemnon, king of kings, whose majesty is sullied, as it were, by the monstrous crimes of the Atrides, and that of Klytemnaestra, 'the two-footed lioness', as the chorus calls her, who avenges her cruelly sacrificed daughter by murdering her husband in cold blood, after entangling him in the inextricable net. In the middle of the stage stands Kassandra, the sublime seeress, dragged as a victim into this catastrophe—Kassandra, who, before dying foretells the punishment of the guilty. The dreadful Erinyes, whose black robes, bleeding faces and serpent locks terrified Athens, represent the spectres of atavistic vengeance. Apollo and Pallas, in all the majesty of divinity, intervene at the end, and force the Erinyes to become the Eumenides, protectors of the city-state wherein reign justice and mercy.

THE GENESIS OF TRAGEDY

In this trilogy, Aeschylos succeeded in presenting to his public the fulness of his conception. This is proved by its immense popularity throughout Graeco-Latin antiquity. For us also, it has remained the type of tragedy. It is a surprise to learn that, shortly after this triumph, Aeschylos, then aged sixty-six, left for Sicily where he spent the last three years of his life. For this, the most diverse reasons have been given. The anonymous biographer of the poet asserts that the departure of Aeschylos was brought about by the judges' preference for Simonides in an elegiac competition upon those who died at Marathon. According to Plutarch, the cause of the bitterness felt by Aeschylos was the noteworthy success obtained by Sophokles with his *Oedipus Tyrannus*. It is the opinion of Suidas that the Athenians proscribed their favourite poet because of the collapse of the wooden amphitheatre, for which they regarded its architect as responsible. All these reasons, however, rendered improbable by their dates, are of themselves too futile and trivial to throw the faintest light upon the end of the life of the great tragic writer. His doubtless voluntary exodus into Sicily is due to more profound causes, related to the great secret of his life. We shall attempt to unravel these causes.

Throughout Greek history, Sicily played the part of a remarkable annex, similar to that which Holland and Switzerland played in French literature. Its merit consisted in being for the Hellenes a sort of drain, and also a stimulating rival. In long-past ages, Greek colonies had peopled South Italy called Greater Greece or Magna Graecia and Sicily with city-states where an extreme form of tyranny alternated with an extreme form of

THE GENESIS OF TRAGEDY

democracy. Sicily was a land of excess of every kind, a refuge for exiles, adventurers, daring thinkers. Such men as Dionysius and Hiero of Syracuse were formidable despots and intelligent protectors of the arts. The philosopher Empedokles reigned for a time as a sort of demi-god over the city of Agrigentum. Pythagoras of Samos found no refuge for his esoteric school except at Kroton and Metapontum, on the gulf of Tarentum, not far from the volcanic island.

This island of Sicily, with its gigantic Etna, is a romantic and more grandiose Greece, alike seductive and awesome. Here is nothing of the classic Athens, so completely shut in by Hymettos and Pentelikon that these mountains might have been cut out by the gods to protect the daughter of Zeus. The eastern side of Sicily (Trinakria, the three-pointed island) even in these days reminds one of pagan antiquity. Looking down upon the whole of this side from the old amphitheatre of Taormina, on a mountain crag fifteen hundred feet above the sea, we obtain an oblique view of the Greek coast of Sicily. The three gulfs with their capes resemble three eagles' feathers fallen from the sky into the deep blue of the sea. On the west we see Calabria and the toe of the Italian boot. Opposite, the white cone of Etna raises its snowy mass above an ocean of lava covered with vineyards and scores of villages. Behind Acireale and Catana, the harbour and promontory of Syracuse shine in the distance. Of the old town there remain only the rows of steps of the vast theatre and a rustic hill where shady pines and elms make one think of the shepherds of Theokritos. From the ruins of the ancient citadel Euryalus, the cone of Etna—with its moving plume, 'the white column', as Pindar calls it—may again be seen on the horizon. Here it is seen from another aspect, but it has not changed, it is in eruption all the time. Etna is everywhere, not only the king, but the father, of the island. I have never had the fortune to ascend Mongibello through the sulphur fumes issuing from its crater and mingling with the tempest, nor to see, from the top of the volcano, the whole of Sicily rising from the sea, mountain after mountain, town after town, at sunrise. It is quite sufficient to wander along the coast and become permeated with the sumptuous melancholy of Syracuse, to feel that the whole Cosmos is one eternal tragedy with its creative energy and its destructive powers.

Such a place might well attract an Aeschylos, for it responded to his exuberant and Titanesque genius. The town of Gela (afterwards Agrigentum and now Girgenti) was enthusiastic over his works and made splendid proposals to him, promising to perform his tragedies in their theatre as well as in that of the neighbouring town of Syracuse. The old poet allowed himself to be tempted, and finally settled at Gela. At the end of three years, however, he felt an urgent longing to return to his native land. He reviewed the whole of his career and wondered if he had attained his goal. He had struggled mightily with Destiny and with the gods themselves, though, less fortunate than Prometheus, he had not penetrated their ultimate secret. Was this because his initiation was incomplete? Was it because he lacked the requisite courage and strength?

A great and unfathomable longing for the temple of Eleusis took possession of him. He remembered the

THE GENESIS OF TRAGEDY

priestess who had played the rôle of Persephone in the sacred drama; he remembered her cry: 'To my aid, Dionysos!', when she would tear herself from the embrace of Pluton. What had become of her? He would never know; the Eumolpides themselves even would not tell him. In his terror, there came to his mind a secret entrusted to him by the guide of the mystae. In ancient times, certain virgins sought a voluntary death in the third act of the sacred drama which he had not seen, and which represented the reunion of Persephone and Dionysos in the divine world. Those priestesses died stifled beneath waves of incense on the appearance of the god Iacchus (the risen Dionysos). The spectators did not notice this, for the maidens disappeared in a seething mass of dazzling lights and murky clouds. In reality, however, they sacrificed their lives to the manifested God, and it was the belief of the Eumolpides that their souls were the protectors of the temple, guardians of the great mystery. Was one of these the prophetess whom Aeschylos had seen in the days of his youth? It then appeared to the old man that all his brilliant tragedies written in the course of a stormy life, were nothing in comparison with that . . . and he was almost overcome by despair.

Shortly afterwards, he had a dream. The Seeress appeared before him, but she was no longer the same. She wore a white robe, instead of a violet one, and her whole form seemed alive with a solar radiance. An expression of perfect joy was on her countenance. At this sight, the old flame was kindled anew in the heart of the old poet. He was on the point of flinging himself into her arms when she arrested him with a forbidding

THE GENESIS OF TRAGEDY

gesture and said: 'Touch me not . . . for I am beloved of a god!' In heart-rending accents, the old man murmured: 'Then how is deliverance to be found?' Persephone raised her hand, pointed to Etna, and disappeared.

But dimly aware of what had happened to him, Aeschylos awoke with a foreboding of death. A strange melancholy, blended with a serenity he had never before experienced, filled his soul. What did this dream mean? Was he to fling himself into the crater like Empedokles who, the report ran, had wished in its depths to discover the secret of things? No, such was not his destiny. After reflection, he wrote, within a few days, a tragedy on Etna. The title alone has come down to us, and the play was given after the poet's death, but the subject matter has never been known. A short time afterwards, Aeschylos suddenly died. If the friend watching by his bedside could have caught his last inarticulate words, he would doubtless have heard such mysterious expressions as 'O sun of Salamis! O shore of Eleusis! Persephone! Persephone! . . .'

For many years, poets from Greater and Lesser Greece came to Gela to visit the glorious tomb of Aeschylos on which could be read the following epitaph, composed by the poet himself and preserved for us by Plutarch: 'This monument covers Aeschylos, son of Euphorion. An Athenian by birth, he died on the fertile plain of Gela. The renowned field of Marathon and the long-haired Mede will tell of his bravery, for they have seen it!'

Was it from affectation that the poet did not wish that the inscription on his tomb should state that he was the father of tragedy, or was this haughty modesty

THE GENESIS OF TRAGEDY

anything more than elegant irony at a certain lack of comprehension on the part of his fellow-countrymen? However it be, after his death, the Athenians rendered him almost divine honours. They erected a statue in his memory at the Keramikon, and set his old tragedies to compete with those of the more recent writers. After glancing at the work of Sophokles and Euripides, we shall attempt to throw some light on the mystery of Eleusis which had so great an influence upon his inner life.

The drama of Eleusis—complement and crown of Greek tragedy—will reveal to us its deepest significance, its transcendent range and importance.

With the initiates of Eleusis, we shall endeavour to pierce the cosmic mystery by way of the history and the trials of the Soul.

CHAPTER IV

THE LIFE AND WORK OF SOPHOKLES— OEDIPUS AND THE SPHINX—ANTIGONE AND THE ETERNAL-FEMININE

The Athens of Perikles and the Genius of Sophokles

IN Sophokles, Athens produced not only her favourite poet, but the flower of her race. Physical comeliness, moral greatness, gentleness of manners and the higher gifts of genius—everything combined to make of him the finished type of the Athenian. His statue in white marble, which may be seen in the Lateran museum at Rome, is one of the most life-like bequeathed to us by antiquity. He is elegantly draped in a perfectly fitting toga which he holds tightly to his well-shaped body. His beard is trimmed and his hair curly, while his broad forehead betokens amazing serenity. The smile on the face seems superior to the assaults of Destiny. He would appear to be receiving the visitor with that exquisite Athenian welcome Χαῖρε, which means: Be glad, and may the Graces companion thee.

We must remember that the middle years of Sokrates' life and the crowning period of his work correspond to what has so fittingly been called the incomparable century of Perikles. Paul de Saint-Victor gives us a vivid picture of it in the following striking lines: 'When

THE GENESIS OF TRAGEDY

Sophokles comes on the scene, Greece is in Athens and Athens is in the light. From the lips of Perikles a golden chain descends upon the people. He commands by his intellect and eloquence. Persuasion is the sole power he wields. Athens is reborn beneath this tutelary guardianship: she emerges from her ruins in a triumph of masterpieces. The Akropolis is wreathed with the wonders of human art: the Parthenon and the Propylaea, the Temple of the Wingless Victory and that of the Erechtheion. For the first and the last time, the veil is lifted from perfection, and absolute Beauty appears before the gaze of men. The city is transformed into a huge workshop where tribes of artists fashion bronze, marble and ivory, gold and precious stones. In their hands, Athens assumes the form of a monumental group, with Pallas Polias, from the top of her rock, overlooking the gulf. To her shining plume the sailors over two leagues of sea-waves pay their homage.

Statues are as numerous as citizens; they are to be seen everywhere.

. . . .

The life of Sophokles accords perfectly with these noble and dignified surroundings. Whereas the life of Aeschylos offers a sequence of violent contrasts, titanic efforts and unassuaged aspirations; in that of Sophokles, all is moderation, grace and harmony. Like Aeschylos, he belonged to a family of the Eupatridae. He was born 495 B.C. near Athens at the village of Kolonos, on the banks of the Kephisos, a beautiful spot 'where nightingales sing beneath the dense overhanging ivy and pine-branch'. At the age of sixteen, he was chosen, because

THE GENESIS OF TRAGEDY

of his beauty, to be the choryphaeus of the youths who, with naked and perfumed bodies and lyre in hand, sang the hymn of victory and danced around the trophies of Salamis. He was twenty-eight when he won his first victory in the tragedy competition. Aeschylos was at that time sixty years of age. The scene is well known, but it must be recalled to mind, for it cast a rhythm of success upon the poet's whole life. Kimon had just overcome the pirates of Skyros and carried off the bones of Theseus. 'Nothing,' says Plutarch in the *Life of Kimon*, 'could give the people more pleasure than this event. To commemorate it, they instituted games, in which the tragic poets were to try their skill; and the dispute was very remarkable. Sophokles, then a young man, brought his first piece upon the theatre and Aphepsion, the archon, perceiving that the audience were not unprejudiced, did not appoint the judges by lot in the usual manner. The method he took was this: when Kimon and his officers had entered the theatre, and made the due libations to the god who presided over the games, the archon would not suffer them to retire, but obliged them to sit down and select ten judges upon oath, one out of each tribe. The dignity of the judges caused an extraordinary emulation among the actors. Sophokles gained the prize; at which Aeschylos was so much grieved and disconcerted, that he could not bear to stay much longer in Athens, but in anger retired to Sicily, where he died, and was buried near Gela.'

Sophokles had been awarded the prize of tragedy before the legal age. He was only twenty-eight, and the law required that the winner should be thirty. We can

THE GENESIS OF TRAGEDY

well understand the chagrin of the author of *Prometheus* at this triumph. Precocious success, however, did not turn the head of the young Sophokles: he continued to show Aeschylos deep respect and sincere admiration. He quietly continued his career, ever trying to follow out the Delphic maxim: 'Extremes are evil; moderation in all things.' His long life was a continuous series of triumphs. The weakness of his voice prevented him from conforming with the practice which required that the poet himself should play the principal part, a practice which fell into disuse after his death. He appeared only in rôles which exacted a special degree of gracefulness. We find him representing Thamyris playing the lyre, and the virgin Nausicaa playing ball with her companions. Nevertheless, he introduced great reforms into tragedy, e.g., a third speaker; he also made the dialogue more flexible and brought the chorus into the action. All the same, his tragedies retain their religious character; we are conscious of the presence of the Gods, whether visible or invisible, shedding their beneficent rays over the whole play.

Seven years before the outbreak of the Peloponnesian War, Sophokles was fifty-seven years of age. To reward him for his Antigone, the Athenians appointed him to lead the expedition against Samos. One had the extraordinary spectacle of the famous Athenian poet, in a great battle, in command of a trireme, between Perikles and Thucydides. There was only one thing that cast a shadow over his old age. His son Iophon, jealous of a bastard whom the old man favoured, presumed to arraign his father before the court in an attempt to have him interdicted under the pretext that he had lost his

THE GENESIS OF TRAGEDY

reason. For sole reply, the defendant read aloud to the judges the celebrated chorus from the *Oedipus at Colonus* which he had just finished. It was received with warm applause. The poet concluded with the words: 'If I indulge in senseless talk, I am no longer the man you have known, but since you give me your applause, it would appear that I am still Sophokles.' He died at the age of eighty-nine, shortly before the death of Euripides. His biographers relate that his death took place during a performance of *Antigone*. We may imagine him in the vast amphitheatre, his head reposing on the lap of a disciple seated on one of the higher rows. At the time when the sublime virgin, after being condemned by Kreon, had descended into her tomb, after bidding a moving farewell to life, her creator had already given up his soul to Pallas Athene. No one had noticed the change. The heroine's swan song had borne away the poet's last sigh.

The Theatre of Sophokles. The Law of Nemesis and the Wisdom of Delphi

Like Aeschylos, Sophokles had been initiated into the Mysteries of Eleusis. More prudent, however, than the impetuous Titan-hearted father of tragedy, Sophokles guarded against revealing in his works those transcendent truths entrusted to adepts under the oath of silence. He contented himself with applying these truths to the morality and the psychology of his plays. For these keys—to one who knows how to handle them—are universal master-keys. They thus became for the masses a salutary revelation, a kind of first degree of initiation.

THE GENESIS OF TRAGEDY

Only towards the end of his dramatic career do we find some of these divine truths filtering through his tragedies, like faint rays of light through a thick curtain.

Indeed, what made Sophokles highly receptive of these truths, was, apart from his great intuitive powers, his intense consciousness of human frailty and his profound understanding of human suffering, in spite of his own exceptionally happy life.

We have seen that the work of Aeschylos, who was inspired by Dionysos, is dominated by two outstanding ideas: on the one hand, the fatality of the Destiny overshadowing humanity and even the gods by the inevitable law of life; and on the other, the Promethean idea, the expression of man's revolt against Destiny, and, when occasion calls for it, against the Gods themselves. The Theatre of Sophokles, who was inspired by Apollo, is dominated by two correlative ideas: first, Nemesis, the punishment of crime and wrong-doing by a kind of immanent justice, a return impact of the passions, in which is manifested the will of providence (this is but one application of the idea of Destiny according to Aeschylos); and afterwards, the idea of Pity and universal Love (an idea whose germ is found in the *Prometheus Bound* of Aeschylos, and to which Sophokles gave added force by introducing the idea of the Eternal-Feminine and its creative potency). Only in the latter part of his work, and especially in *Antigone*, do we find the glorious blossoming of this idea which, moreover, is met with in Greece only episodically, and as though apart from all the accepted ideas in Plato's Diotima.

THE GENESIS OF TRAGEDY

To return to the idea of Nemesis.

In their allegorical statues, the Greeks represented the goddess Nemesis with raised forearm to indicate the cubit, an ancient measure, and holding a curb in her other hand. Nemesis was the enemy of the proud, the avenger of arrogance and injustice. Agent of the high decrees of Pallas, she shares the feelings of this goddess. She detests and punishes insolent presumption, iniquitous violence, ostentation of power, insult at misfortune, scorn for suppliants, outrage on the dead, ingratitude of children towards their parents: in a word, whatsoever disturbs the sacred and eternal order of things. Paul de Saint-Victor remarks that the sin against Nemesis in Greek religion plays a part analogous to the sin against the Holy Ghost in Christian doctrine. Both are alike inexpiable. 'Moderation in all things' is the basis of Delphic and Apollonian morality; it is also that of Sophokles. He formulates it as follows: 'The Gods chastize all those who, born as men, do not think as men.' Such is the morality that dominates the entire theatre of Sophokles, and more particularly his four tragedies: *Ajax, Electra, Philoctetes* and *Trachiniae*.

It would be possible, in these four dramas, to set forth various applications of Nemesis, and also to show how vividly Sophokles grasps the reality of life. I prefer, however, to examine the masterpiece in which the full genius of the poet is exhibited.

The trilogy of *Oedipus Tyrannus, Oedipus at Colonus* and *Antigone* shows us how, by searching into the depths of the most stupendous tragedies in history and legend, and tearing away the blood-stained veil in which they are enveloped, the poet may afford us a glimpse into the sublime truths of a Beyond which dominates this life and explains it by the light which it sheds.

The 'Oedipus Tyrannus' and the Riddle of the Sphinx

If we pass from the cycles of Argos and of the war of Troy to the Theban legends, we are struck by a complete change in tone and colour. The snowy peaks of Olympos and shores strewn with wrecked ships, give place to verdant glades bathed in rose-tinted light that remind one of Fauns and Nymphs. Solemn-toned cithers are succeeded by the languorous and passionate strains of the flute. Boeotia, peopled by a Lydian race from Asia Minor, had been from pre-historic times the favourite home of the cult of Dionysos. It was not the risen and spiritualized Dionysos of the Orphic and Eleusinian initiation, but the popular Bacchus, the impetuous God, full of the frenzy of life, and accompanied by troops of Bacchantes, who was celebrated at Thebes. In his name the Theban women held their secret assemblies on Mount Kithaeron. This cult was originally very solemn and of a character which we should now call psycho-physiological, for it taught women the secret of favourable conception, along with such disciplines and rites, prayers and ceremonies as were calculated to attract noble and pure souls to the wombs of the mothers. For in these feminine initiations, as in all others, the principle of past lives was formally taught. Subsequently, these ceremonies, of high and lofty order, degenerated into strange and cruel

THE GENESIS OF TRAGEDY

orgies. The Lydian race was a sensual and passionate one. Initiations founded with the object of disciplining woman and controlling birth, in order to produce a superior humanity, degenerated into dangerous vices and excesses.

The popular imagination, over-excited by these orgiastic cults, caught hold upon the Egyptian Sphinx and transferred it to Thebes. The deity of the Nile, however, underwent a transformation in passing into Hellas: the Sphinx became the Sphinge. In changing sex, it changed its nature and signification. The male Sphinx, whose monumental figure still exists at the foot of the great pyramid of Gizeh, has the body of a bull, the paws of a lion, the wings of an eagle and a human head wearing either the 'pschent' or the sign of deity. He was a majestic and beneficent god. Egyptian initiation regarded him as the symbol of the entire cosmic evolution proceeding from the animal, through man, on to deity. By giving the symbolical animal a woman's head and bust, by changing the Sphinx into the Sphinge, the Hellenic legend made of it a monster of cruelty and licentiousness representing feminine perversity in its most inauspicious form. She became the devastating scourge of the whole country. Living in a wild cave on Mount Kithaeron, she attracted men to it by her womanly beauty and asked them the question: 'What creature walks in the morning on four feet, at noon on two and in the evening on three?' As no one could answer this puzzle, the treacherous Sphinge hurled into a pit her imprudent visitors after clasping them to her lovely bosom and rending them with her claws.

Now, there came along a stranger, who was stronger

THE GENESIS OF TRAGEDY

and more discerning than these feeble victims. Defying the disquieting glance of the Sphinge, he succeeded in solving her puzzle. He replied that the unknown creature was Man.* Whereupon, the vanquished Sphinge is compelled to fling herself into the pit.

Thebes, finding itself without a master, offered the crown to its liberator who married Jocasta, widow of the late king. The fortunate victor raised to the throne by a stroke of fortune, was named Oedipus. He did not know that he was the son of the deceased king and that he had married his own mother. An oracle having foretold that this son would kill his father, his parents, immediately after his birth, had caused him to be exposed on Mount Kithaeron. They believed him to be dead. Hence the terrible fate in store for this man, once his true origin should be discovered. From the height of his power and fortune, he is suddenly to fall to the lowest depths of shame and degradation under the dual stigma of parricide and incest.

Such is the popular legend which appears to have regarded the case of Oedipus merely as an example of the unjust fatality which apparently afflicts human destiny. The subject is one which Sophokles greatly enhanced and magnified. He depicted Oedipus as the man of desire who subjects the world to himself by the might of his intellect and his will, though he knows nothing of the essence of things. For he is still ignorant of the Soul, of the Gods, of the great mystery of the Beyond. He has no need of these in order to ride rough-

* The Theban legend seems to say that Oedipus, although not an initiate, had guessed the great puzzle of life by his intellect alone. But he had only half solved the puzzle, as Sophokles proved.

THE GENESIS OF TRAGEDY

shod over his fellow-men and taste the delights of existence. Like a raging torrent, he has overthrown all the obstacles in his way. And now he has reached the height of power and is intoxicated with his good fortune. On attaining this stage, the Gods reveal to him the true meaning and purpose of life. Already his past and involuntary crimes—his own passions disguised as wild beasts on his track—lay siege to his throne and lie in wait for him. They will hurl him into a pit more awful than that of the Sphinge. There he is to learn what human destiny is, and after passing through the school of trial and suffering, the old man will die as a beneficent initiate.

We shall now consider the principal stages of this drama.

. . . .

The scene is Thebes, between the palace of the Labdacides and the temple of Apollo. The square is crowded with wailing old men, women and children, suppliantly carrying branches of olive trees. In their distress, they implore Oedipus to help them. A terrible scourge, a mortal pestilence ravages the city. Death assails the seeds of plants beneath the soil, destroys the flocks and removes life from the unborn child. Heaps of corpses encumber the streets of the city of Kadmos, bent beneath the curse of an unknown deity. By the mouth of the priest of Zeus, the people invoke their king, the victor of the Sphinge, praying that he may deliver them from this new scourge.

Oedipus, majestic as a god, appears on the top of the stairs, between the Doric columns of his palace. In eager response to the voice of the priest who invokes his aid, he has anticipated the public wishes and sent his brother-in-law to Delphi to consult the oracle of Apollo. Kreon brings the answer of the Pythia. As a bearer of good news, the messenger is crowned with laurel. The oracle declares that the cause of the evil is a monster that pollutes the city. Punishment must befall the murderer of the deceased king, who has not yet been discovered. By a solemn oath, Oedipus promises to try and find the guilty man, pronouncing against himself an awful curse, should he fail in his mission. On the advice of Kreon, Oedipus has sent to consult Teiresias, the famous soothsayer who must know the great secret. We see the approach of the blind old man, bending beneath an augur's staff and led by a child. He advances with slow and apparently regretful steps. Then we witness the most extraordinary scene in the whole theatre of Sophokles, affording the most amazing perspectives on the esoteric background of the tragedy.

In this purple-clad king, who speaks to his people in all the pride of his power, and in this blind old man before whom the crowd respectfully gives way, as though afraid of touching him, two contrasted worlds are face to face. The King is confronted with the Prophet. On the one hand, the whole material power; on the other, the whole moral force. Here, Reason gropingly tottering in the darksome labyrinth of Effects; there, the Spirit-Seer who dominates this gulf and fathoms it by dwelling in the light of Causes. In Oedipus and Teiresias, the visible and the invisible Worlds face, measure and defy each other.

At first, the king welcomes the prophet with all the honours due to his rank. 'O Teiresias,' he says, 'thou

THE GENESIS OF TRAGEDY

who judgest all the signs that are in the earth—the secret things and all that men may learn—though thou art blind, yet canst thou feel our city's plight whereof thou art the champion, in whom alone, Prophet and Prince, we find our saving help!' The old man, however, evades these questionings. 'Ah me!' he murmurs with bowed head. 'It is but sorrow to be wise when wisdom profits not. All this I knew, yet missed the meaning. Else had I not come!' And as the king presses him he answers: 'Dismiss me home, be ruled by me.' The chorus also makes its appeal: 'In the name of the Gods, keep not from us that which thou knowest; thou seest us suppliant at thy feet.' Teiresias answers: ''Tis you, not I, who are mad; I shall not reveal my sorrows so as not to reveal thine.' 'What, thou know'st all and wilt say nothing?' says Oedipus. 'This fatal secret will be revealed of itself, notwithstanding the silence wherein I shroud it,' sadly answers the disciple of Apollo. But Oedipus is impatient and irascible. No sooner is Teiresias unwilling to be his humble servant than he regards him as nothing but a traitor and a charlatan. Angrily he accuses the would-be soothsayer of being the author—or at least the accomplice—of the crime.

Smarting beneath this insult, Teiresias suddenly raises himself to his full stature and a flash streams from the blind man's eyes. His timidity has gone, the prophet is about to speak, and his words will be terrible: 'Indeed? And I command thee to conform with the decree thou hast pronounced, and, from this day to speak neither to me nor to any of the Thebans, for thou art that impious one who pollutes this earth.'—'Darest thou utter such impudent words, thinkest thou to escape

THE GENESIS OF TRAGEDY

the punishment they deserve?'—'Yea, for I have on my side the might of truth.'—'Repeat what thou hast just said.'—'I tell thee that thou art this murderer of Laïos* whom thou seekest.' Thereupon the fury of Oedipus knows no bounds. He believes himself in the presence of a vile impostor, accuses Teiresias of having been bribed by Kreon to rob him of his crown. Tieresias, however, who becomes calmer in proportion as the anger of Oedipus increases, answers with the serenity of one who sees things from above, because he scarcely belongs any longer to this world.

Teiresias:

Though thou be master, thou must brook one's rights.
Equality—reply! Speech yet is mine,
Since I am not thy slave, nor Kreon's man
And client, but the slave of Loxias.†
I speak then. Thou that tauntest me for blind,
Thou who hast eyes, and does not see the ill
Thou standest in, the ill that shares thy house—
Dost know whose child thou art? nor see that hate
Is thine from thine own kin, here and below.
Twin-scourged, a mother's Fury and thy father's,
Swift, fatal, dogging thee, shall drive thee forth,
Till thou, that seest so true, see only night,
And cry with cries that every place shall harbour,
And all Kithaeron ring them back to thee,
When thou shalt know thy marriage . . . and the end
Of that blithe bridal-voyage whose port is death!
Full many other evils that thou knowst not
Shall pull thee down from pride and level thee
With thine own brood, aye, with the thing thou art!

* Father of Oidipous, or Oedipus.
† Loxias, or Apollo.

THE GENESIS OF TRAGEDY

So then, rail on at Kreon: if thou wilt,
Rail on at me who speak: yet know that thou
Must perish, and no man so terribly.

After uttering these words, spoken without any trace of anger though solemnly and in tones of profound pity, Teiresias departs as he came, led by the child playing on a flute a kind of funeral march in which one seems to hear the dull sinister tread of approaching Nemesis. After stammering an impotent protest, Oedipus returns to his palace in consternation. A secret horror has frozen his furious rage.

The germ of the entire drama is contained in this masterly scene. Event follows rapidly upon event as the occult facts of the past are revealed, imprisoning the unhappy king in their cruel chains. We shall briefly sum up the three scenes in which Sophokles exhibits the working of destiny with all the dexterity of a modern theatrical manager.

During a dispute between Oedipus and Kreon, when the king accuses his brother-in-law of treason and threatens him with death, Jocasta interposes and separates them. Alone with her husband, she attempts to reassure him. She has no faith in seers and makes mock of the oracles of Apollo, claiming that she can prove them false. For the oracle has predicted that Laïos would be killed by his son. Now, this son has been exposed at birth on Mount Kithaeron, where he died. Consequently, the oracle has lied. But when Jocasta tells her husband that Laïos was murdered at the cross-roads near Delphi, Oedipus is smitten with terror. He suddenly remembers that, years previously, he himself killed on this spot a tall majestic man, seated

THE GENESIS OF TRAGEDY

in a chariot, who had obstructed the path and struck the king on the forehead. Jocasta's description of her first husband applies to this man. Thus Oedipus might unwittingly have slain the king of Thebes in this fatal encounter. On this point also, Jocasta reassures him. For, it is asserted, no one man killed Laïos. Public report states that he and his followers were assassinated by a band of brigands. This is the account given by the only servant who survived the massacre. This man, a shepherd, is still living on Mount Kithaeron. Contrary to the advice of Jocasta, Oedipus sends for him. For now that fear, as well as doubt, has entered his soul, he is determined, even at the cost of death, to throw light upon the enigma of his birth.

Meanwhile a fresh incident brings another terror: a messenger announces the death of his adoptive father Polybus, king of Corinth, whose son Oedipus believes himself to be. At first, he joyfully welcomes this news: there is now no danger whatsoever of Oedipus killing his father, as the oracle has foretold. All the same, there is one obscure point. The wife of Polybus is still living, and the oracle has stated that Oedipus would marry his mother. Thereupon the messenger, in order completely to reassure Oedipus, reveals a great secret which he had hitherto entrusted to no one. Oedipus is not the son of Polybus; he is a foundling whom the king has adopted, and, being himself childless, has acknowledged as his own. It was the messenger himself who took the child to the king of Corinth. He had received him from a shepherd of Mount Kithaeron. But whence came this hapless babe? A mystery! The old shepherd of Mount Kithaeron is the only one who knows from what royal

THE GENESIS OF TRAGEDY

hands he received it. . . . And this shepherd is the one for whom Oedipus has sent . . . and who will shortly appear. But even now, on listening to the messenger of Polybus, the terrible truth illumines with a flash the night of the past. The pit gapes to receive Oedipus: Jocasta has already fallen into its depths. The details regarding the child, his poor feet pierced and tied by cords,* have brought back to memory her own crime: the child given up to death through dread of the oracle. No longer is any doubt possible. The oracle was right; destiny has spoken. The being she wished to destroy stands before her as an avenger . . . and this accursed son has become his mother's husband! Oedipus, braving all, is determined to question the old shepherd who is about to come; he must have irrefutable proof of his birth, whether it is royal or infamous. In vain Jocasta tries to dissuade him. 'In the name of the gods, I beseech you, yield and ask no more.' As he furiously persists, she breaks out: 'Unhappy man, may you never know who you are. Alas! O Wretched Wretched utterly! That name I give you and henceforth no other name!' Whereupon Jocasta returns to her palace from which she will never again come out alive.

The shepherd, who had hitherto guarded the secret of the birth of Oedipus in the wild solitudes of Mount Kithaeron, now arrives, trembling with dread. He is aware that the dreadful secret for long years hidden within his breast, and which he would gladly keep undivulged, will bring him no reward. Confronted with his accomplice, the messenger of Polybus, he still

* The name of Oedipus comes from ὀιδίπους meaning swollen-footed.

THE GENESIS OF TRAGEDY

attempts to deny the truth and to steal away. Oedipus flings him to the ground and threatens him with death. By these means he extorts from the shepherd the confession that he received the child from the queen's hands, for the purpose of exposing it to death. 'Then why did you give it to this old man?' asks Oedipus. The shepherd replies:

> 'Twas pity, sir, I thought: he dwells afar.
> And takes him to some distant home. But he
> Saved him to suffer! If you are the child
> He saith, no man is more unfortunate.

Whereupon Oedipus exclaims:

> Alas! It comes! It comes! And all is true!
> Light! Let me look my last on thee, for I
> Stand naked now. Shamefully was I born:
> In shame I wedded: to my shame I slew.

And so the past actions of Oedipus, his involuntary crimes resulting from the crime of his parents and from his own passions, have come back, like the larvae of Tartaros, to twine their phantoms around him and hurl him into a slough of despond. With his own hands, he had unloosed the viperous knot of his destiny. It leaves him thunderstruck, bloodstained and horrified. This is the *ne plus ultra* of tragedy, though even in all the excess of terror and pity, the drama retains the lines of beauty by reason of the melodious genius of Sophokles and the superhuman thought which inspired his work.

We know the end of the tragedy which takes place behind the scenes, within the palace. It is related to the

THE GENESIS OF TRAGEDY

chorus by a weeping servant. After throwing herself sobbing on to the marriage bed, Jocasta has hanged herself above it, on a column of the gunaeconitos (women's apartments). Oedipus rushes into the room and tears away, from the still warm corpse of her who was both his mother and his wife, the clasp from her breast. With it he tears out his own eyes, so that he may no longer behold what he ought not to see at all, and may conceal from himself in everlasting darkness his own crimes. One ought to have seen Mounet-Sully play the last scene of Oedipus Tyrannus to form an adequate idea of the most poignant production in the whole of Greek tragedy. The unhappy Oedipus, blind and with blood streaming from his eyes, was seen to grope his way down the royal staircase and stretch out his arms into the black night which now surrounds him for ever, whilst his moaning and laments are lost in space. One ought also to have heard his words to Kreon:

> Leave me to haunt, mountains, where the name
> Is known of my Kithaeron—proper tomb
> By mother and by father set apart
> For me, their living child. So let me die
> Their victim still that would have slain me there.

Then he fell on his knees and for the last time embraced his children whom he can no longer see and from whom Kreon is forced to tear him away because his arms, in a convulsive thrill of tenderness and despair, could no longer release their hold. The white peak of Mount Kithaeron showed on the horizon its snowy dome in the sombre twilight, and the fallen king departs into gloomy exile, led by the same child, and to

THE GENESIS OF TRAGEDY

the sound of the same funeral melody which, that very morning, had brought to that spot the soothsayer Teiresias. One ought, I repeat, to follow the *crescendo* of these multiplied impressions, interpreted by an actor of genius, to understand how far human sympathy can extend and what Racine called 'the majestic sadness of tragedy'.

The 'Oedipus at Colonus'. *Purification by Suffering*

Were there no sequel to *Oedipus Tyrannus*, it would be the most pessimistic of dramas. Notwithstanding the beauty of form and the genius of Sophokles, there would be left behind the doleful impression that human destiny is controlled by chance and that life is a sinister snare. Oedipus committed parricide and incest, but he did not know this; therefore, in the eyes of human justice, he is not guilty. But we must consider the whole of the trilogy if we would fathom the profoundest elements of the work which are to be found in the arcana of divine justice. Then, the question assumes another aspect. Oedipus is, as it were, the inheritor and expiator of the sins of all his race. He owes his misfortunes as much to crimes committed in his former lives as to the passions to which he is still subject. The first drama of the trilogy has shown us, with tragic impetuosity, the awakening of conscience beneath impending catastrophe. The second part of the work, written in the poet's old age in a mood of serene melancholy, shows us the purification of the soul by the magic power of suffering heroically borne. For Oedipus, in the enduring of his misfortunes, now shows the same energy that he had

THE GENESIS OF TRAGEDY

previously shown in the satisfaction of his desires. And so evil is overcome by the victory of the man over himself. Enlightened by grief, the man of passion, brute force and lust, now almost a saint, enters by deliberate death into a state of higher consciousness. His end is a revelation, a kind of transfiguration.

Briefly, let us see the stages of this interior drama as scenically represented.

Years have passed since the events that cast a gloom upon the palace of the Labdacides. Fresh catastrophes are in store for Thebes. The two sons of Oedipus are rivals for the throne. They have prevented their father from finding a refuge in the city which has rejected him with feelings of horror. And now the hapless king wanders, a beggar, from land to land. All the same, he has found in his daughter Antigone an admirable companion. She guides his tottering footsteps, protects him on the rough paths of exile and consoles him with her steadfast affection.

The immortal group, which has carved for all time the image of Pity leading Misfortune, appears at the outset of the tragedy, and we hear these words spoken by Oedipus: 'Antigone, child of a blind old man! To what spot of earth or whose city are we come? Who will now receive the wanderer Oedipus, that asks but little, yet than that little, still less obtaining? But I am satisfied with even this. For my past trials, my long experience with them and my noble nature all teach me to acquiesce.'

They are now close to Athens, at Colonus, the sacred wood of the Eumenides. These terrible goddesses are greeted by Oedipus as his liberators. For the oracle of

THE GENESIS OF TRAGEDY

Apollo has declared that here he would find death and deliverance. Oedipus is not afraid of the Furies; no longer does he feel remorse. He has flung off the burden of the catastrophes that overwhelm him, by understanding them. He has overcome Nemesis by calmly submitting to every kind of affront. Now, a dazzling ray has pierced the darkness; on the other side of the tomb he glimpses a marvellous light.

In this second part of the trilogy, Oedipus, a majestic old man, noble-browed and blind, a king in rags, appears before the city gates, his hand leaning on the shoulder of his daughter, like a god driven from Olympos and led by a compassionate Muse. The terrified citizens draw back before this unwonted apparition, but the women weep and the children bring flowers. It appears as though this moving sight had brought a beam of divine gentleness into the city. The voices of the sanctuary at Delphi have proclaimed that the body of Oedipus will protect the land that possesses it, will make it flourishing and invincible. His tomb, more powerful than an Akropolis, will defend the city that guards his remains. It is in the name of this oracle that Oedipus asks of Theseus, king of Athens, a refuge for his body in the wood of the Eumenides. Theseus, who understands the greatness of this gift, gratefully accepts it. In vain does Kreon, who has become tyrant of Thebes after having banished Oedipus, now claim him as a gage of the duration of his own power; in vain does he attempt to carry off Antigone with an armed band in order to compel her father to follow her. Theseus restores the maiden and drives away the shameless ravisher.

But thrice has been heard the thunder-roll in the

heavens. Oedipus recognizes the omen: the Gods are calling him. Enthusiasm for death now takes possession of the old man who has already bid farewell to life. He says to his daughters Antigone and Ismene: 'Follow this way, my children—move on—for I have once more appeared, as ye were to your father, a new guide to my children. Move on and touch me not, but let me e'en find this sacred tomb where fate declares that Oedipus must be hidden from mortal eye in Attic earth. This way, move forward, for this way my conductor Hermes leads me, and the goddess of the shades below.' Accompanied by Theseus they disappear in the sacred wood, and it is a messenger who relates what took place before the cave where, according to the legend, Pluton disappeared with Persephone when carrying her off to hell. Oedipus has entreated his daughters to leave him. On returning after a few minutes, they see no trace of their father. Theseus was standing there motionless, his hand over his eyes which were fixed on the cave, in the attitude of a man dazzled by a flaming vision. Has Oedipus been destroyed by lightning, or has the earth suddenly opened and swallowed him up? Theseus, the sole witness of the miracle, does not reveal what has happened.

What did Theseus see, according to Sophokles? The messenger says: 'Know for sure that he has left his long, long life on earth.' 'Oh, how?' 'By providential interposition and without a pang.' Antigone adds: 'A new kind of death has ended his life.' Had the Eumolpides of Eleusis been questioned on this matter by one of their disciples, they would doubtless have answered: 'Theseus must have seen the physical body of Oedipus consumed instantaneously by a flame of the Fire-Principle coming from the bowels of the earth, and his transfigured soul, clad in its astral body, leap forth from the cast-off body of flesh to rejoin the Gods. This is why Theseus after witnessing the prodigy, flings himself on to the ground, as the messenger relates, in adoration alike of Earth and of Olympos, the abode of the Gods.

Assuredly, in this end of the drama of expiation, Sophokles raised a corner of the veil of the Mysteries, signifying, by this image which was both symbolical and real, the complete liberation of the soul from its earthly chains through the fire of suffering and the energy of the will.

The 'Antigone', *Revealer of the Eternal-Feminine and of Universal Love*

We may now attempt to pierce the secret of the tragedy of *Antigone*, the conclusion of the great Theban trilogy.

This drama represents the blossoming of the thought of Sophokles. It brings before us the most extraordinary psychological evolution that has ever been represented on the stage. This evolution not only comes about in the heroine, it spreads all around and affects the whole city. Let us follow the stages of this metamorphosis which seems miraculous, though the magic of art makes it inevitable.

The city of Thebes is emerging from the horrors of a civil war which has grafted itself upon the disasters of the family of Oedipus. The sons of the incestuous

THE GENESIS OF TRAGEDY

king have provoked this war in an attempt to usurp the reins of government. The besiegers have been repulsed, but the two rival brothers have inflicted deadly blows each upon the other. Thebes is freed from her external enemies, though as completely crushed by her misfortunes as if she had been vanquished. Only apparently now does she believe in her Gods, in divine justice. Two powers alone rule over men's hearts and cause them to bow their head: Hatred and Fear. Kreon, an ambitious upstart, a clever and intriguing tyrant, crafty and obstinate, has attained to power. No longer having another master, the city of Thebes trembles before him. Straightway he intends to give the people a proof of his absolute authority. The body of Eteokles, the defender of Thebes, has been buried in accordance with the usual rites; but the body of Polyneikes, the enemy of his country, whose sole representative Kreon henceforth wished to be, is deprived of funeral honours, his body rots in the sunlight, a prey to dogs and vultures. And such is to be the lot of those who dare to disobey the tyrant of Thebes. We must remember that the Greeks believed the souls of the unburied dead to be condemned to endless wanderings, to eternal sufferings. Only one person, Antigone, in all the city dares to oppose the decree and confront the tyrant. What is it that gives such extraordinary courage to a defenceless virgin, of royal blood, true, though owing her birth to the crime of incest?

Strange to relate, no one has ever more fully elucidated the deep mystery of the soul of Antigone than Richard Wagner. Here is a truly remarkable passage from his *Opera and Drama*:

THE GENESIS OF TRAGEDY

'In this State, there was just one solitary mournful heart to be found—one to which humanity had flown for refuge. . . . It was that of a sweet young girl, and, from out its depths, the flower of Love had grown into all-powerful beauty. Antigone knew no politics. She loved.

'Did she seek to defend Polyneikes? Did she seek to find reflections, relations or legal points?—so as either to explain, to excuse, or to justify her action?

'No! She loved him. Did she love him because he was her brother?—and were not Oedipus and Jocasta her parents? Could she, after her frightful life-experiences, think otherwise than with horror of her family ties? Can she be supposed to have gained strength for her love from this frightful tearing asunder of Nature's closest ties?

'No! She loved Polyneikes because he was unhappy, and because nothing but love's utmost power could free him from his curse.

'Now, what kind of love could this be, on her part, which was neither sexual, parental, filial, nor sisterly? It was Love's most beautiful blossom, for, from out of the wreck of all these loves (which Society had refused to recognize and the State had expressly denied) there grew up—nourished by the inextinguishable seed of all of them—the richest love of all, the flower of purely human love.'

It must be acknowledged that the true character and psychology of Antigone could not be explained more luminously. But we must now return to the drama of Sophokles. Day has not yet risen upon the sleeping city. In the semi-darkness of the approaching dawn, Antigone

THE GENESIS OF TRAGEDY

and Ismene, the two daughters of Oedipus, stealthily leave the palace of Kreon. News of the sinister decree which condemns to the gibbet the body of Polyneikes, has reached them. For fear of eaves-dropping, they have left the palace to consult together. One trembles with indignation, the other with fear. The courageous elder sister informs the younger of her resolve to confront the tyrant, and, in spite of him, to bury the body of her brother. She asks Ismene to join her in the act. The timid and gentle Ismene, however, lacks her sister's fine courage. She shrinks from the project, alleging the folly and danger of such an act undertaken by two feeble women. Whereupon Antigone answers with cold disdain: 'I would neither urge thee nor, if thou wert still willing to act, wouldst thou do it pleasingly with me at least. But be thou of what sort it seems good to thee, I however will bury him. It is glorious for me to die, doing this. Here shall I be with him, with my dear one, having wrought holy deeds, since longer is the time during which I must please those below than those here. For there I shall always be: but if it seem good to thee, do thou hold in dishonour the things which are honoured by the gods.' Antigone is conscious of being sufficiently strong to act alone. From this moment, a wide gulf separates her from her sister. Subsequently, when the feeble though kind and faithful Ismene, moved by her sister's tragic fate, wishes to follow her in death, the latter proudly replies: 'No, thou hast chosen to live and I to die.'

Thus is outlined, from the first scene, the character of the heroine and the nature of the conflict in which she is engaged. On the one hand, egoism and hatred hold sway, armed with all the resources of political power and with the crushing weight of material things. On the other hand, a solitary ardent soul is seen reduced to its own resources, to that might of disinterested love in which dense egoism and frivolous scepticism do not believe, but which is conscious of its infinity because it draws its strength from the unfathomable depths of the interior world and from a great Beyond! Which of the two will gain the victory? The various episodes of the struggle follow rapidly upon each other in thrilling *crescendo*.

A radiant morn has risen upon the city of Thebes. The hymn to the Sun, sung by the old men of the Chorus, sounds forth as a proud challenge to the plan of Antigone, for it proclaims the striking victory of Thebes over her enemies, to the rhythm of a crash of arms and chariots drawn by prancing steeds. In honour of the day, the Chorus, along with the entire city, seems to be prostrating itself before its new master. But no sooner has Kreon, in an ambiguous and hypocritical speech, attempted to justify his decree against Polyneikes, than he is interrupted by unexpected news. One of the guardians appointed to keep watch over the body of Polyneikes and to prevent its burial, in order that it may be devoured by wild beasts, comes and relates the strange scene which he has witnessed. In the full blaze of noon, beneath a hurricane of blinding dust which veiled the burning rays of the sun, a maiden has been seen approaching the already putrefied body of Polyneikes. 'She shrieks aloud the wailing cry of a sad bird, as when she has seen the bed of her empty nest bereft of her young ones; and so likewise this woman, when

THE GENESIS OF TRAGEDY

she sees the corpse bare, cried out with wailings and was cursing forth bitter curses upon those who had done the deed. And in her hands she straightway bears thirsty dust, and from a well-wrought brazen urn upraised with libations thrice-poured she crowns the corpse.' Kreon cannot believe his ears. Who has dared to make the sacramental libation of milk, wine and honey upon the wretched body? Who has come to snatch the soul of the accursed man from its punishment and carry it off to the Elysian fields through this downpour of tears, sweeter than celestial balm?

Here she comes: it is Antigone herself, led by the guardians! Gently she bows her head in profound sadness, though her eyes shine with a secret joy. Kreon questions her. Fearlessly she confesses the hideous crime. 'And then didst thou dare to transgress these laws?' asks the tyrant in amaze. She answers in disdain: 'It was in no wise Zeus that proclaimed these things to me, nor Justice that dwells with the gods below, who ordered these laws among men. Nor did I think that thy proclamations were so mighty as that, being a mortal, thou shouldst override the *unwritten* and infallible laws of the gods. For by no means now at least or yesterday, but always do these live and no one knows the time at which they appeared. For these I was not likely to pay the penalty among the gods, having feared the will of any man: for I knew that I should die, and why not? Even if thou hadst not proclaimed it first. But if I shall die before the time, I count it gain. For whosoever lives as I do amidst so many ills, how does he not win gain by having died? . . . And if to thee I seem now to happen to be doing foolishly,

THE GENESIS OF TRAGEDY

almost methinks I incur the charge of folly from a fool.'

At these words, Kreon is beside himself with anger. To be railed at by his victim, to see her smile and triumph beneath his threats, is intolerable. 'Surely now,' he says, 'I am not a man, but she is a man if this power shall rest with her with impunity. . . . I hate also when one, having been caught in wickedness, then wishes to gloss this over.'

'I am thy captive,' says Antigone. 'Dost thou desire anything greater than to put me to death?'

'I indeed desire nothing greater,' says Kreon, 'having this I have everything.'

'Why then dost thou delay?' ironically retorts Antigone. 'Since to me naught of thy works is pleasing, nor may they ever be pleasing? And so also to thee my acts are displeasing. And yet, whence could I have won more glorious renown at least, than by laying my own brother in the tomb? This would be said to be pleasing to all of them, if fear did not lock their tongue. But tyranny is both fortunate in many other things, and it is lawful for it to do and say what it wishes.'

Kreon cannot contain himself with passion, but he is also growing uneasy. He does not understand this force which paralyzes and exasperates him. The end of the dialogue between the furious tyrant and the audacious virgin is an exchange of curt retorts which cross one another like piercing arrows. Those of Kreon, like feeble reeds, fall broken against the quivering breast of the enthusiastic maiden. Those of Antigone, on the other hand, pierce the darksome soul of the tyrant like

THE GENESIS OF TRAGEDY

darts of light, carrying with them disturbance and unrest. When finally he calls upon her to hate the enemy of Thebes even in the realm of Pluton, she answers in those immortal words which have crowned her with a halo of fame down the ages: 'Truly I was not born to join in hating, but in loving.'

In this important scene, Antigone shows herself at the height of her combative power to love and believe. The tender weeping virgin has become transformed into an inspired prophetess, showing herself before the astonished tyrant, as an intrepid warrior maid whose armour is invulnerable.

. . . .

Antigone's words: 'All the Thebans would be on my side, did not fear stop their mouth,' have cast doubt into the soul of Kreon. The following scene proves to him how correct she was. The tyrant's son is desperately in love with the daughter of Oedipus. Greek morals, while allowing men the utmost freedom, were very strict against women in the home, forbidding relationships of every kind between the young of both sexes previous to marriage. Haemon, however, has seen Antigone in his father's palace. Divining that a celestial flame was smouldering in the breast of this silent passionate virgin, volcanic fires were kindled in his own. Sophokles does not tell us whether Antigone returns this passion, absorbed as she is by love for her brother, but in all probability she too is in love with the youth. The father has consented to the marriage. Distracted by the death sentence pronounced upon his betrothed, Haemon pleads her cause with his father. Saying nothing of his

THE GENESIS OF TRAGEDY

love, he relates the things that are being noised abroad. Throughout the city, commiseration is felt for the unfortunate girl, so unjustly condemned. Haemon implores the king to pardon her, but Kreon is inflexible. He can think of nothing but his compromised authority, his power that has been flouted. Antigone must die; Haemon will find some other wife. The dispute becomes embittered. 'O loathsome disposition weaker than a woman's!' exclaims the king. 'It is impossible that you ever marry her while still alive.' 'Then she will die, and having died will destroy someone,' says the son, as he leaves the king.

. . . .

In the eyes of Kreon, Antigone has become the very incarnation of revolt, the obstacle to tyranny, the negation of his sovereignty. He does not dare to shed her blood; but he will do worse. Hers shall be the punishment reserved later for Roman vestals who have been unfaithful to their vow of chastity. She shall be confined and immured alive. In a cave which shall be her sepulchre, she shall expiate her crime by dying of hunger. Then Kreon, having freed himself of the only soul that has had the audacity to oppose him, will reign as absolute master and in all the splendour of his pomp and glory over the city of Thebes and its submissive inhabitants. Kreon is the perfect representative of absolute materialism, hardened by egoism and hatred. He imagines that he can reign openly by brute force. In this drama, Sophokles shows us how profound is the error of this genius of darkness who would set himself up as a torch for the whole world. He imagines

THE GENESIS OF TRAGEDY

himself the bearer of light and yet produces only black night. In seizing the reins of power, he piles up around him dense clouds from which catastrophes will come forth like thunder-bolts to strike him, while from the very tomb in which he wishes to imprison the only free and living soul in the whole city, will flash a light that will change the aspect of things.

From this moment, the tragedy expresses with growing intensity the interior drama of the various characters. By means of stage effects and impassioned melodies, it colours, externalizes and strengthens their emotions. Thus the final scenes give the sinister impression of a cloudy sky which darkens more and more until the lightning flashes forth.

Antigone leaves the palace like a victim prepared for sacrifice. From her head, wreathed with narcissus and asphodel, a violet veil falls over her shoulders and envelops her white form. In low thrilling tones, she bids farewell to life. All the tenderness in her soul, all the emotions hitherto confined in her breast, now find expression in this swan song. She is not afraid to go down alive into the cavern which is to be her tomb. It is a proud thing to be the only free soul in the city. All the same, she sorrows at leaving behind the light of day and the city in which she was born; she laments over the marriage joys she has not experienced. She compares herself to Niobe, stifled beneath a vegetation of stone, and changed into a rock, weeping in eternal silence. To crown her misfortunes, not a voice is raised to lament her lot. The chorus of cowardly old men even mocks at her for presuming to vie with deity by opposing the law of the stronger, they reproach her for effecting her own downfall by reason of the independence of her character. . . . Kreon is impatient; he fears that his victim will escape him. Antigone, following her jailors, disappears at the back of the theatre, apparently abandoned both by the Gods and by men, wrapped about in her solitude, like a swan of dazzling whiteness on the surface of a dark lake.

The sky is black as night; the still heavy air now seems laden with the wrath of the Gods. The measure is full, misfortune is at hand, the rumbling of thunder begins in the person of Teiresias, the gloomy soothsayer. He announces that, in the city, birds of prey with frightful shrieks are rending the body of Polyneikes, and that the altars are being profaned. Teiresias calls upon the tyrant to bury the body and save the innocent Antigone. At first, Kreon attempts to resist, then, appalled at the prophet's terrifying predictions, he hurries to the sepulchre to prevent disaster. . . . In the prevailing anguish, minutes become hours. The drama proceeds, devouring space and time alike.

In presence of Kreon's frenzied condition, the trembling and servile old men who make up the Chorus in their turn seem to become demented. Not knowing what is to become of them, some crouch on the altar of the orchestra like a flock of timid birds. Others dash to the back of the stage for further news. Soon they return, livid and pale, accompanied by a panting messenger who relates the catastrophe.

As they drew near the fatal cavern, Kreon and his followers have heard inarticulate cries and groans. Entering, the king sees a pitiable sight. The stone which formed the sepulchre had been unsealed. Inside,

THE GENESIS OF TRAGEDY

Haemon lay stretched near the lifeless body of Antigone, who was hanging by the neck to a jutting crag. Haemon, after untying the fatal knot, had vainly attempted to restore his betrothed to life. The father now wishes to drag away his son from the dead maiden, but Haemon threatens him with his sword, and then falls heavily upon its point, breathing his last upon the still warm though lifeless bosom of the virgin, whom he calls his beloved spouse for the first and last time. Kreon, returning half demented to his palace, completely gives way on learning that his wife Eurydike has also committed suicide at the news of her son's death.

In this way Antigone, the ideal sister, and Haemon, the distracted lover, have found a marriage bed on their funeral couch. Regarding things from the highest plane, one might say that, in this double suicide, earthly and heavenly love have tried to embrace each other, but have been shattered as by a thunderbolt in a mortal kiss.

There is something oppressively overwhelming in this termination, though, in spite of everything, there emerges a superior kind of harmony, a thought truly divine. For Antigone, by her death, has gained the victory. Living, she would be less noble, less powerful. Her heroic death liberates, raises and transfigures everything around her. It constitutes the tragic though brilliant victory of soul over body, of mind over matter, of justice over injustice.

One additional word regarding the place of this tragedy in the psychic history of mankind.

In his poetical order, Antigone is the first manifestation of an ideal which has developed throughout the ages and has been called the Eternal-Feminine by Goethe at the end of the second *Faust*. This ideal is found in Plato's Diotima and Dante's Beatrice, in Petrarch's Laura and in the inspired and inspiring lovers of modern times, in Christian saints and in heroines passionately devoted to their fatherland. This superior Eternal-Feminine may be called the reflection of the Divine, and at the same time the expression of feminine sensibility in its loftiest and most intimate essence. Here we may behold Woman exalted to the entrancement of sacrifice. Then the Love, whichever it be, that burns in the glowing furnace of the feminine heart, reacts upon the heart of man himself, producing therein a strange enthusiasm wherein the desire for possession becomes blended with the creative flame and with the highest of all virtues.

If it is true, as I hope has been proved by this study of the soul of Sophokles' masterpiece, that Antigone is the first of these heroines of disinterested love, one would like this moving tragedy to have an epilogue. This is absent, though the plot imperiously suggests it. The drama ends with the dual suicide of Antigone and Haemon, and the curtain falls upon this funereal impression, though the action is continued in the mind of the strongly moved spectator.

Night has fallen upon the sinister events of the day. The people have placed on a litter the bodies of Haemon and Antigone. They have covered with flowers the unfortunate lovers who have found their nuptial bed in the tomb, and now they bring them in front of Kreon's palace, where they have erected a triumphal funeral pile. The tyrant himself is utterly crushed in spirit as

THE GENESIS OF TRAGEDY

he utters the words: 'No longer do I belong to the world of the living.'

The vitiated atmosphere of Thebes would appear to have been purified by the holocaust. And now, around the flaming pile, the chorus sings a new hymn invoking 'Love! Invincible Love!' This however is not the ill-starred love which produces only delirium and disaster, it is creative Love which bestows grace and harmony, opening tombs and raising the dead to life. Before the flames of love leaping upwards from this consuming pile, it would appear that the fabled founders of Thebes, Kadmos, Harmonia and Amphion, who built its walls with the music of his lyre, had returned. The crimes of the Labdacides are forgotten. Worship of the dead has once more paved a way to the gods. Family and city may be reborn after a new mode. No longer is it the perfidious Sphinge, it is the living soul of Antigone, that reigns over Thebes. . . .

I do not know if any of the ancient spectators of this masterpiece had such a vision. Still, it seems to me to contain the eternal signification of this noble tragedy: the contagion of Enthusiasm by the might of Love.

CHAPTER V

THE MYSTERY OF ELEUSIS—PSYCHE IN THE THREE WORLDS—THE FUTURE OF THE THEATRE

The Sacred Drama of Eleusis

THE summary we have made of the dramas of Aeschylos and Sophokles has proved to us that the Athenian tragedy, at its highest, had a moral and religious object which consisted in a kind of soul purification by the spectacle of its passions and in an elevation to the soul's higher destinies. It also proves that the most famous tragedies of these poets, such as the *Prometheus* and the *Oresteia*, the *Oedipus* and the *Antigone*, contained a profound hidden meaning which could be understood by none but initiates.

A study, had it been possible, of the tragedies of Euripides, would have shown us that this profound hidden meaning is totally absent from the third of the great Greek tragedians. The great difference between him and his two predecessors is that he was not an initiate of Eleusis. A disciple of Sokrates—and even more so of the Sophists—Euripides is a sentimental sceptic, perpetually wavering between doubt and faith and lacking in that which constituted the power of his illustrious rivals: a luminous conception of the origin and the end

THE GENESIS OF TRAGEDY

of life. This does not prevent Euripides from being a great poet after his fashion. He is the inventor of a new pathetics, being unequalled in emotional scenes, cries of suffering and the melodious expression of passion. This misogynist who, according to Sophokles, 'insults women on the stage and worships them in his gynoeceum', this man who has said so much evil of the other sex, has drawn for us exquisite figures of maidens and wives, Iphigeneia and Polyxena, Adromache and Alkestis. He may be said to have introduced into poetry the voluptuousness of tears. As such, he is the precursor of the modern theatre, upon which he has exercised as great an influence as he did upon his contemporaries. The male heroes of Euripides, however, have lost their grandeur and their dignity; they have descended to the position of ordinary citizens. The higher aims of tragedy are no longer attained. In the case of Aeschylos and Sophokles, the *mise en œuvre* of the passions is but a means of purifying them, of creating a new tranquillity and harmony in the soul. Euripides, on the other hand, looks upon man as the sport of chance, or the victim of divine caprice. In such a conception of life, terror and pity assuredly become more poignant, but they lose their power to ennoble and to educate. One comes away dignified and restored to serenity after a tragedy of Aeschylos or Sophokles; a melodrama of Euripides leaves one affected, though crushed or depressed. In spite of the poet's genius, it lacks the divine afflatus which Aeschylos and Sophokles obtained from the teachings and the spectacles of Eleusis.

We shall now attempt to penetrate to the heart of these mysteries, in order to learn something of that spring of eternal youth from which these great dramatists obtained their invincible faith and power.

Origin of the Sacred Drama of Eleusis

The origin of this drama casts a radiant light upon its bearing and its inner meaning. It sprang from the blending together of two myths, that of *Dionysos* and that of *Demeter* and *Persephone*. The former, originating in Thrace and the initiation of Orpheus, is a *cosmogenic* mystery, dealing with the origin and the end of the world. The latter, developed at Eleusis by the Eumolpides, is a *psychic* mystery, and tells the story of the human soul, of its birth, death and resurrection, which are shared between earth, hell and heaven. Although the problem of cosmic evolution and that of the evolution of the soul are closely united and inextricably intertwined with each other, these two myths for a long time developed separately. Their origin dates back to the night of time. Only at a comparatively late period, in the sixth century before Christ, did these myths and mysteries blend in a powerful synthesis under the influence of the Eumolpides. Then was born, with the bay of Eleusis and the dimly outlined temples as a background, that sacred drama which must have entranced Graeco-Latin antiquity for nearly one thousand years, on to the day when the Emperor Theodosius abolished its performance.

Our object will now be to try and reconstruct the principal scenes of this drama, finding our material in the irrefutable testimony of antiquity and the excavations of Eleusis. The Homeric hymn to Demeter shall be the magic wand of our evocation. But before raising

THE GENESIS OF TRAGEDY

the curtain of this mystic theatre, we shall briefly trace the history of the origins of Dionysos and Persephone, as related by the Eumolpides. This is, as it were, the prelude of the drama. Like two shining stars emerging from a cloud, we here see Man and Woman born of the loves of the gods. As the plot proceeds we shall find these twin stars grow dim in a series of avatars and then rise in dizzy ascent towards the heavenly Light, on to the gods also transfigured by their painful odyssey. The prelude affords a glimpse of their strange birth, their quickening in the womb of things.

'In the immemorial origin of bygone times,' said the Orphics, 'the unfathomable God whose out-breathing and in-breathing bring about the appearance and the dissolution of the worlds, awoke from deep slumber. He was then in act what he is always in potentiality. The ineffable God became Thought. Zeus-Jupiter the Demiurgos, God the Creator, the Eternal-Masculine became self-manifest. But immediately he made himself dual. He saw himself enveloped with a marvellous veil, like some vast mirage. This moving multi-coloured veil, with innumerable folds, the mirror of his thought, over which floated the astral images of all beings, was his Feminine-Double, increate Light, Demeter, the Soul of the World. Then, before the dazzling though inapprehensible beauty of his Spouse, a sublime desire flashed like lightning through the mind of Jupiter (Zeus)—that of creating a perfect being who should sum up all others within its own harmony. The Archetype of Man had its birth in the thought of Zeus. But how was it to be realized? In order to hold his scattered and fleeing bride, to possess her in one complete

THE GENESIS OF TRAGEDY

embrace, Zeus changed himself into an astral serpent. With his innumerable folds he encircled Demeter in a cloud of flame. From this ardent embrace was born the charming infant, fresh as a rose, Dionysos of seductive and irresistible smile. This was the speaking Word, the incarnate Desire of his father, and from his very birth he was devoured by a desperate craving after life. By reason of this desire he became the Dionysos-Zagreus—Dionysos rent and torn in pieces.

'One day the divine child happened to behold himself in a mirror. He remained lost in contemplation of his charming reflection. Then the Titans (the unleashed elements or inferior forces of nature) threw themselves upon him, rending him in seven pieces which they flung into an immense boiling cauldron. Pallas Athene (divine Wisdom, born of the pure thought of Zeus) saved the heart and head of Dionysos, and took them back to his father. Zeus received them into his own bosom to give birth to another son, and destroyed the Titans with lightning. Of their burning bodies mingling with vapours which issued from the lacerated body of Dionysos, mankind was born. But of the purest part of Dionysos, his heart remoulded by Zeus, are born heroes and men of genius. He is also to give birth to the new, the resurrected Dionysos.'

Thus relate the Orphics when explaining allegorically the origin of the world. To this cosmogonic myth the Eumolpides determined to link the history of the human Soul and of its destiny. Supplementing the myth of Dionysos by that of Persephone, they continued as follows the story related by the Orphics: 'Demeter could not console herself for the lamentable destiny of

THE GENESIS OF TRAGEDY

her offspring and for the fate of a world distracted by pain and death. In compelling her to give birth to the son of his desire, Zeus had failed in his audacious undertaking to create perfect Man. In her turn, the queen of Heaven determined to realize her own dream. The master of the gods had subdued her against her will; she would now seduce him against his will. Her desire was to bring into the world an immortal daughter, who could not be rent in pieces like the unfortunate Dionysos, and who, after imbibing the beauty and glory of her mother, would resist all temptations by the virgin purity of her invincible love. In the ethereal vaults of heaven, beneath the constellations of Virgo and Leo, Demeter drew Zeus into her arms for the conception of this divine daughter, the Archetype of the human Soul. She received the name of Persephone, she who plunges into the abyss, but also that of Soleira, she who saves.

'Thus was born Persephone from the tears of her mother over the death of Dionysos.' Such are the mythical bases of the doctrine of the Eumolpides, the origin of their cosmogony and their psychology. In this teaching, Dionysos and Persephone appear as creations of divine thought, who seek each other in the other's being. The sacred drama, worked out at length down the centuries by the Eumolpides, was the plastic *mise en scène* of their adventures and their history. This mystery took place in the three worlds. It began in heaven and descended, by way of earth, to the depths of hell, ascending once again to the empyrean after undergoing a marvellous transfiguration. The great secret of the mystery, the prime motive of this action, concentrated

THE GENESIS OF TRAGEDY

in superhuman types of intensest passion, lay in the fact that Dionysos and Persephone, Spirit and Soul, Desire and Love, Man and Woman can fulfil and save themselves only through each other with the help of the Initiate, represented by Triptolemos. Thus, on the one hand, Persephone succeeded in leaving her hell by the remembrance and the contemplation of her predestined Ideal; on the other, Dionysos, torn asunder by the Titans, rose again in radiant beauty through the unprecedented sufferings and the boundless love of Persephone.

Let us now try to form some idea of the external scenery which formed the accompaniment and framework of the sacred drama.

. . . .

The mysteries of Eleusis, which in Greece were called the sacred festivals or holy orgies, lasted nine days, and were celebrated at first every five years, and afterwards every year, in the autumn. They consisted of a series of instructions and ceremonies, of prayers, purifications and ablutions, of hymns sung by the Eumolpides or the participants, and of magic visions. But it was the sacred drama, the last act of which was performed after the ninth day, during the holy night, that formed the important element. The ensemble of these mysteries was at once a religious cult, a philosophical revelation, and a journey to the other world; an initiation by vision, speech, and effort of will. Here, the spectators became actors. As human fractions of the divine drama, they came in gradually and ended by taking full part in it. The principal characters were played by the priests and

THE GENESIS OF TRAGEDY

priestesses of the family of the Eumolpides. None other had the right to usurp these high functions, and strict prescriptions were imposed to effect their worthy performance. Absolute chastity was required of the hierophant. In the drama, the Eumolpides represented the Gods, i.e., the cosmogonic powers. Neophyte spectators entered as Greeks or Athenians, but they were expected to gain, in the sacred drama, another loftier and more intimate personality, that which had shared in the universal and divine life, the remembrance of a past and the shadowing forth of a future existence.

The sacred drama had a prologue, which was celebrated at Agrae, during the months of February, six months before the great Eleusinia. It was played in the open air on a theatre of verdure. Persephone, seated before a grotto and surrounded by nymphs, was embroidering a long veil on which were woven the actions of the gods. Demeter had ordered her daughter to finish the veil and await her return. She had promised her that she would evoke all the gods except the dangerous Eros, the god of Love and Desire, who might compass her ruin; besides, Demeter had strictly forbidden her daughter to gather the lovely flowers of the meadow, as their distracting perfume might obliterate her memory of the celestial world and drag her down into the Pit. At first Persephone abandons herself to the chaste felicity of her divine dream, through which she glimpses, like a distant star, the celestial bridegroom, the marvellous Dionysos. But when, in her embroidery, she has reached the war with the Titans and the birth of mankind, she stops, troubled and uncertain. She knows not how to continue; her memory fails her. Still, she

THE GENESIS OF TRAGEDY

remembers having heard the gods say that it is Eros who gives birth to mortals, that he is at once the most formidable and the most beautiful of the gods. Overcome with curiosity and desire, she invokes him, in spite of her mother's prohibition and the entreaties of the nymphs. The cunning Eros-Cupid appears under the form of a handsome youth, whose insinuating smile and apparent innocence reassure the virgin. He promises to help her in her embroidery on condition that she plucks the finest flower in the meadow. At the same time, he strikes the earth with his bow and there springs up a magnificent narcissus whose golden heart exhales an intoxicating perfume. Eros promises that if Persephone will pluck this magic flower, she will immediately see, as on a vast screen, the monsters of the deep, and that the great secret of heaven and hell will be revealed to her.

In dazed bewilderment, Persephone yields to the temptation. She plucks the narcissus and raises it to her lips. At once the earth is rent asunder and Pluton appears, riding a chariot drawn by two black horses. Irresistible in his violence, he carries off the virgin in spite of her cries, and disappears with his prey. Eros has departed with a laugh, and the nymphs now call in vain: Persephone! Persephone!

This scene, skilfully conducted in subtle and rapid dialogue, symbolized to the Mystae the Soul's descent from the heavenly and spiritual life to the earthly and material one, in the lower world. It was a mythological and suggestive image of its incarnation. All the same, this was no more than a prelude of the Greater Mysteries.

THE GENESIS OF TRAGEDY

The Sorrow of Demeter and the Initiation of Triptolemos

(First Act of the Sacred Drama)

On the fifteenth of the month Boedromion (September), in the presence of the people, the Archon-King proclaimed the opening of the Eleusinia at the Peokile of Athens. During the nine days of the festival, all war was to cease throughout Greece. At the same time, the sacred herald who had come from Eleusis, uttered a curse against the profane. The following day, the Mystae, who had kept vigil at the Eleusinion of the Akropolis and received the instructions of their guides, met at the Keramikos, or the Potters' Quarter, before proceeding to Eleusis. Then there were seen processions of men of all ages, in linen robes and crowned with myrtle passing along the *Via Sacra* which leads to the sanctuary through the plain of Attica and the hill of Daphne. At Eleusis there began religious ceremonies and exercises of all kinds. On the fifth day, in the temple of Hekate, the first act of the sacred drama was played.

The scene represented the cavern of Hekate, the goddess of metamorphoses, conceived as the daughter of Night and the Twilight. In this gloomy cave of bare and forbidding rocks, Demeter was seen to enter hurriedly. The Great Goddess, clad in a white peplos, her large blue star-spangled mantle floating behind, her faun-coloured hair fastened with azure bandlets, holds a lighted torch in each hand. Repeatedly she calls upon Hekate, who appears wearing a black robe embroidered with red dragons and a flame-coloured mantle. Her dark hair falls back in scattered locks upon her neck. The yellow crescent of the moon serves her as a diadem. She holds a caduceus, whose interlaced and confronting serpents shine in the dim light of the cave. Hekate is beautiful, but there is a look of malevolent curiosity in her eyes, while the enigmatical smile seen on old statues appears on her lips. Demeter, who has heard the heart-rending cry of her daughter rise from the pit, has vainly sought her on earth. No God has been willing to tell her what has become of Persephone. In despair, the world Mother appeals to Hekate, who knows the tortuous paths and secret designs of Zeus, that she may learn the awful secret. After making her swear that she will not avenge herself on the messenger of ill-tidings, Hekate informs her that Pluton has carried off her daughter to his subterranean kingdom. And it is Zeus himself, sovereign lord of heaven and earth, who has given her to him to be his wife.

Demeter is overwhelmed by the news. She drops her two torches which flicker out on the ground, and sinks on to a rock. The kingdom of Pluton is the only place in the world where she cannot go. Hekate tries to persuade her that Pluton is not a God to be despised, that the Queen of the dead will be a great Goddess. She does not succeed in calming the Mother of the Gods in her despair. Then Hekate draws near to Demeter, and, with ambiguous smile, utters words of mystery.

This beginning of the sacred drama shows that Demeter, in the Mystery of Eleusis, played the part of a *mater dolorosa*. Her grief at the loss of her daughter Persephone is as heart-rending as that of the Virgin Mary, in the Christian tradition, at the death of her Son,

THE GENESIS OF TRAGEDY

the divine Word, incarnate in her flesh and dying on the Cross. The sole difference is that the sorrow of Demeter, Mother of the Gods, is so to speak cosmic in its nature. It represents the suffering of the higher worlds in presence of the cruel destiny of the human Soul, when leaving the natal sphere of the Archetypes, it descends into the lower world of dense matter. This grief, however, so poignant that it seems to be inconsolable, will none the less become the means of her redemption, of her return to heaven.

Indignant with her implacable spouse, Demeter will henceforth live on earth. All she now thinks of is to lament for her daughter, mingling her grief with human tears. With a stroke of the caduceus, the magician Hekate gives her the appearance of an old woman, wrinkled and lame. In this disguise, the Great Goddess goes to Eleusis and presents herself to Metaneira, widow of King Keleus, who takes Demeter for a highway beggar, and at first would drive her away. But her three daughters and the warm-hearted Triptolemos, her young son, intercede and give her shelter. Humbly the old woman crouches by the fireside, saying that she is an exiled Cretan seeking her daughter who has been carried off by a pirate. The ambitious Metaneira, seeing that the stranger is of royal race and acquainted with magical secrets, hopes that she will be able to persuade her son Triptolemos to appear in the public market place to claim the royal heritage of his defunct father—and leaves her alone with the youth. Here takes place the scene representing the initiation of Triptolemos. It is of vital importance for the meaning and understanding of the drama of Eleusis. The Mystae are still in the

THE GENESIS OF TRAGEDY

temple of Hekate as spectators, but the scene has suddenly changed. We find ourselves in the dwelling of Metaneira. Doric columns surround the domestic altar of the royal abode; a smouldering fire is burning.

The enigmatical reply of Triptolemos to his sisters calls for an explanation. To the Eumolpides, Triptolemos, the mythical founder of the mysteries of Eleusis, was the type of the perfect initiate, pure-headed and disinterested. Neither because of ambition nor for his own personal safety will he save Persephone at the risk of his life, but rather from a sympathy alike pure and impetuous. And it is because of this superb *élan*, spontaneous as early youth, that Demeter straightway offers the generous youth the bath of the fire of enthusiasm which inspires the souls of true heroes with invincible faith, and clothes them, so to speak, with diamond armour. What then is this Persephone whom Triptolemos has never seen, but whose ineffable beauty he divines when he hears her sweet name uttered? Persephone, as already stated, is the Archetype of the human Soul, and it is because Triptolemos has power to conceive her sublime image that his own soul has already won its wings.

Intelligent spectators of the drama of Eleusis must thus have been taught two lessons by it. The first was that man can become great only by rising to an Ideal above himself, by contemplation of the Archetypes whose images he bears within the depths of his own being. The second lesson was that even the superior man cannot really save himself except by saving others. Thus it was that the true initiates present at the sacred

THE GENESIS OF TRAGEDY

drama of Eleusis were highly privileged to contemplate —in the bath of fire given by Demeter to Triptolemos— the glorious birth of an immortal soul.

Persephone in the Lower World
(Second Act of the Sacred Drama)

The two preceding scenes occupied an entire afternoon. This was succeeded by the first *holy night*, a formidable test for neophytes. Like Triptolemos, they too were to descend into hell. Now hell, at Eleusis, had a dual meaning. In the adventure of Persephone, there was an objective continuation of the drama of the soul, bound to matter, in the circle of life on earth. Afterwards, in the personal tests that awaited the Mystae, they experienced subjectively the terrors of death, the fright, the wanderings and the struggles which await imperfect souls shrouded in darkness when they leave the physical body. Would they succeed in evading the dreadful currents and oppressive heaviness of the atmosphere and in reaching the gates of the celestial abodes by stripping themselves of this fluidic body—still wholly steeped in the defilements of earthly life—and clothing themselves with a more ethereal one? Were they about to be swallowed up and dissipated in the whirl of the elements, in the pit of Hekate, between the earth and the moon, or to become elect individuals in the higher, the eternal life? Such was the problem—an imperious one—for, as Eleusis taught, the soul can live only by its own effort. It is free to be or not to be, to perish or to rise again. The Second Act of the Sacred Drama now begins.

THE GENESIS OF TRAGEDY

The scene, the temple of Pluton, represented Tartaros. The Mystae found themselves in Hell, a place of darkness, of sinister and murky depths. In its centre rose the Tree of Dreams, with wide-spreading foliage. Through the inter-twining branches faint glimpses could be caught of the moving forms of fantastic creatures: Lamiae and Harpies and Gorgons.

After this violent scene, in which the wrath of Pluton was unleashed in the pit of Hekate, there was a feeling as though a hurricane had swept over the shades. Here took place the episode frequently mentioned by such ancient authors as Lucian, Plutarch and Apuleius. The objective drama of the other life once more became subjective. The Mystae personally went through the terrors of hell, or rather the trials of purgatory, according to Christian terminology. Dense night enveloped them. Hands laid hold upon them, and dragged them away in the darkness. Then, like blinding flashes of lightning, sinister visions pierced the blackness. Some caught glimpses of Sisyphos crushed beneath a rock, others of Ixion broken beneath his wheel. Men were seen hurled to the ground by monstrous serpents which encircled their bodies, or stranded in a bog. A voice exclaimed: 'Thou art in the pit of Hekate. Here, the passions thou hast created are living entities. The beast which thou hast fostered chooses thee for its prey. Ye who are ambitious, cruel, lewd, wicked and hypocritical, defend yourselves against your offspring!' And hideous larvae appeared and disappeared, barring the way. Were they going forward or backward? No one knew. Around the groping and distracted Mystae, the unbroken hissing of the wind mingled with plaintive cries.

THE GENESIS OF TRAGEDY

No longer were they in a temple; it was a boundless Erebos, streaked with dull flashes of light. 'The soul at the moment of death,' says Plutarch, 'experiences the same sensation as do those initiated into the mysteries. First, there are haphazard courses, painful detours, a disturbing and goalless procession through the darkness. Then, before reaching the end, dread is at its height: shivering and trembling, cold sweats and horrors.'*

Suddenly, a door of light opened in the darkness. Through it they hurried. Along a narrow passage, the Mystae, who had not fallen unconscious on the road or retreated from fear, reached the peristype of a vast Doric temple where the torch-bearer (the Dadouchos) awaited them. 'You have now reached the threshold of Demeter,' he said. 'But to-day only for a moment will you be permitted to contemplate the image of the Goddess. In three days, you shall enter into her light, after having seen the return of Persephone.' And through the open door, in the temple shining with candelabra, the Mystae admired the colossal statue of Demeter in gold and ivory, standing in all her majesty and leaning upon a sceptre. Her very presence seemed to express the peace of Elysium, but she awaited in awesome silence.

The Sacred Marriage
(Third and Last Act of the Sacred Drama)

The three following days were devoted to gymnastic games and theatrical performances, in commemoration

* Plutarch, *Fragments*.

of the heroes of Titanesque and Argonautic legend: Prometheus, Herakles, Jason, Theseus, etc.—characters in which the Eumolpides recognized various manifestations of the mystic Dionysos. On the ninth day of the festival was the procession of Iacchos. The statue of an infant god, his head wreathed with ivy, was solemnly carried from Athens to Eleusis. He had been named Iacchos (born of the Light) so that he might not be confused with the popular Bacchus, and so exposed to profanation. To the initiates he symbolized the second Dionysos. His mysterious rebirth and meeting again with Persephone constituted the last act of the sacred drama. The Mystae were present, all through the holy night, at the temple of Demeter.

The scene represents a grotto on the summit of Olympos. Here is seen a bed of ivory and gold, adorned with lilies and roses, and half enveloped in a cloud. Some distance away stands Zeus, in profound meditation. Suddenly, a hurricane sweeps the mountain tops and shakes Olympos to its foundations. Demeter enters like a Fury, waving a torch in each hand. She reproaches her husband for cowardly delivering up her daughter to Pluton and all the defilements of Tartaros. In vain is it that Zeus attempts to exculpate himself, alleging that Persephone is free and that he has tried to rescue her through the heroes sprung from the blood of Dionysos. The Mother of the Gods answers him in accents of fierce irony. But a voice from the abyss is then heard, it is the voice of Persephone calling on Dionysos; and we are led to the climax.

THE GENESIS OF TRAGEDY

We have thus attempted to form a living and plastic idea of the drama of Eleusis, judging by the ruins of destroyed temples and the valuable testimony of the philosophers of Alexandria, in the days of declining Hellenism.

CONCLUSION

There is nothing to say of the symbolical ceremonies which concluded the celebration of the mysteries, nor of the supernatural apparitions concerning which the most illustrious authors of antiquity, such as Plato, have spoken with rapturous interest. In this epoptie* or *direct vision*, according to Porphyry and Proklos, Demeter herself, i.e., condensed astral Light, became manifest to the initiates, revealing to them in flashes, through clouds of incense, its inhabitants: archetypes and souls. One may discuss endlessly as to the authenticity of these phenomena. The only thing which here concerns us is the sacred drama, the speaking *résumé* of the cosmic and the psychic doctrine of the Eumolpides. A summary of the drama, enables us to judge of its manifold and transcendent signification.

Only a few words remain to be said regarding the moral effect produced by the mysteries upon those who took part in them. Let us glance briefly at the position

* The third and highest grade of initiation into the Eleusinian mysteries.

THE GENESIS OF TRAGEDY

held by Greek tragedy in the history of the theatre, and at the luminous perspectives opened to us by the sacred drama of Eleusis for the reconstruction of the initiatory theatre in the modern world. We shall thus see that Greek tragedy, combined with the drama of Eleusis, already contains, in striking epitome, the entire subsequent history of the theatre, and offers us, as it were, a schematic plan of its future evolution. The synthesis of the Promethean idea and the Eleusinian idea will give us the key to the initiatory theatre, for it is both a summary of the past and a vision of the future.

MORAL IMPRESSIONS OF THE SACRED DRAMA UPON THE SPECTATORS. Plato said: 'There are many who bear the torch and the thyrsus, but there are few initiates.' This is true for the time of Plato, as for our own and for all time. Only those who have experienced transcendent truths in their own interior life, accompanied by a fundamental upheaval of their entire being, can understand all that is contained in the drama of Eleusis. But it is easy to picture—as indeed is proved by numerous contemporary testimonies—the divers impressions produced by the strange though moving spectacle upon the *élite* of the Mystae.

This consisted in a kind of purification of their inmost being, a rising to ethereal spheres, a marvellous sense of harmony with the Cosmos. The world seemed to them more transparent and they themselves to have undergone a metamorphosis. New revelations can be comprehended only by a new soul. And this had been awakened in them by images, words and songs, which delighted their eyes and charmed their ears. It had

THE GENESIS OF TRAGEDY

greeted things hitherto unheard and undreamt of as truths that were age-long and eternally young. Recognizing them, it had attained to self-revelation. Is greater certitude possible? When the mind reasons, it splits up or readjusts the scattered fragments of the true; but when the soul identifies itself with the thing contemplated, it discovers that it has reached the very centre of truth itself. What Eleusis had produced in its initiates was—through successive emotions and a final inundation of light—*the cessation of separate life and the consciousness of the one life.*

Now, the one life consists in the organic communion of the soul with the universe, with humanity, with God. Was not this revelation of the intimate relationship of the innumerable beings who all descend from the Archetype and the universal Soul,—multiple representations, evolved, degenerescent or reintegrated forms of the Eternal-Masculine and the Eternal-Feminine,—a new communion with the universe? In vain is Dionysos torn to pieces, in vain are his limbs scattered throughout the world, in vain does Persephone suffer a thousand deaths,—once they become aware of their origin, they know that, at the end of their cosmic Odyssey they must meet again in the bosom of the infinite Father-Mother. Was it not communion with the divine heart of mankind—to have contemplated the prototypes of Man and Woman reintegrated in all their power and beauty, through suffering and struggle? The second Dionysos had mingled the pure drops of his blood with the sweet tears of a resurrected Persephone. Streams of light had flashed forth at their embrace, and the Mystae, having become seers, had perceived the vast refraction of the

THE GENESIS OF TRAGEDY

God in the Argonautic legend, the glorious garland of his liberating incarnations. With what a new glow did Herakles and Jason, Perseus and Prometheus then shine! By the side of this magnificent fractioning of the god into his radiant manifestations, Apollo, who simply decreed justice, appeared cold and harsh, almost selfish. This was the motto of the second Dionysos: 'At the height of being and consciousness, taste the intoxication of life in the sacrifice of self!' Neither mutilation nor abnegation, but the supreme affirmation of the self in a proud holocaust. Such was the complete unfoldment of the Hero offering himself to men, to the universe, to God—on the altar of Beauty, Truth and Love.

DUALISM OF TRAGEDY AND OF THE DRAMA OF ELEUSIS. The stupendous exaltation of this feeling shows how different was the impression produced by the mystery of Eleusis and by tragedy. Absolute was the contrast between these two impressions. The performances of Athenian tragedy took place in open daylight, amid all the tumultuous life of the city-state of Pallas. Their aim was to glorify the national heroes of Greece, and also, according to Aristotle, to effect the purification of the passions by terror and pity; but the origin and end of life, the nature of the Gods and the mystery of the Beyond remained unexplained. At the end of the tragedy, the uninitiated spectator found the sombre portal of death.—Now, this was the very problem which the drama of Eleusis claimed to solve. In the myth of Dionysos and the Great Goddesses, it introduced the spectator into the secret of life, i.e., into the interior

THE GENESIS OF TRAGEDY

realm of the soul and that mysterious Beyond from which, according as it attempts or gives up the struggle, the soul is able to rise to a higher or sink into a lower sphere. From the full blaze of everyday life, the mysteries projected man into the twilight of the other world where shines in the darkness the midnight sun, the star of the spirit, the risen Dionysos. Briefly to summarize the difference between Athenian tragedy and the drama of Eleusis, we may say that the former represented the Promethean idea—the realization of the divine in the life on earth—and the latter the Eleusinian idea—the realization of the divine in the other life through the deliverance of the soul which has reached perfection. And so the tragedy of Athens and the mystery of Eleusis were separated by the yawning abyss which stretches between the Ephemeral and the Eternal.

Nevertheless, they were inseparable from—and an admirable complement of—each other. For we cannot conceive of the earth without the heavens, nor of the heavens without the earth.

THE SYNTHESIS OF THE TWO IDEAS. We have condensed into precise formulae the quintessence of the Greek tragedy and that of the drama of Eleusis. From these outposts we may see the rays which these two beacons with their revolving lights cast upon the entire subsequent history of the theatre, searching its most distant horizons.

After the fall of Hellenism and the Graeco-Latin world in the fifth century, the theatre lay dead for a thousand years. For, indeed, the crude and puerile

THE GENESIS OF TRAGEDY

mysteries of the Middle Ages do not count in the history of art. In the Western world, the theatre reappears only at the Renaissance. Consciously or unconsciously, it conforms more or less to the technique of Greek tragedy, adding thereto a new sense of human responsibility which it owes to Christianity. It however lacks its complement, the divine mystery, which Greece possessed under the form of the sacred drama of Eleusis. For our world is deprived of one possession of antiquity: progressive initiation. No wonder therefore that we are now experiencing, in theatrical life, two tendencies which began in the sixteenth century. The first is a tendency to plunge with a sort of frenzy into the realities of life; the second is a vague though invincible aspiration towards a divine world, towards that cosmic and psychic synthesis which antiquity, after its own fashion, found in the mysteries. These tendencies are seen alike in the laic theatre of Shakespeare, the father of the entire modern theatre, in the catholic theatre of Calderon and Lope de Vega, in the classical theatre of Corneille and Racine, and in the romantic theatre which followed. The mystical tendency is even found intermittently in the chaos of contemporary pessimism and realism, which somewhat resembles that dreadful cauldron into which Macbeth's witches wildly fling fragments of dead bodies gathered from the four corners of the world. Aspiration after the divine persists, inscrutable though invincible, in the worst of deviations.

The situation is a formidable and a menacing one. Is any restoration of the initiatory theatre possible amid these convulsions of a perverted aesthetic sense? I firmly believe that it is, notwithstanding every difficulty,

THE GENESIS OF TRAGEDY

because such restoration is a postulate of the whole previous evolution of the theatre. All the same, it appears to me possible only under the aegis of a controlling idea: that its founders and organizers seriously intend to bring about an harmonious synthesis and a new blending between the Promethean idea and the Eleusinian idea which were embodied separately by the Greeks in tragedy and in the drama of Eleusis. Manifestly this pre-supposes an organic conception of the Cosmos and a clear idea of the transcendent destiny of mankind,—a conception in which the individual soul, having recovered all its powers, would evolve freely in the three worlds.

I should have liked to continue these studies throughout the entire history of the theatre, to demonstrate how the divine world—which flashes its rays upon the tragedy of antiquity—suffers eclipse in the modern classic and romantic drama, and how it recovers, in spite of everything, after endless efforts, aspiring after a wider horizon wherein the struggles of earth shall be the preludes of the celestial victories of the Soul and thus effecting the synthesis of its life in the three worlds. This will be the task of the future creator of the idealist theatre. Meanwhile some of the ideas contained in this work may yet be realized in unexpected forms.

A restoration of the idealist theatre! These words seem like a fantastic chimera in the present materialistic chaos, an unmeaning challenge to the powers that be. And yet, this restoration will come about, if only after terrible trials and cataclysms, because it is the logical consequence of the past and of the forces latent in mankind. Here we shall mention only the one

THE GENESIS OF TRAGEDY

preliminary essential condition. We want no miracle, opposed to the eternal laws of the Cosmos, but simply an act of faith, worthy of the powers already won by man.

The light of the Divine is not dead in this world, though it now seems powerless because it is scattered and divided. Once more Dionysos has been rent and dismembered by the Titans. He awaits the liberator who will restore him to life. Faith is crystallized Love; let us have Faith. Let there be shining within us the torch of Enthusiasm which can be lit by none but ourselves,—and the spiritual sun will rise upon the horizon. It may be, at the present time, that this is the only way to prepare, in view of a still uncertain future, the coming of that theatre where the human soul, at present crippled and abased, will recover its might and employ its sacred rights in the advancement of synthetic art—of redemptive and initiatory drama.

THIRD PART

THE SACRED DRAMA OF ELEUSIS

AUTHORIZED TRANSLATION
by
BERESFORD KEMMIS
AND FRED ROTHWELL

ACT ONE

THE SORROW OF DEMETER

Scene I
Hekate's Cavern

Scene II
The Palace of King Keleos at Eleusis

Scenes III, IV, V, VI
The Same

ACT TWO

PERSEPHONE IN THE LOWER WORLD

Scene I
Tartaros: The Temple of Pluton

Scene II
The Same

ACT THREE

THE SACRED MARRIAGE

Scenes I and II
A Grotto on Mount Olympos

CHARACTERS

Demeter: Goddess of the Earth

Hekate: Mystic Goddess

Metaneira: Widow of Keleos, King of Eleusis

Triptolemos: Her Son

Kallirhoe:
Phaino: } Her Daughters
Rhodope:

Pluton: Pluto or Hades, king of the lower regions

Persephone: Daughter of Demeter

Zeus: King of Gods and Men

Dionysos.

Chorus of Demons, Mystae, Invisible Spirits, Invisible Heroes.

ACT ONE

THE SORROW OF DEMETER

SCENE I

(*The scene represents Hekate's Cavern, set amid massive gloomy rocks, scarcely visible in a wan light shining from the back.*)

DEMETER, *then* HEKATE.

DEMETER. (*Clad in a white peplos, a blue mantle spangled with silver stars floating on her shoulders. She carries a diadem and a golden sceptre. Her tawny hair is fastened with azure fillets. She rushes in with a torch in each hand and searches at the back of the cavern.*)

Hekate! Hekate! where art thou? She is hiding. Will she refuse to answer me like the others. Hekate! Come hither. It is the Mother of the Gods that calls thee!

HEKATE. (*Steps forward slowly from the back of the cavern. She is clad in a black peplos, embroidered on the hem with golden dragons and a red cloak. Her dark hair falls in a tangle of ringlets on her*

---

* This Drama had a Prologue entitled 'The Rape of Persephone by Pluton' which was performed at the Minor Mysteries of Agrae in the spring. See the Chapter on 'Plato and the Mysteries of Eleusis' in my book *The Great Initiates*.

THE GENESIS OF TRAGEDY

neck. The yellow crescent of the moon serves her for diadem. In her hand she carries a caduceus, whose interlaced and confronting serpents seem made of fire. She is beautiful, but her eyes gleam with a disturbing curiosity and the enigmatic smile seen in ancient statues plays about her lips.)

The queen of the world calls me and I hasten to come at her summons. This is the first time that sublime Demeter deigns to enter my cave. I await her commands.

Demeter. Daughter of Twilight and Night, hitherto I have ever shunned thine equivocal glance which haunts ill-omened places. But to-day, forsaken by all the gods I am come to entreat thine aid. I allowed my daughter Persephone to go playing with the Nymphs, the daughters of Okeanos, to gather acorns and hyacinths in a meadow. Supposing her happy, I had returned to the Empyrean, to rejoice in the brilliant light which no season dims and which can never be quenched. But all at once a heartrending cry pierced the Ether and echoed in my heart. It was the voice of Persephone crying out as though under violence. Thrice her beloved voice rent the bottomless Ether, and thrice I trembled to the depths of my being . . . until her moans died away to silence in the Abyss. Then seizing these two lighted torches I came down to earth, searching it in all directions, filling the mountains with my cries, entreating all the gods. But all remained dumb to my prayers, and even all-seeing Helios refused to answer me. Is it then some secret so terrible that no one dare reveal it to me? Answer me, Hekate, thou goddess of tortuous ways and subtle disclosures, thou who divinest the hidden purposes

THE DRAMA OF ELEUSIS

of Zeus, answer me! Thy knowing smile tells me that thou hast the secret!

HEKATE. I know it and will acquaint thee with it. But before I speak, promise me that thou wilt not curse me as a bringer of ill tidings.

DEMETER. I promise thee the fairest gifts from my kingdom of light—I swear it by the Styx—and shall ever be thy friend if thou wilt but tell me where Persephone is. For when I know that, I shall be able to find her—and to bring her back!

HEKATE. Well, then, it is Pluton who, in collusion with thy husband, the Lord of Heaven and Earth, has seized thy daughter. Zeus has given her to him as his wife.

DEMETER. (*Dropping her two torches which go out.*) Pluton? The King of the Lower World! . . . the only region into which I cannot descend!

(*She sits down on a rock; her head droops upon her breast.*)

HEKATE. Consider that the illustrious Lord of Hades is not a husband unworthy of thy daughter. He is brother to Zeus and owner of immense wealth. Trust my penetrating knowledge, the Abyss has its own joys. It is a better lot to live a queen among the shades than a slave among the gods.

DEMETER. (*Still in the same attitude.*) The immortal one dragged down among the dead! The pure Virgin deflowered in the arms of the insatiable Pluton! Her memories of Heaven effaced in those starlike eyes, those eyes of hers which would close under my kisses and reopen to reflect the whole firmament! Parted for ever from my daughter! Infinite grief and bottomless horror! What are the miseries of men beside ours? Clouds that pass, shadows cast by shadows ephemeral as they! They forget—but we do not forget; they die, but we are immortal! The grief of a man is like the plaint of a reed, but the grief of a god shakes the universe. Our capacity to suffer is eternal like our capacity for joy. To put an end to our griefs a world would have to crumble and another to be born out of its wreck!

HEKATE. Listen. . . . Thou knowst not everything. . . . Listen to the inmost thought of Zeus! For I have detected it, I who detect all things. . . . As Persephone, in tears, was disappearing in the Abyss, carried off in a chariot drawn by prancing steeds, and desperately struggling in the arms of her passionate husband, the mouth of hell gave a shout of triumph while a murky cloud issued from it. But I, who had spied out everything, was carried by my desire to the heights of Olympos. It was empty; the gods had deserted it. Thereupon guided by the fiery serpents of my caduceus, who know all paths, I continued forthwith to the Empyrean, to Zeus all-powerful. For my thought incessantly travels from the depths of the Abyss to the heights of Heaven, and these agile serpents guide me where I will. I found the king of the universe upon his clouds seated deep in meditation. Terrified he seemed at what he had done, for the fall of Persephone had afflicted all beings and had filled the gods with horror. I appeared before him in a purple light, with wild straggling locks, and I greeted him with my caduceus, the serpents darting forth flames in the presence of the lord of the lightning. Overjoyed to see me he uttered winged words: 'The radiant Demeter has deserted the heavens. I am alone; the gods are undecided and the world is dismayed. But Demeter shall never more see her

THE DRAMA OF ELEUSIS

daughter unless she returns to Olympos to conceive a new god. There I shall await her. Go, dear Hekate, and carry her this message.' Straightway I returned to seek thee, Great Goddess, with flaming torches as at a marriage. . . .

DEMETER. (*Rises trembling with indignation.*) Conceive a new god to this cruel and implacable Zeus who leaves Persephone to perish! Have I not already given him Dionysos, the son of his desire! . . . and he allowed him to be torn in pieces by the Titans. . . . It would be the same with the new god of whom he dreams, insensate as he is! No, never will I return to Olympos! In horror I hold the all-devouring Abyss, as also the Heaven which supplies it with victims. Did I but wield the thunderbolts of Zeus, I, Mother of the Gods, would break in pieces this universe, so that he might give me back my daughter, the divine Virgin! . . . I will have no more celestial insignia! . . . I am only a despairing mother.

(*She tears off the azure bandlets round her head and flings them to the ground. Her fawn-coloured tresses roll over her shoulders.*)

HEKATE. Mighty Demeter, where wilt thou dwell henceforth?

DEMETER. Among the wretched.

HEKATE. In what land?

DEMETER. In the freest.

HEKATE. With what nation?

DEMETER. The proudest.

HEKATE. In what home?

DEMETER. In the most afflicted. There will I weep my immortal tears and defy the lord of the thunderbolt, now the cowardly accomplice of his infamous brother! Knowest thou, Hekate, such a free land,

THE GENESIS OF TRAGEDY

such a proud nation and grief-stricken home as I seek?

HEKATE. In the land of Attica, not far from the majestic peak of Pallas, there is a peaceful and hospitable shore shielded by the heights of Megara and by the white girdle of Okeanos. Its name is Eleusis. The wild waves reach that coast only as the soft murmurs of the azure Nereids, under the gentle breath of the south wind. It is inhabited by a people of free and upright husbandmen. They honour thee under the name of the all-nourishing Earth who, beneath the burning glance of Helios, teems with golden grain and rustling harvest fields. In that land dwells a mourning family, the household of King Keleos, who has just gone down among the dead. His widow, Metaneira and his three daughters weep for the dead king, and the young Triptolemos, who loves only his plough and horses, is too weak to defend the household. Grief, silence and fear rule in the king's palace as in a grave.

DEMETER. That is the door at which I will knock; there is the home where Demeter will seek shelter. But help me, subtle Hekate, to change my appearance and assume the form of an infirm wandering old woman.

HEKATE. (*Smiling*.) I will honour thee, venerable goddess, with nimble hands. Am I not the queen of metamorphoses who delights in moulding the changing masks of beings? Is it not I who give a delicate vesture to souls passing through the moon and descending to earth and who disrobe them when they ascend again to Ouranos? I shall be able to disguise the Great Goddess just as well. Come with me to my Cavern. Within a few moments this magic caduceus will have veiled thy splendour and wrinkled thy face so completely that neither god nor man will recognize thee.

DEMETER. Oh, cruel degradation, shameful mask for the features of an Immortal. . . . But beneath it I shall be free to weep for Persephone!

(HEKATE *and* DEMETER *disappear at the back. The scene is darkened and then lights up again to represent the interior of the palace of Keleos at Eleusis. To the* RIGHT *and* LEFT *Doric columns. At the back a niche like the cella of a temple with the household altar, on which a fire is still just smouldering in the ashes.*)

SCENE II

THE PALACE OF KING KELEOS AT ELEUSIS.

(QUEEN METANEIRA *seated, in mourning. Her three daughters, in funeral attire, are grouped on the steps of the altar. To* RIGHT *and* LEFT PHAINO *and* KALLIRHOE *have set down on the ground their libation urns. They are lying near the urns which they envelop with their arms and loosened hair.* RHODOPE, *seated in the middle holds her urn on her knees in meditation.*)

KALLIRHOE. Oh, King Keleos, our father, when once thou didst reign in this palace we used to tread joyous measures before thee in honour of Artemis and the Graces, under the sacred olive tree. Now that thou hast gone down among the dead, we have poured the holy libations on thy tomb, invoking thy name and praying in our distress for a sign from thee, but thou hast not answered.

PHAINO. Oh, beloved father, at the evening festival I used once to adorn myself to offer thee the golden cup, full of pure wine and garlanded with vine leaves. Then thou wouldst call me the light of thine eyes, sweeter than the Dawn which brings the wonders of Day. Now we have draped thy tomb with grass and flowers for a table-covering and set on it fruit and cakes for the funeral meal. But thou wert there no more to smile to us. Father, dost thou feel my tears? I am weeping over thee.

RHODOPE. Oh, father, what has become of thee? Thy body was burned with thy weapons and clothing. Thy ashes lie in the urn beneath the mound. But where is thy weary shade? Has it stayed in the tomb, or does it haunt the earth or the banks of the Kokytos? Ye alone can tell, mighty spirits, deities of the lower world. But let us pour the sacred libations and pronounce the prayers according to the rites.

METANEIRA. They weep, while I am consumed with rage. They are calling upon pale shadows, while I am seeking in vain to rouse the living.

SCENE III

(THE SAME, *then* TRIPTOLEMOS, *a youth of eighteen. In one hand he has a horse's bridle and in the other a goad in the form of a lance. His bearing is grave and modest.*)

METANEIRA. Whence dost thou come?

TRIPTOLEMOS. From my father's tomb.

METANEIRA. What hast thou done to-day?

TRIPTOLEMOS. I have broken in a horse and ploughed my field.

METANEIRA. Dost thou not know that to-day the people are meeting in the Agora to elect a King of Eleusis? It is thou who shouldst be the successor to thy father. I bid thee go to the assembly to plead thy cause.

THE DRAMA OF ELEUSIS

Unless thou speakest there in the name of thy father, showing them thy youth and strength and promising them all that they desire, they will not elect thee.

TRIPTOLEMOS. I have no mind to beg for the people's votes. I have proved in battle my strength and the justice of my cause. They know me by my words and acts. Let them choose me freely if they want me; if not, let some other take the crown.

METANEIRA. Why then, it is thine uncle Dolikos whom they will choose. Once King, he will strip us of our possessions and expel us from this palace.

TRIPTOLEMOS. Let him take the city, the palace and the throne. He will not dare to take the furrow made by my plough. Mother, I repeat, I will only be King of Eleusis if a god bid me.

METANEIRA. Demented and ungrateful boy! Woe, woe to us!

SCENE IV

(THE SAME. *Enter* DEMETER *in the guise of a bent old woman, wrapped in a grey mantle, with a stick in her hand. She halts at the door and stretches out her hand, like a suppliant, towards the hearth.* TRIPTOLEMOS *remains motionless leaning on his lance. The three maidens rise.*)

METANEIRA. (*Still seated.*) Who is this strange woman?

PHAINO. An old woman broken by age.

KALLIRHOE. But still of noble bearing.

RHODOPE. A foreigner. Her dress is not of this country.

METANEIRA. Some roadside beggar.

PHAINO. Oh, mother! Let us welcome her. She can walk no further.

KALLIRHOE. She seems exhausted with hunger and thirst.

THE GENESIS OF TRAGEDY

Rhodope. And no doubt her woeful heart weighs her down even more than her limbs.

Metaneira. I dislike strangers who slink in to our hearth, without a word, to spy upon us. We do not know from what enemy they may come, nor what misfortune they may bring in the folds of their cloak. Stranger, if thou hast some message to bring us, utter it. If thou hast a favour to ask of us, speak. If thou comest on behalf of some man or some god, tell us who it is. If not, go thy way.

(Demeter *stretches out her hands towards the hearth, then clasps them over her face and seems to sob in silence.*)

Phaino. She is begging shelter. . . .

Kallirhoe. She is weeping bitterly. . . .

Rhodope. It is some noble person in distress!

All Three. Mother! Be merciful and let us welcome her!

(Metaneira *remains motionless on her seat and is silent.*)

Triptolemos. Whoever thou mayst be, venerable and afflicted lady, be welcome under this roof in the name of Zeus the hospitable, friend of outcasts. Take thy rest by this fireside.

(*The three sisters hasten to support* Demeter *and lead her to a seat near the hearth, where she sits down slowly with bowed head, in an attitude of desolate sadness.* Triptolemos *puts down his bridle and lance, fetches a cup of wine and presents it to* Demeter.)

Triptolemos. Accept, noble stranger, this cup of hospitality. Drink from it and be our guest. If then thou wishest to speak, we will listen. If not, we will respect thy silence. Unspoken griefs are sacred.

(Demeter *takes the cup and drinks a mouthful beneath her veil, then returns it to* Triptolemos, *clasps her hands in token of gratitude and relapses into her attitude of dejection.*)

METANEIRA. Now that thou art our guest under the shelter of our roof, I invite thee, stranger—it is my right—to tell us who thou art and whence thou comest, what is thy native land and what destiny has led thee to these shores?

DEMETER. (*Raises her head slightly and speaks in a majestic tone which contrasts with her rags.*) I come from Crete with her hundred cities, where I dwelt in a palace of gold and marble. For I had charge of a king's children and I had myself a daughter, tender as a fawn and gentle as a woodland nymph. A pirate stole her from me. Since then I have been wandering from shore to shore in search of her, but in vain. Now I am old, weary and homeless, and I have lost my all. My heartache has not been stilled and my strength is leaving me. If thou art willing to take me into thy house, Metaneira, I will teach thy daughters to work the fine fabrics which are woven with the ivory shuttle, and many other wonders. For I know the secrets of royal palaces and the potions which soothe the blackest griefs—all save mine own—and the magic herbs from the flanks of Mount Ida which almighty Zeus descended.

(*At the name of Zeus a faint flame flickers on the hearth.*)

PHAINO. Her voice is soft and mysterious.

KALLIRHOE. It sounds like the plaint of a lyre in a temple.

RHODOPE. She speaks like a queen.

METANEIRA. Truly thou hast spoken like a king's daughter, O stranger; and I will receive thee in my dwelling, though perchance we may soon be driven from it. For thou must know that Dolikos is scheming to

THE GENESIS OF TRAGEDY

seize the crown from my son. Wise and aged woman, the graces of eloquence dwell on thy lips. I will leave thee alone with my son Triptolemos that thou mayest teach him wisdom. Persuade him to go to the Agora to claim the crown before the people in the name of his father.

DEMETER. Very well, I will question him.

METANEIRA. (*To her daughters.*) Go ye and get ready a repast for the stranger. Thou, Triptolemos, stay with her. I am going out to consult the elders of the city.

(EXIT *with her daughters.*)

SCENE V

THE SAME.

DEMETER. What gloomy sorrow overshadows thy youthful brow, Triptolemos?

TRIPTOLEMOS. My father is dead.

DEMETER. Less painful is it for a son to lose his father than for a mother to lose her daughter. Is it of men or of Gods that thou hast to complain?

TRIPTOLEMOS. Of no one; my destiny is that of all men. But death is even more cruel for those who depart than for those who remain.

DEMETER. How knowst thou this?

TRIPTOLEMOS. (*In a low voice.*) One evening, in accordance with the rite dear to Pluton, in order to call forth the soul of Keleos, I sacrificed a lamb on his tomb. In the vaporous fumes of black blood, his shade, pale and terrifying, appeared before me. He said to me through the murky smoke: 'I am no more than an unhappy wandering shade, assailed by larvae in the kingdom of darkness. For Pluton

THE DRAMA OF ELEUSIS

is an implacable master and enfolds in denser darkness those who have lived in the enjoyment of insensate pleasures. Unless an immortal genius protects us, we dead no longer live except by the love of the living . . . and when they forsake us . . . we pass away like empty vapour. I wander about in darksome terror, a larva hunted by other larvae. Thou who alone on earth still lovest me, my son, couldst give me Elysian peace.' 'I am willing,' I said to him, 'but how can I come to thee?' The shade became paler and moaned anew: 'Forget me not, my son . . . for I suffer . . . I suffer. . . .' And the phantom disappeared.

DEMETER. (*Aside.*) Terrifying is the realm of Pluton, where Persephone moans in despair. . . .

TRIPTOLEMOS. Thou seemest troubled, thy hands tremble on thy staff; I see tears flowing, in spite of thy veil. What is the matter, unhappy woman?

DEMETER. What hast thou done for the accursed shade of thy father?

TRIPTOLEMOS. I have crowned his tomb with flowers and then returned to my plough. I have wrought and sown, invoking Demeter.

DEMETER. Wherefore Demeter?

TRIPTOLEMOS. I know her not, but she is said to be the greatest of the Goddesses, the Mother of the Gods. Is it not she who lives in Heaven and reigns over the Earth? Is it not she who makes the corn and flowers to grow?

DEMETER. And why thinkst thou that she will set free the soul of thy father?

TRIPTOLEMOS. When the grain is sown, the earth covers it over and no one sees it any more; but with the warm breath of spring there appears the green sprout which ripens into golden ears. If Demeter causes

THE GENESIS OF TRAGEDY

the corn to germinate in the soil, she must also bring back into her light the souls of men who descend into the underworld. Wherefore hope sings in my heart like the lark in my path.

DEMETER. (*Apparently moved and weeping beneath her veil, then continuing in trembling accents.*) How fine he is, this proud young stripling! More beautiful in his hopeful courage than the Olympians in their placid security. With a soul so heroic, he should be a god. If Zeus, alone, and without my aid created the virgin, Pallas, why should not I, alone, and without the aid of Zeus, create a boy, a god! Yes, I will him to be immortal. It is he who shall give me back my daughter.

TRIPTOLEMOS. What is the matter, stranger? Thou seemest to toss thy old age as a burden light to bear! Sparks play across thy mantle, and two torches are alive behind thy veil.

DEMETER. (*Sits and resumes the attitude of the old woman.*) They are but the reflections of the hearth upon my gown, and thou takest a mother's tears for flame. But listen; come near to me! I have learnt much, and I know many secrets, for I am old. And I have many remedies, for I am a good magician. Thou bewailest the accursed soul of thy dead father, while I lament over my lost daughter. I swear to set free the soul of thy father, if thou will rescue my daughter from the brigand who stole her from me.

TRIPTOLEMOS. Did I but know him, I would not hesitate.

DEMETER. Didst thou know him, thou wouldst not dare.

TRIPTOLEMOS. I have mastered horses with my bridle and the wild beasts of the mountains with my lance. Wherefore should I fear a brigand?

DEMETER. Know that my daughter is dead, and that

THE DRAMA OF ELEUSIS

her ravisher is Pluton. Darest thou descend into Tartaros?

TRIPTOLEMOS. He who feels himself the friend of the Light of day, dreads not the darkness. Open to me the gates of Hell, and I will enter!

DEMETER. Without knowing that thou wilt return?

TRIPTOLEMOS. (*Calm and solemn.*) What matter! Before I start, I will invoke the great Demeter on the sacred furrow of my cornfield. I know that she will hear my voice in far-away Ouranos.

DEMETER. (*Rising and clasping* TRIPTOLEMOS *to her breast.*) O, noble blood, thou whelp of a lion fed on woman's milk, the piety of a child dwells in thy heart, the honeyed words of sages flow from thy lips, and the flame of the valour of heroes flashes from thine eyes. . . . I love thee with a mother's love! Thou art more than a man, thou art my son! . . . Therefore I shall reveal to thee mysteries unknown to mortals, I shall tear away every veil from thine eyes and make thee more powerful than any king on earth. Thou shalt sing divine melodies; thou shalt tread the paths that span the worlds—and, one day, in despite of Tartaros and treacherous men, in despite of Zeus himself, thou shalt rise to the light of heaven with my daughter Persephone, in Hekate's chariot drawn by fiery serpents. Such shall be the destiny of Triptolemos, sacred tiller of the soil amongst men, hero divine amongst the gods!

(*She takes the head of* TRIPTOLEMOS *in her hands and kisses him on the brow.*)

TRIPTOLEMOS. Who art thou, adorable and powerful Mother, greater than she who bore me?

DEMETER. One day thou shalt know. Now, however, I would render thee invulnerable for thy terrible and life-giving task. With mine own hands, I will fashion for thee subtle and unbreakable weapons, so that thou mayst cross the gates of heaven and hell without receiving any hurt.

(*She passes her hands over the arms and breast of* TRIPTOLEMOS. *A radiant light flashes forth, and* TRIPTOLEMOS *appears in glowing splendour, his delighted eyes fixed upon those of the Goddess. Lightning flashes all around.*)

SCENE VI

THE SAME.

METANEIRA. (*Enters suddenly.*) Help! The palace is burning. Wicked and accursed witch, why did I leave thee on my hearth? May the three-formed Hekate destroy thee and thy fire! It is our enemies who have sent thee to strike my son blind and draw upon my house the curses of the people. Depart, witch!

(*When* METANEIRA *has finished speaking, the flames suddenly disappear and the fire dies out.* DEMETER, *flinging aside her veil and her old woman's mantle, stands erect and radiant. Her countenance is that of a Goddess. The staff in her hand changes into a burning torch.*)

METANEIRA. Who among the Immortals makes sport of us? My strength has left me.

(*She sinks to the ground, her head supported by the seat and her face in her hands.*)

THE THREE DAUGHTERS OF METANEIRA. (*Kneeling.*) Zeus, have pity on us!

TRIPTOLEMOS. (*Still standing and lost in ecstasy.*) Who art thou, Goddess?

DEMETER. I am Demeter. (*Turning towards* METANEIRA, *in a calm majestic voice.*) Thou hast had no kindly welcome for the stranger and the exile. Thou

THE DRAMA OF ELEUSIS

hast forgotten, woman, that unknown gods occasionally hide themselves beneath the tears of grief and the tatters of distress. Nevertheless, because thy daughters received me kindly, and because thou art the mother of this child, I pardon thee; but because thou hast disregarded and outraged me, the Great Goddess, there shall be eternal war between the children of Eleusis and the profane who resemble thee. As for thee, son of Keleos, henceforth I love thee as I love my daughter Persephone, whom thou art to rescue from Hades. Go into the public market-place, declare that it is my decree that a temple be built at Eleusis on the hill of Kallichoros. Thou shalt be my priest, and thy renown and that of thy descendants shall surpass the glory of kings. There I shall initiate thee into my mysteries and instruct thee regarding thy work; celestial springs shall flow for men at the sanctuary of Eleusis. Let the temple be dedicated to Demeter and her daughter Persephone.
(She disappears.)

METANEIRA. (*To* TRIPTOLEMOS, *as she rises furiously to her feet.*) Thou hast caused me to lose the royal mantle and all the glory of my old age. Cursed be thou! No longer am I thy mother.
(EXIT.)

THE THREE SISTERS. (*Rising to their feet, they approach their brother. They place their hands on his shoulders, and in thrilling accents ask.*) Who is this Persephone?

TRIPTOLEMOS. (*Pensive and with arms folded across his breast since the disappearance of* DEMETER. *At his sisters' question, he gravely raises his right hand and answers.*) She is the one who must be delivered —in order that she may set us free also!

ACT TWO

PERSEPHONE IN THE LOWER WORLD

SCENE I

The Palace of Pluton in the Lower World.
(Pluton, *sceptre in hand, is seated by the side of* Persephone *who is asleep on her throne, her head leaning against the trunk of the Tree of Dreams. The mystae silently place offerings of flowers at the feet of the Queen of the dead, who remains sunk in profound slumber.*)

Chorus of Demons. Glory to Pluton, the victor of Persephone! To celebrate thy wedding Hell rejoices and Tartaros is alight with countless flames. Hitherto the children of earth have evaded us; they were innocent and too insubstantial for our pit. But now that we possess the Goddess from above, souls will come in crowds, attracted by her beauty and her sin, and this kingdom will soon become peopled with empty shades. Monsters and Harpies, rejoice in the Tree of Falsehoods. Glory to Pluton! Hell thrills with delight and Tartaros holds its prey!

Pluton. (*Holding a black goblet and gazing upon the sleeping* Persephone.) How beautiful she is in her slumber! Daughter of Heaven, thou, fragrant bloom of the Gods, art mine. None of the Immortals will ever see thee again. But that thou mayst

THE DRAMA OF ELEUSIS

be wholly mine, thou must quaff this potion of oblivion and blind desire. Therefore I strain out into the goblet this blood-red fruit, this fruit of darkness. (*He squeezes into the goblet the pulp and juice of the pomegranate.*) Then will be effaced within thyself the remembrance and desire of Heaven which thou still retainest and through which thou mightst escape me. Afterwards, none can remove thee from Hades, though Zeus himself were to conceive a new Dionysos! . . . But wert thou to summon him, were thy divine spouse to be reborn of thy free desire, within the womb of celestial Demeter, he alone could rescue thee from me! . . .

PERSEPHONE. (*Awaking.*) Where am I? . . . Oh! this dull torpor in the arms of a terrible master. . . . Who am I? . . . The sinister queen of a mournful kingdom . . . endless night that wraps me about . . . a people of shades . . . and on my head monsters of frightful mien . . . dreams and falsehoods!

CHORUS OF MYSTAE. We are unhappy souls, wandering on this shore. Save us, gentle Queen, lead us back to the Elysian Fields.

PERSEPHONE. Alas! my brothers and sisters, how can I, myself a captive, set ye free? I hear thy laments and accept thy tears as a memory of the world above. Weep over me as I do over ye; that is the only gift we can make one another.

PLUTON. Look upwards, spouse of Pluton and Queen of the dead! Where is there a finer empire than mine? Who receives such homage as I do? On earth they fear me and seek my favour. My altars stream with the blood of victims. To thee shall be paid like homage with myself. (PERSEPHONE *covers her face with her hands.*) Here the dead throng about thy feet more frantically than the living round the temple of the Olympians. See how they implore thee! Here thou art Queen even more than Demeter in Heaven. Eternal are the dwellings thou wilt assign to them. Now, however, quaff this potion which will make known to thee the joys of Hades and of my marriage-bed. . . .

(*He offers the goblet to* PERSEPHONE, *who first hesitates to take it and finally grasps it with mingled curiosity and uneasiness. At the same moment, in the Tree of Visions, the screech-owls, sphynxes and harpies begin to gleam with a magic brightness, open wide their eyes and protrude their claws.*)

PERSEPHONE. O strange draught that makes my hand quiver. A terrifying desire lurks in its red liquid. The stones of the fruit glisten like the knowledge of evil, or like the fertile seed of infinite torments. . . . No, I will not drink! . . . Whoever looks once into that black depth has to look again. (*She looks into the goblet a second time.*) It is strange, now I see myself there with my eyes gleaming with a lurid glow. It is the same fire which gleams in the eyes of my terrible lord. It is burning in my veins! . . . Ah! what an arrow has pierced my heart! . . . Oh! dreadful torment! It is the remembrance of past happiness, the remembrance of the world above! When I used to play on the lap of my heavenly mother, I was the divine virgin, and yet I had a husband. . . . But I no longer know his name. . . . His image is fading. . . . Was it only a dream? Alas! Alas! I can no longer go back there. Must one then forget?

THE CHOIR OF INITIATES. Forget not, O Persephone! Drink not of the red blood from the black goblet,

THE DRAMA OF ELEUSIS

but lead us out of Hekate's pit into the Elysian Fields!

THE CHOIR OF DEMONS. Forget, forget! Drink and give us to drink from thy cup. It is the cup of life! For we are consumed with thirst, the unquenchable thirst of Hell!

PERSEPHONE. I too am athirst now . . . dreadful torment. . . . Oh this remembrance, faint as an expiring hope. . . . Could I but re-kindle it . . . or blot it out!

(*She looks into the cup a third time.*)

PLUTON. The spell is working. . . . She will drink from the goblet.

PERSEPHONE. (*Turning to* PLUTON.) What a mirage! What an unknown intoxication! Thy colour is changing, O King, thine eyes grow wider, thy golden diadem is gleaming. There are blue stars in thy dark hair. Dusky Pluton is turning into handsome Aidoneus! I have not then lost my husband. Breathless in amazement, I am finding him again, handsomer and more awful than ever! Is it real?

PLUTON. It is real. I am the eternal lord given by Zeus to the maiden Persephone. Only drink, and thou wilt be queen of the dead, and all Hades will celebrate the sombre joys of our marriage-bed, which will make even high Olympos pale before them!

(PERSEPHONE *closes her eyes and lifts the goblet to her lips. But a clap of thunder is heard, followed by a clash of cymbals. In the darkness appears a chariot drawn by fiery dragons, with* HEKATE *as driver. At her right sits* TRIPTOLEMOS, *carrying in his hand like a lance his ploughman's goad.*)

THE SAME.

PLUTON. (*Rises and waves his sceptre.*) Who dares enter the gates of Hell? A living man! May he perish by fire!

HEKATE. Thou hast no power over Triptolemos. Demeter has laved him in her flames of fire and I have brought him here. Spare thy lightning, for he is invulnerable.

PLUTON. Wretched Hekate! Hast thou done this, siren-faced bitch, shameless and suspicious spy? Since thou hast such audacity, I shall make yellow thy smiling mask which deceives men and gods alike. Thou shalt be the horror of the earth. They shall call thee witch and perjuress and I shall brand thee with the wrinkles of the Lemures!

HEKATE. I do the bidding of the Great Goddess. And now, god of the dead, listen to the voice of a living man.

TRIPTOLEMOS. Stay, Persephone. Drink not of that goblet. Remember thy Mother!

PERSEPHONE. (*Puzzled, and as if aroused from a dreadful dream.*) Who art thou, O mortal, bolder than the gods?

TRIPTOLEMOS. A king's son, Triptolemos, ploughman of Eleusis, foster-child and initiate of Demeter, one who despised a crown that he might come and seek thee here.

PERSEPHONE. O pure and dauntless youth, thy very sight rouses me from a frightful dream. Looking upon thee, I seem to behold once more the earth in springtime and my divine Mother, and the sacred Spouse, so long ago betrothed to me . . . and forgotten! Like a spring again beginning to flow, celestial voices softly murmur in my heart. . . .

THE DRAMA OF ELEUSIS

TRIPTOLEMOS. Mount then on this chariot . . . and follow me!

PERSEPHONE. Alas, thou art not the one able to break open for me the gates of this kingdom! No man has that power; a god alone could wrest me from the hands of a god. He who of old stirred with me in my mother's womb and whom the Titans tore to pieces. . . . He who still lives in the ineffable thought of Zeus . . . he alone could deliver me. . . . It is thou upon whom I call, Dionysos! Dionysos!

(*She throws down Pluton's goblet.*)

PLUTON. Death to Triptolemos! Now he belongs to me. Hades will hold him fast!

(*Another peal of thunder.* PLUTON, PERSEPHONE, HEKATE *and* TRIPTOLEMOS *disappear.*)

ACT THREE

THE SACRED MARRIAGE

SCENE I

ZEUS, *soon after* DEMETER.
(*A grotto on Mount Olympos. A couch of ivory and gold strewn with lilies and roses, half wrapped in a cloud.*)
ZEUS. (*Standing at some distance from the couch, leaning on his sceptre in deep meditation.*)

> The appointed time has elapsed. Demeter must return. Her frantic course through the world is drawing to an end. Triptolemos, her nursling, has passed the gates of Tartaros; but, himself Pluton's prisoner, has been unable to bring back Persephone. Golden-haired Demeter, the Mother of the Gods, the uncreated Light, wanders over the earth like a Fury armed with her burning torches, but cannot recover her daughter. Before her terrible eyes men recoil in fear from her path. For her heart is enraged against me. And yet . . . without me . . . could she give birth to him who shall deliver Persephone? Thus I also am subject to the inexorable fate of the world which is my own creation. Though my thunderbolt can shatter men, they are still free to live and die at their own will, but their thoughts once translated into actions have consequences that even I cannot arrest. As to the gods I have begotten,

THE DRAMA OF ELEUSIS

nothing binds them; they act each in his own sphere, with the power I have conferred on them, and are eternal like myself. If Persephone were to drink from Pluton's goblet, neither my thunderbolt nor my sceptre could bring her back. . . . And now my heart yearns for my daughter, nought can take her place and I am weary of my solitude. But without Demeter I can do nothing for her. . . . But what is this unaccustomed sound? The Ether vibrates and hums . . . and from the depths of space a whirlwind is beating against the flanks of the mountain. It is the Mother of the Gods returning to Olympos to assail me like a furious wave. . . . (*The roar of rushing water is heard.*)

ENTER DEMETER *carrying two torches.*

DEMETER. Oh heartless and cruel Zeus, when wilt thou cease to wrong me? Dwelling unchangeable in thy splendour and strength, thou hast no care for the evils endured by thy creatures and by myself who am half of thee. Thou hast let Persephone our daughter fall into the Abyss and against her will hast yielded her to thy brother Pluton.

ZEUS. Pluton has taken her against my wish, but I could not wrest his prey from him. She is his legitimate conquest. When Persephone went to play with the nymphs on the borders of Okeanos, her curiosity was already drawing her towards the lower spheres, and in secret her heart invited . . . her captor!

DEMETER. Treacherous one! Thy deep-laid ruse is only a screen for thy cruelty. By letting her descend thou hast planned her ruin.

ZEUS. Persephone is the daughter of thy desire; she is immortal and free as thou art.

DEMETER. Death were better than such an immortality!

THE GENESIS OF TRAGEDY

What hast thou done to deliver her from her bondage? I at least have sent Triptolemos into Tartaros to rescue her. The ploughman of Eleusis has awakened Persephone from her slumber, but Pluton has both of them bound in his chains.

ZEUS. No man can break them.

DEMETER. Relentless spirit. Wilt thou not then set thy daughter free?

ZEUS. (*Sombre.*) Alas, has not my son Dionysos followed his sister into the Abyss to save her?

DEMETER. Yes, Dionysos, the son of thy desire! . . and the Titans tore his limbs asunder. . . . No more than thyself was he able to bring Persephone back to me. But now, if thou knowst of no remedy, if thou wilt not restore my daughter to my arms, I will go myself to the underworld, and with these torches will set thy universe aflame!

ZEUS. Listen to me, Persephone can be saved only by a new God. . . .

DEMETER. Which one?

ZEUS. A God conceived by my flame and born of thy light; a son of my will and of thy love!

DEMETER. His name?

ZEUS. The dream of my supreme desire . . . the new Dionysos!

DEMETER. For the Titans to rend him once again?

ZEUS. The Titans will have no power over him. He will be stronger than they, though not invulnerable, and will offer himself to men, to the universe, to the gods. He will do combat in his frenzy and beauty; with shouts of triumph will he see his own blood and tears. On his stainless breast he will bear no longer the nebris made of the skin of a slain fawn—but the radiant star of invincible Love!

DEMETER. More blood! More tears? No, I will not

THE DRAMA OF ELEUSIS

agree. By the eternal virginity of my light, better that this universe should perish than that there be another made again in its likeness! . . . Rather eternal slumber in the night from which we emerged. . . .

(*A prolonged cry of pain is heard coming from the depths of the Abyss.* DEMETER *drops her torches, which die out on the ground.*)

ZEUS. Listen to the voice calling thee from the Abyss.

A VOICE FROM THE ABYSS. Dionysos! Dionysos!

DEMETER. (*In frenzied joy.*) The voice of Persephone!

ZEUS. Dost thou hear? 'Tis no longer thee on whom she calls, but Dionysos, the son of my desire!

DEMETER. (*Raises her hands to her temples and remains in a state of ecstasy.*) What is this dream that wraps me about, this divine slumber that lulls me to peace and calm? Again I hear the music of the spheres. . . . O all-pervading light . . . through which pass white steeds and shining bucklers, proud heroes and flaming virgins . . . and in the far distance . . . thy gentle flashing splendour. . . . O Dionysos!

(*Closing her eyes, she sinks gently on to the couch.*)

ZEUS. (*Without moving from the spot, extends his sceptre over Demeter.*) The final charm overcomes her . . . slumber streams from my sceptre . . . my thought descends into her bosom. . . .

(*Clouds rise from the ground, conceal the group and fill the cavern.*)

CHORUS OF INVISIBLE SPIRITS. When Demeter slumbers, the gods meditate and men thrill with an unknown joy. For from her dream there comes forth a new god.

Oh men, bow down before the holy mystery of the gods.

THE GENESIS OF TRAGEDY

One of their glances brings to birth millions of lives;
One of their days covers myriads of years;
One of their nights is a slumber of the universe, in which time and space, holding their wings, brood over future ages.

SCENE II

THE SAME.

(*The clouds that fill the cavern have become luminous. On the* RIGHT *appears the chariot of* HEKATE. TRIPTOLEMOS *holds the reins of the fiery dragons. By his side is seated* PERSEPHONE *wearing a peplos of diaphanous white, gold-tinted. The garment seems illumined from within. She wears a wreath of narcissus, shining like stars. Hyacinth-coloured gauze falls from her locks on to her dress like a bride's veil.*)

PERSEPHONE. Triptolemos, child of Eleusis, haughty ploughman and fearless tamer of steeds, who overpowerest the flaming dragons which crush the rocks and split the Ether, with sure hand hast thou led me here through boundless space. On the day that a celestial ray pierced Tartaros, I tore myself away from the arms of vigilant Pluton, sunk in dark slumber. I mounted thy chariot. Of themselves the gates of Hell opened before thee and we traversed the Empyrean. While this marvellous journey has lasted, however, I know not how many centuries have passed, for the light of Helios no longer illumined us, the stars alone were our guides. . . . But what is this divine spot? What are these perfumes, these celestial chants that fill my soul like the golden-hearted crocus? . . . I recognize the Olympos of my birth. Dazzling beams flash from the cavern. No longer can I tear away mine eyes. . . .

THE DRAMA OF ELEUSIS

TRIPTOLEMOS. Look, O Goddess, thou art now to behold him thou hast sought throughout the worlds.

(DIONYSOS *issues from the incandescent centre of the clouds which immediately disperse, and the shining god appears in the depths of the cavern again plunged in darkness. The horses of Dionysos resemble flames of gold. In place of the nebris, a star shines like a helmet upon his breast.*)

PERSEPHONE. O, brother divine, appearing before me so sad and beautiful in thy splendour, I greet thee with trembling heart, not daring to approach thee.

DIONYSOS. Persephone, my sister who hath finally escaped from the pit, for weary centuries hast thou been before me, a living dream, as thou art at this moment, shining with everlasting youth beneath thy bridal veil and thy wreath of narcissus.

PERSEPHONE. Alas, I have plucked the narcissus of desire; black Pluton has taken me. . . . I have plunged into the pit . . . and have forgotten! But it only made me more unhappy than ever; black were my tears in the darkness where I found myself.

DIONYSOS. And I was in search of thee. Though the Titans rent me limb from limb, I did not forget thee. They tore away my flesh, cast my body to the tigers and my head into the pit; but ever did my flesh, my heart and my head, cry out: Persephone! Persephone!

PERSEPHONE. And all the time I, defiled by frightful dreams, bound to the arms of Pluton, queen of the dead, myself dead, heard nothing!

DIONYSOS. (*Approaches the chariot of* TRIPTOLEMOS, *in which* PERSEPHONE *is still seated.*) Oh, the craving for life, the longing for rebirth in order to find thee . . . amongst mortals. I was that Bacchus of earth,

THE GENESIS OF TRAGEDY

who thinks he enjoys, but who enjoys in order to suffer himself and make others suffer. I watched the Bacchantes die, wounded by my glance when dreaming of thee! . . . I lived . . . and tore myself into a thousand parts; I was born again . . . to scatter myself into millions of pieces. . . .

PERSEPHONE. Oh, the craving for love and death by giving myself. I struggled in the arms of Pluton, calling for rescue and clasped none but phantoms and shades. . . . Then, unable to die, I cried out. . . .

(*She rises.*)

DIONYSOS. At that cry I rose from the dead . . . and I came.

(*He takes her by the hand and leads her down from the chariot.*)

PERSEPHONE. Thou camest in the shape of those heroes, touched with the kiss of the thunderbolt, who are of thy race and blood; Herakles, Jason and Prometheus!

DIONYSOS. I flowed in their blood, I strove in their body, I spoke by their voice that thou mightest recognize me . . . and thy lips uttered cries of joy and grief, yet thou couldst not break the gates of thy hell! Then I came myself!

PERSEPHONE. In the Abyss a ray of thy light reached me. Then I ascended . . . and I am now here! (*She throws her arms around Dionysos' neck and gazes at him.*) Through my desire the Brother has become the Lover.

DIONYSOS. Through my sorrow the Sister has become the Bride.

PERSEPHONE. In thy dark hair the ivy has blossomed. What are these red berries?

DIONYSOS. They are the drops of my blood shed for

THE DRAMA OF ELEUSIS

thee. . . . Thy narcissus flowers have wept; what is this dew in their eyes?

PERSEPHONE. Those are the tears of Persephone!

DIONYSOS. How beautiful art thou, daughter of celestial Light!

PERSEPHONE. How beautiful art thou, son of immortal Desire!

DIONYSOS. Thine from all time past!

PERSEPHONE. Thine for all time to come!

(*On the threshold of the cavern appear* ZEUS *and* DEMETER. PERSEPHONE *throws herself into her mother's arms, while* DIONYSOS *places himself by the side of* ZEUS.)

ZEUS. Triptolemos, thy courage and thy purity have given thee to see what no mortal has ever beheld. Return to Eleusis, but reveal nothing of these mysteries to the profane. Among men thou shalt be known as the son of Demeter; among the heroes and the gods, as the saviour of Persephone!

(*The chariot of* TRIPTOLEMOS *descends; the gods disappear.*)

CHORUS OF INVISIBLE HEROES. All ye who have beheld this holy mystery, whence gods and men have issued, take the remembrance of it with you to earth. May it be thy solace during life, thy guide after death. But hide it in the depths of thine heart like a diamond in a rock. We can receive Truth in our inner selves and carry her radiations through the world, but whoever betrays her sublime source will lose her for ever.